NEW CENTURY BIBLE COMMENTARY

General Editors

RONALD E. CLEMENTS	MATTHEW BLACK
(Old Testament)	(New Testament)

Philippians

THE NEW CENTURY BIBLE COMMENTARIES

Other titles in preparation

NEW CENTURY BIBLE COMMENTARY

Based on the Revised Standard Version

PHILIPPIANS

RALPH P. MARTIN

Grand Rapids

WILLIAM B. EERDMANS PUBLISHING COMPANY

IN MEMORIAM
PATRIS

Library of Congress Cataloging in Publication Data

Martin, Ralph P
    Philippians.

    Reprint of the ed. published by Marshall, Morgan & Scott, London which
was issued in the New century Bible series.
    Bibliography: pp. ix, xv.
    Includes index.
    1. Bible.   N.T.   Philippians — Commentaries.
I.   Title.   II.   Series: New century Bible.
BS2705.3.M33   1980   227'.6077   80-10643
ISBN 0-8028-1840-4

CONTENTS

EDITOR'S NOTE

This New Century Bible *Philippians* by Professor Ralph P. Martin, completes the plan, announced in the foreword to *Colossians and Philemon*, to replace the single volume *Ephesians, Philippians, Colossians and Philemon*, modelled on the old series and now out of print, by three separate volumes on Ephesians, Colossians and Philemon, and Philippians.

MATTHEW BLACK

PREFACE

'It is most probable, it is almost certain indeed, that Paul wrote letters subsequent to his Epistle to the Philippians. And yet, from many points of view . . . the Epistle to the Philippians may be justly regarded as Paul's Last Will and Testament.' So wrote John A. Hutton in a book (*Finally, With Paul to the End*, London, 1934, p. 218) which, while in no sense a commentary on the letter to Philippi and while unencumbered with technical apparatus, may still be claimed as being one of the most illuminating and helpful contributions to our understanding of the historical Paul.

This epistle has a distinctive place within the corpus of apostolic writings. It gives us a window into Paul's personal and pastoral character. It equally provides data for a case-study of one early Christian congregation with whom Paul cherished fond and enduring relationships. Something of their hopes and fears, their problems and opportunities, comes through as we try sympathetically to enter, *via* Paul's letter, their world of long ago.

These matters will continue to engage the interest of teachers and ministers in the Church, irrespective of the more scholarly debate over the letter's composition and place of origin.

A modicum of information regarding this discussion will be found in the following pages, with more attention given to two more central concerns: the nature of the sectarian teaching against which Paul warns in ch. 3, and the meaning of the great christological passage in ch. 2:5–11. The present commentator has tried to sum up the state of the matter in both areas and has drawn gratefully on recent studies, notably by J. Gnilka (1968) and J.-F. Collange (1973).

As with the commentary in this series on *Colossians and Philemon*, which appeared in 1974, the introductory note by Principal Matthew Black explains how these supplementary volumes came to be written. It remains once more to express appreciation for a renewed opportunity, given to few students, to take a second look at a biblical text and to see their (hopefully) more mature reflections captured in printed form.

Since this Preface is being written during sabbatical leave at Spurgeon's College, London, it is appropriate to acknowledge the opportunity that such a freedom from teaching responsibility affords, and also to recall the congenial atmosphere of the college for the writing of this commentary.

Fuller Theological Seminary   R.P.M.
Pasadena, California

PREFACE TO REVISED EDITION (1980)

The reprinting of this commentary gives the opportunity to correct several typographical and other errors that have been discovered in the 1976 edition. But it has not been possible to alter or update the commentary itself. Nor would the writer wish to do so, except in some marginal ways.

Some reviewers have considered that the commentary has made too much of the alleged polemical intention of Paul in his Philippian letter. The present writer has reflected further on these points but sees no reason to change his mind.

Recent studies appearing since 1975 are, however, listed below, and alert students of Paul may wish to consult some of these titles that offer a more traditional way of regarding this epistle as Paul's almost benign attitude to Philippian problems.   R. P. M.

SUPPLEMENTARY BIBLIOGRAPHY
(1975-1979)

PHILIPPIAN STUDIES (1975-1979)

Baumbach, G. 'Die Zukunftserwartung nach dem Philipperbrief,' in *Die Kirche des Anfangs,* ed. R. Schnackenburg, Leipzig, 1977, pp. 435-57.

Caird, G. B. *Paul's Letters from Prison* (New Clarendon Bible), Oxford, 1976. He maintains the unity of the letter and its setting in Rome.

Collange, J.-F. *The Epistle of Saint Paul to the Philippians.* Translated from the French by A. W. Heathcote, London, 1979. This is a translation of Collange's edition in *CNT,* 1973, which is referred to in this commentary. It remains the most up-to-date and incisive treatment of Philippians available.

López, E. Fernández, 'En torno a Fil 3, 12,' *Estudios Biblicos* (Madrid) 34 (1975), pp. 121-3. He chooses the reading of P^{46} referred to on p. 136.

O'Brien, P. T. 'The Fellowship Theme in Philippians,' *Reformed Theological Review* 37 (1978), pp. 9-18.

Palmer, D. W. '"To die is gain" (Philippians 1, 21),' *NovT* 17 (1975), pp. 203-218.

Pedersen, S. '"Mit Furcht und Zittern" (Phil. 2, 12-13),' *Studia Theologica* (Oslo) 32 (1978), pp. 1-31. He understands the phrase 'with fear and trembling' to mean 'with obedience' to God, and so it is related to the hymn of 2:6-11 as providing an ecclesiological response.

Tyson, J. B. 'Paul's Opponents at Philippi,' *Perspectives in Religious Studies* (Danville, VA) 3 (1976), pp. 82-95, claiming that Paul's enemies were a Christian group, leaning to docetism and perfectionism.

de Vogel, C. J. 'Reflexions on Philipp. 1, 23-24,' *NovT* 19 (1977), pp. 262-74. He wants to assert a valid Pauline dichotomy between body and soul.

Walter, N. 'Die Philipper und das Leiden. Aus den Anfängen einer heiden-christlichen Gemeinde' in *Die Kirche des Anfangs*, ed. R. Schnacken-burg, Leipzig, 1977, pp. 417-34.

ON PHIL. 2:5-11

Hofius, O. *Der Christushymnus Philipper* 2, 6-11 (Wissenschaftliche Unter-suchungen zum NT, 17), Tübingen, 1976. A valiant effort to oppose Käsemann's position, and to relate the hymn's genre to that of the canonical psalms and the confession of Isa. 45:23.

Howard, G. 'Phil. 2:2-11 and the Human Christ,' *CBQ* 40 (1978), pp. 368-87.

Losie, L. A. 'A Note on the Interpretation of Phil. 2:5,' *ExpT* 90 (1978-79), pp. 52-54.

Murphy-O'Connor, J. 'Christological Anthropology in Phil., II. 6-11,' *RB* 83 (1976), pp. 25-50.

Wilson, R. E. '"He Emptied Himself,"' *Journal of Evangelical Theological Society* 19 (1976), pp. 279-81. He reverts to the classical pre-Lohmeyer understanding.

OTHER STUDIES

Casson, L. *Travel in the Ancient World*, Toronto, 1974, ch. 9, expressing in popular form the theme of the article referred to on p. 42.

Ellis, E. E. 'Paul and his Opponents: Trends in Research,' in *Christianity, Judaism and Other Greco-Roman Cults: Studies for Morton Smith at Sixty*, Part I, ed. J. Neusner. Leiden, 1975, pp. 264-98 (reprinted in *Prophecy and Hermeneutic in Early Christianity*, Grand Rapids/Tübingen, 1978, pp. 80-115).

Hengel, M. *The Son of God. The Origin of Christology and the History of Jewish-Hellenistic Religion*, London/Philadelphia, 1976. This small book is im-portant for NT christology, emphasizing its Jewish setting and the early appearance of claims regarding Jesus' pre-existence and exalted status.

Sanders, E. P. *Paul and Palestinian Judaism*, London/Philadelphia, 1977. The discussion of Paul's background and his teaching on 'righteous-ness' throws fresh light on the exegesis of Phil. 3.

Smallwood, E. M. *Jews under Roman Rule*, Leiden, 1976, is important for Paul's heritage in the Dispersion and the status of Philippi as a colony.

ABBREVIATIONS

OLD TESTAMENT (*OT*)

Gen.	Jg.	1 Chr.	Ps.	Lam.	Ob.	Hag.
Exod.	Ru.	2 Chr.	Prov.	Ezek.	Jon.	Zech.
Lev.	1 Sam.	Ezr.	Ec.	Dan.	Mic.	Mal.
Num.	2 Sam.	Neh.	Ca.	Hos.	Nah.	
Dt.	1 Kg.	Est.	Isa.	Jl	Hab.	
Jos.	2 Kg.	Job	Jer.	Am.	Zeph.	

APOCRYPHA (*Apoc.*)

1 Esd.	Tob.	Ad. Est.	Sir.	S 3 Ch.	Bel	1 Mac.
2 Esd.	Jdt.	Wis.	Bar.	Sus.	Man.	2 Mac.
			Ep. Jer.			

NEW TESTAMENT (*NT*)

Mt.	Ac.	Gal.	1 Th.	Tit.	1 Pet.	3 Jn
Mk	Rom.	Eph.	2 Th.	Phm.	2 Pet.	Jude
Lk.	1 C.	Phil.	1 Tim.	Heb.	1 Jn	Rev.
Jn	2 C.	Col.	2 Tim.	Jas	2 Jn	

DEAD SEA SCROLLS (DSS)

1QS	The Rule of the Community (Manual of Discipline)
1QH	Hymns of Thanksgiving
1QM	War of the Sons of Light against the Sons of Darkness

GENERAL

Aboth	*Sayings of the Jewish Fathers*
Adv. Haer.	*Against all Heresies* (Irenaeus)
AG	W. Bauer, *A Greek-English Lexicon of the New Testament and Other Early Christian Literature*, translated by W. F. Arndt and F. W. Gingrich, Cambridge, 1957
AJT	*American Journal of Theology*, Chicago

AV	*Authorized Version* (King James version, 1611)
BA	*Biblical Archaeologist*
Barn.	Epistle of Barnabas
BC	*The Beginnings of Christianity*, i–v, edited by F. J. Foakes-Jackson and Kirsopp Lake, London, 1920–33
BJRL	*Bulletin of the John Rylands Library*, Manchester
BDF	F. Blass and A. Debrunner, *A Greek Grammar of the New Testament*, translated and edited by R. W. Funk, Cambridge/Chicago, 1961
BZ	*Biblische Zeitschrift*, Paderborn
CBC	*Cambridge Bible Commentary*
CBQ	*Catholic Biblical Quarterly*, Washington, DC
1 Clem.	First Epistle of Clement
CNT	*Commentaire du Nouveau Testament*, Neuchâtel/Paris
EGT	*Expositor's Greek Testament*
Ep.	Epistle
EQ	*Evangelical Quarterly*, Exeter
ET	English Translation
ExpT	*Expository Times*, Edinburgh
Geogr.	*Geographica* (Strabo)
Gr.	Greek
HE	*Church History* (Eusebius)
Heb.	Hebrew
HTR	*Harvard Theological Review*, Cambridge, Mass.
HzNT	*Handbuch zum NT*, edited by H. Lietzmann and G. Bornkamm
IB	*Interpreter's Bible*
ICC	*International Critical Commentary*
Ignatius *Eph.* *Magnes.* *Polyc.* *Rom.* *Smyr.* *Trall.*	Ignatius to the Ephesians, Magnesians, Polycarp, Romans, Smyrnaeans, Trallians

JBL	*Journal of Biblical Literature*, Philadelphia
JThC	*Journal for Theology and the Church*, Tübingen/ New York
JTS	*Journal of Theological Studies*, Cambridge
KEK	*Kritisch-exegetischer Kommentar über das NT*, edited by H. A. W. Meyer, Göttingen
LXX	Septuagint
MNTC	*Moffatt NT Commentary*
Moulton	*A Grammar of NT Greek*, vol. 1, Edinburgh, 1908; vol. 2, edited by W. F. Howard, 1919–29; vol. 3, edited by N. Turner, 1963
Moulton–Milligan	*The Vocabulary of the Greek Testament*, by J. H. Moulton and G. Milligan, London, 1914–30
NEB	*New English Bible*, 1970
NovT	*Novum Testamentum*, Leiden
n.s.	New Series
NTD	*Das Neue Testament Deutsch*, Göttingen
NTS	*New Testament Studies*, Cambridge
o.s.	Old Series
Polyc. *Phil.*	Polycarp to the Philippians
RB	*Revue Biblique*, Jerusalem
RHR	*Revue de l'historie des religions*, Paris
RSPhTh	*Revue des Sciences philosophiques et théologiques*, Paris
RSV	*Revised Standard Version (NT, 1946; OT, 1952; rev. 1973)*
RV	*Revised Version (NT, 1880; OT, 1884)*
SB	H. Strack and P. Billerbeck, *Kommentar zum Neuen Testament aus Talmud und Midrasch*, Munich, 1922
SE	*Studia Evangelica*, edited by F. L. Cross, Berlin
SJT	*Scottish Journal of Theology*, Edinburgh
s.v.	under the word (entry)
TynB	*Tyndale Bulletin*, London
Test. Asher	*Testament of Asher* in *The Testaments of the Twelve Patriarchs*
TDNT	*Theological Dictionary of the New Testament*, Grand Rapids, 1964–75

ThStK	*Theologische Studien und Kritiken*, Hamburg/ Gotha
ThZ	*Theologische Zeitschrift*, Basel
TR	Textus Receptus
Vermes	G. Vermes, *The Dead Sea Scrolls in English*, Harmondsworth, 1962
ZNW	*Zeitschrift für die neutestamentliche Wissenschaft*, Giessen/Berlin

BIBLIOGRAPHY OF COMMENTARIES

✓Barth   Karl Barth, *Erklärung des Philipperbriefes*, Zürich, 1928 (ET *The Epistle to the Philippians*, London, 1962).

Beare   F. W. Beare, *A Commentary on the Epistle to the Philippians* (Harper-Black series), London, 1959.

Benoit   P. Benoit, *Les épîtres de Saint Paul aux Philippiens*, etc., (*La Bible de Jérusalem*), Paris, 1949.

Bonnard   P. Bonnard, *L'épître de Saint Paul aux Philippiens* (*CNT*), Neuchâtel/Paris, 1950.

○Collange   J.-F. Collange, *L'épître de Saint Paul aux Philippiens* (*CNT* new edn), Neuchâtel/Paris, 1973.

Dibelius   M. Dibelius, *An die Thessalonicher, i, ii; an die Philipper* (*HzNT*), 1937.

Friedrich   G. Friedrich, *Der Brief an die Philipper* (*NTD*), Tubingen/Göttingen, 1962.

Gnilka   J. Gnilka, *Der Philipperbrief* (*Herders Theologischer Kommentar zum NT*), Freiburg-im-Breisgau, 1968.

Grayston   Kenneth Grayston, *The Epistles to the Galatians and to the Philippians* (*Epworth Preacher's Commentaries*), 1957.

——   *The Letters of Paul to the Philippians and the Thessalonians* (*Cambridge Bible Commentary*), Cambridge, 1967.

Heinzelmann   G. Heinzelmann, *Die kleineren Briefe des Apostels Paulus*, 8 (*NTD*); *Der Brief an die Philipper*, Göttingen, 1955.

Hendriksen   W. Hendriksen, *A Commentary on the Epistle to the Philippians* (*Geneva Series*), London/Grand Rapids, 1962.

Houlden   J. L. Houlden, *Paul's Letters from Prison* (*Pelican New Testament Commentaries*), Harmondsworth, 1970.

Kennedy   H. A. A. Kennedy, *The Epistle to the Philippians* (*EGT*), Edinburgh, 1903.

Lightfoot   J. B. Lightfoot, *Saint Paul's Epistle to the Philippians*, London, 1896 ed.

Lohmeyer   E. Lohmeyer, *Der Brief an die Philipper*, ed., W. Schmauch (*KEK*), Göttingen, 1956.

Michael   J. H. Michael, *The Epistle of Paul to the Philippians*
               (*MNTC*), London, 1928.

Michaelis   W. Michaelis, *Der Brief des Paulus an die Philipper*,
               (*Theologischer Handkommentar zum Neuen Testament*),
               1935.

Moule   H. C. G. Moule, *The Epistle to the Philippians*
               (*Cambridge Greek Testament*), 1906.

Müller   J. J. Müller, *The Epistles of Paul to the Philippians
               and to Philemon* (*New London/International Commen-
               tary on the New Testament*), London/Grand
               Rapids, 1955.

Scott   E. F. Scott, *The Epistle to the Philippians* (*IB*),
               Nashville/New York, 1955.

Synge   F. C. Synge, *Philippians and Colossians* (*Torch Bible
               Commentaries*), London, 1951.

Vincent   M. R. Vincent, *The Epistles to the Philippians and
               Philemon* (*ICC*), Edinburgh, 1897.

INTRODUCTION
to
Philippians

INTRODUCTION

I. PHILIPPI: CITY AND CHRISTIAN COMMUNITY

A. PHILIPPI: STATUS AND HISTORY

Paul's intention to enter the Roman province of Asia, in the course of the second missionary journey, was momentarily checked. He therefore took the road northwards to Pisidian Antioch, crossed the Sultan Dagh mountain range, and continued in a northerly direction until he and his party reached the borders of Bithynia, a senatorial province in NW Asia Minor (Ac. 16:6).

As he tried to enter Bithynia by taking the north road to Nico-media, he was once more thwarted (Ac. 16:7), with the result that he turned westwards. He came down to the coast at Troas, where the apostolic party stopped. It was here that Paul received a night vision in which there came to him the invitation: 'Come over to Macedonia and help us' (Ac. 16:9). Responding immediately to this summons, and in company with the author of Acts (Ac. 16:10 marks the opening of a 'we-section', as the narrative is cast in the first person plural of the verb, 'we concluded . . . God had called us'), Paul sailed directly to Samothrace. Since travel by sea along this coast line was often delayed by unfavourable winds, the mention of direct and speedy journeys is probably Luke's way of indicating divine approval. (Contrast Ac. 20:6.) Then he sailed to Neapolis (modern Kavalla), the port of Philippi. At Neapolis the Roman road *via Egnatia* ran to Philippi, some eight miles inland.

The Lucan description of Philippi in Ac. 16:12 is noticeably full. The city is called 'the leading city of the district of Macedonia, and a Roman colony'. This translation, however, is uncertain and the Greek text underlying it is difficult. (For a discussion, see especially A. N. Sherwin-White, *Roman Society and Roman Law in the New Testament*, Oxford, 1963, pp. 93ff.) The issue centres on the fact that the Roman province of Macedonia had the unusual characteristic of being divided into four *regiones*, 'sub-provinces'. *Regio* corresponds to the word (*meris*) rendered 'district' in this verse. Each sub-province had a 'leading city', but in the case of the district of Macedonia in which Philippi stood, the capital city was Thessalonica. It is called *prōtē Makedonōn* (*Corpus Inscript.*

Graecarum no. 1967). Ac. 16:12 does not state in so many words
that Philippi was *the* leading city of its region, though it comes
near to saying it. A possible submission is that Luke's verse should
be translated 'a leading city of the district of Macedonia', in which
case the Greek *prōtē* ('leading') is used as a title of honour
(H. J. Cadbury, in *BC* iv, p. 188), or it may be that Luke is classi-
fying Philippi as a city of the 'first district of Macedonia' (reading
prōtēs, a conjecture for which there is support in some Alexandrian
MSS: cf. C. S. C. Williams, *Alterations to the Text of the Synoptic Gospels
and Acts*, Oxford, 1951, pp. 61f., and H. Conzelmann, *Die Apostel-
geschichte*, Göttingen, 1963, p. 91). There are other variants within
the textual tradition, so certainty of meaning is not now possible.
We shall have to be content with a general sense: Philippi, says
Luke, was 'first city of its region'. More importantly, it was a
Roman colony.

The more significant claim to fame from a Christian viewpoint
lay in its status as a city of the Roman world. The history of the
site where Philippi now stands goes back to the fourth century BC.
About the year 360 BC Philip II of Macedon took it from the
Thracians. He gave the town its name—Philip's city—fortified it
and exploited its mineral wealth (Strabo, *Geogr.* vii, frag. 34). In
167 BC, under the Roman Aemilius Paulus, it was transferred to
the Roman empire; but its distance from the port of Neapolis prevented it from achieving much importance, and Roman administration settled in Amphipolis (referred to in Ac. 17:1).

However, in 42 BC Philippi was the scene of the battle between
the republican forces of Brutus and Cassius and the imperial
armies of Octavian and Antony. Numbers of Roman veterans
from Octavian's victorious army settled here (so Strabo, *Geogr.*
vii, frag. 41, who remarks that 'in earlier times Philippi was called
Crenides and was only a small settlement, but it was enlarged
after the defeat of Brutus and Cassius'). In the city that now became a Roman colony, there was a further intake of soldiers after
the defeat of Antony and Cleopatra by Octavian in 31 BC at
Actium. The full title of the city now appears as *Colonia Iulia
(Augusta) Philippensis*. The civic dignity of Philippi as a Roman
colonia (attested by an inscription to be seen *in situ*) is specially
mentioned in Ac. 16:12 and is important for the background of
the epistle.

Of all the benefits of the title conferred by Octavian Augustus,

which included the use of Roman law in local affairs and sometimes exemption from tribute and taxation, the enjoyment of the
ius Italicum was the most coveted. This is defined as the privilege
'by which the whole legal position of the colonists in respect of
ownership, transfer of land, payment of taxes, local administration, and law, became the same as if they were on Italian soil; as,
in fact, by a legal fiction, they were' (Cadbury, *BC* iv, p. 190). The
ius Italicum accounts for the presence of Roman officials in the city,
and these are mentioned in Ac. 16:22 (*stratēgoi*, 'magistrates', used
to render the untranslatable Latin term *duoviri*: see A. N. Sherwin-
White, op. cit., pp. 92f.) and 16:35 (*rhabdouchoi*, 'police sergeants',
Latin *lictores*). Such civic officers play an important role in the Acts
narrative, and it is an interesting question to enquire why Luke is
at pains to describe in such full detail both the technical status of
the city and the part played by the Roman administrators in the
accusation and release of the Christian missionaries. The best
answer is that Paul's adventures in Philippi can only be understood in the light of the special circumstances of the indictment
brought against him.

Equally notable is the special character of the charge against
him and the refusal of the Romans to accept the accusation; even
when Paul is unjustly beaten, they are compelled to apologize and
to request that he leave the city. That explains Paul's determined
attitude not to go until he had received a full apology (Ac. 16:35–
39). So much was at stake for Paul's future contact with Roman
officialdom that, as Luke is careful to observe, Paul sensed the importance of leaving Philippi with the record set straight. This
meant that the charges levelled against the apostles were un-
founded, and that the Romans had to admit that they made a
mistake in beating and detaining Roman citizens (Paul, Silas)
when their case had not been heard (Ac. 16:37: 'uncondemned',
Gr. *akatakritoi*; probably this word reflects the Latin term *re incog-
nita*, 'the case not having been investigated').

B. The City's Religious Situation

The special nature of the opposition Paul encountered at Philippi
is brought out by A. N. Sherwin-White (op. cit., pp. 78ff.). This
is the first clash between Christians and non-Jewish authorities.
Previously Paul had been involved in religious riots (at Pisidian
Antioch, Iconium). Now for the first time there is a formal indict-

ment before the municipal magistrates, according to Ac. 16:20. The charges levelled are twofold: (*i*) Paul and his company are accused of causing a disturbance; and (*ii*) they are attempting to introduce an alien religion (16:21) which, the Philippian citizens object, is not permitted. These measures were taken chiefly at the instigation of private initiative (see A. N. Sherwin-White, 'Early Persecutions and Roman Law Again', *JTS* 3 n.s., 1952, p. 204).

The several parts of this accusation are worth following up as background to the setting of Paul's later letter.

(*a*) It seems to be clear that Roman patriotism was strongly influential at Philippi. To be sure, the owners of the slave-girl, possessed by a demonic spirit, were probably looking no higher than for a way to safeguard their commercial interest when they invoked the age-old principle of incompatibility. By this a Roman citizen might not practise a cult that had not received the public sanction of the state. But this restriction was overlooked if the practice was not socially unacceptable, i.e., was not immoral or subversive. No such charge was brought against the apostles. So we are led to suspect that the main allegation lay in their being Jews (16:20).

(*b*) The anti-Semitic flavour of the charge may have been brought about by recent events in the Roman world. In AD 49, Claudius had taken steps to discourage the spread of Judaism. Evidence for this comes in his edict to expel Jews from Rome (Suetonius, *Life of Claudius* 25.4; on which see F. F. Bruce, *New Testament History*, London, 1969, ch. 23). See Ac. 18:2. Perhaps there is a further hint of a Philippian intolerance of alien sects in the banning of the Jews to a place outside the gate. Hence Lydia and her women folk met 'by the riverside' (16:3), not primarily because the river provided a water supply for ceremonial washings (see W. Schrage, *TDNT* vii, pp. 814f.), although this river, the Gangites, is the only notable body of water in the entire region (Strabo, *Geogr.* vii, frag. 21). But their choice was more because it was the spot most conveniently situated outside the city limits, as recent archaeological work has shown. (See Paul Collart, *Philippes, ville de Macédonie depuis ses origines jusqu'à la fin de l'époque romaine*, i, 1937, Paris, pp. 319–22, 458–60; W. A. McDonald, 'Archaeology and St. Paul's Journeys in Greek Lands', *BA* 3, 1940, p. 20; J. Finegan, *Light from the Ancient Past*, ii, Princeton, 1959, pp. 350f.) The evidence concerns the discovery of a colonial

arch on the west side of the city. It is thought to be roughly contemporary with the time when Philippi became a colony and to
symbolize and commemorate its status. It may have indicated the
line of the *pomerium* (the empty space outside the walls of the city
within which foreign deities were not allowed). The *via Egnatia*
ran west beneath this arch and so across the river Gangites
(Appian, *Roman History: The Civil Wars*, iv, 13, 106). This may
well be the 'gate' referred to in Ac. 16:13 and this allusion explains why the Jewish women met beyond it, as was required by
law.

Animosity against the Jews at Philippi may also account for
the continuing hatred of the populace directed at the infant
Christian church, especially in view of the close link it had with
these Jewish women (cf. Lydia's house as the first venue for
Christians, Ac. 16:40). From the letter (1:28–30; 2:15) we learn
of the hostility and persecution which the church continued to
endure, presumably from the pagan world. Paul's call to stand
firm is renewed time and again (1:27; 2:16; 4:1); and the church
is assured of Paul's ongoing interest and confidence as it shares
with him in the grace of God given to his people undergoing
trial (1:7).

(*c*) Yet again it is possible to see the sort of environment which
surrounded the church from a reading of the letter in the light
of archaeological and historical study. The religious climate of
Philippi was that of syncretism (see Beare, pp. 7–9; Gnilka, p. 2;
Collange, p. 20).

The Greek and Roman pantheon of the gods merged with cultic
worship imported from the east, and this fusion was imposed on to
a background of the local Thracian indigenous religion. The
Thracian devotion to Artemis under the name of Bendis (see
Ch. Picard, 'Les dieux de la Colonie de Philippes vers le 1er siècle
de notre ère, d'après les ex voto rupestres', *RHR* 86, 1922, pp. 117–
201; Beare, p. 8) is attested by Herodotus, and is mainly concentrated on fertility rites in an agricultural community. Mars, too,
was venerated as lord of both agriculture and of war under his
Thracian name of Myndrytus. Silvanus, an Italian god of the field
and woods, is attested in Macedonia, as well as more widely
known gods and goddesses imported from the orient: Isis (Philippi
was placed under her protection after 42 BC and Antony's victory), Serapis, Apollo, Asclepius, and from Anatolia, Mēn and

the great Mother-goddess Cybele (see *New Century Bible: Colossians and Philemon*, 1974, pp. 4f.). The last named as 'Most High God' (cf. Ac. 16:17) suggests Sabazios, and this has been linked with Yahweh in hellenized Judaism.

Above all, there was the imperial cult, seen in the existing monuments from the city. Inscriptions mention priests of the deified emperor and his genius: Julius, Augustus, Claudia; and monuments were erected to his gifts of peace (Quies Augusta) and victory (Victoria Augusta).

C. PAUL'S VISITS TO PHILIPPI

The precise time of the arrival of Paul has been estimated at any-where between AD 49 and 52. (The proposal to date it ten years or so earlier made by M. J. Suggs, 'Concerning the Date of Paul's Macedonian Ministry', *NovT* 4, 1960–1, pp. 60–8, is not acceptable.) Scholarly opinion on the historical value of the graphically told stories in Ac. 16:11–40 varies considerably. All students recognize that the narratives are wonderfully vivid. 'One cannot help feeling that this'—the account of the jailer—'is the best story Luke has given us so far' (J. A. Findlay, *The Acts of the Apostles*, London, 1934, p. 154). But at that point agreement stops.

For some interpreters the stories simply betray Luke's artistry as a story-teller and the verisimilitude is part of the literary form, embodying legendary elements to arrest attention and drive home his point, e.g., 'Luke has reported this story (involving an exorcism, a conversion of the jailer, a release from prison) with the full array of Hellenistic narrative art, so that the glory of Paul beams brightly' (E. Haenchen, *The Acts of the Apostles*, ET Oxford, 1971, p. 504; H. Conzelmann, op. cit., pp. 93f.). At the other extreme, Sir William Ramsay (*St. Paul the Traveller and Roman Citizen*, London, 1908, pp. 206–26) finds in the account of Paul's Philippian ministry a sign of Luke's own civic pride, assuming that Luke was the 'man of Macedonia' and that he was encouraging Paul to visit his native city. The 'we-section' opens here (Ac. 16:10), and breaks off at 16:40, suggesting that Luke stayed behind in what was his home town. Intimate details of civic status (16:12), the local officials (16:20, 38), and the frequently occurring earthquakes in that part, were all taken by Ramsay to be hallmarks of an eyewitness narrator, with a personal involvement in the scenes he depicted and described.

Perhaps the truth lies in a middle ground. A. N. Sherwin-White has thrown much light on the essential veracity of Luke's account, at the same time admitting that there are outstanding problems, such as the textual difficulties at 16:12, and that the nomenclature of *stratēgoi* ('magistrates') is not quite the correct designation (op. cit., pp. 92f.). And we should note, with Haenchen (p. 503), how Luke has pieced together different materials into a unified narrative. But, as an overall description of the first mission preaching on non-Asian soil and the effects it produced, we may appeal to this narrative, especially since it is confirmed by what Paul writes in 1 Th. 2:2 (cf. Phil. 1:30), viz., that the mission at Philippi was a time of conflict for Paul and that there he underwent some humiliation as he was haled before the rulers (Gr. *archontes*, corresponding to the Latin *aediles*) at the market place (Gr. *agora*)—a location that has now been excavated: see W. A. McDonald, *BA* 3, 1940, pp. 20f.—and put into jail (the traditional site of this small prison is seen on the north side of the excavations).

Also to confirm the basic trustworthiness of the Acts narrative is the way in which the first conversion story (Lydia) centres on a group of women proselytes. We know that the Jewish faith appealed to women (see E. Schürer, *The Jewish People in the Time of Jesus Christ*, ii, 2, Edinburgh, 1893, p. 308: 'in the case of Jewish propagandism, it was found that it was the female heart that was most impressionable'), and also that in Macedonia, of all the Greek provinces, the status and importance of women was well known. W. W. Tarn and G. T. Griffith (in *Hellenistic Civilisation*, 3rd edn, London, 1952, pp. 98f.) write:

> If Macedonia produced perhaps the most competent group of men the world had yet seen, the women were in all respects the men's counterparts; they played a large part in affairs, received envoys and obtained concessions for them from their husbands, built temples, founded cities, engaged mercenaries, commanded armies, held fortresses, and acted on occasion as regents or even co-rulers.

The presence of women members of the congregation at Philippi is attested at 4:2, 3. (Cf. W. Derek Thomas, 'The Place of Women at Philippi', *ExpT* 83 (1971–2), pp. 117ff.)

The religious climate and political sensitivity in Philippi are to be seen in the story of the ventriloquist slave girl, professedly in the grip of the python spirit (16:16), who declares that the Christian missionaries are heralds of the 'Most High God', i.e., the supreme god of a syncretistic cult (see *BC* v, pp. 93–6). The Philippian jailer, too, acts in a typical way, as a soldier who knows what is at stake if the prisoners manage to escape, and who prefers death to a loss of honour and the inevitable disgrace of the penalty he will receive for his lapse of duty (16:27). When we add in the detail of Paul's response to the current pro-Roman feeling (expressed in 16:37) and see that many verses in his letter presuppose exactly that pride and obligation which marked out Roman colonists—e.g. Phil. 1:27; 2:15; 3:20—we may well believe that the historical narrative in Ac. 16 is firmly founded on fact and not spun out of Luke's imaginative reconstruction.

What is indisputable is that, following Paul's initial evangelism in the city, a church was founded in circumstances which left an indelible mark on Paul's mind. He is able to look back on the 'first day' when God's good work began in his converts' lives (1:3–6). In a phrase (in 4:15) which suggests that he had come to see the significance of his gospel's penetration of the Roman world as it turned in the direction of the imperial city, he views his first visit as 'the beginning of the gospel'. Since that day he has had contact with the church there from time to time (see 4:10, 16 in the commentary).

The Acts record mentions a return visit to Philippi. (Ac. 20:1–6 refers to two such visits.) The prospect of a visit in this period is alluded to in 1 C. 16:5, and to judge from 2 C. 7:5 (cf. 2 C. 2:13) one of these trips was far from pleasant, since Paul was in the midst of the Corinthian crisis. Cordial relations with the Macedonia churches were maintained throughout this bleak time in the apostle's life, and he is impressed by their generosity and sincerity (2 C. 8:1ff.). He boasts of them to other churches—a tribute in 2 C. 8:2 which is reflected in Polycarp's letter (*Phil.* 11:3) and in the Marcionite Prologue to the epistle: 'The Philippians are Macedonians. They persevered in faith after they had accepted the word of truth and they did not receive false prophets. The apostle praises them, writing to them from Rome in prison by Epaphroditus.' Already in his letter to this church the warm, affectionate relationship is present. Of them, as of no other church, he writes: 'Brethren, whom I love and long for, my joy and crown . . . my beloved' (4:1; the nearest parallel is 1 Th. 2:19).

2. THE INTEGRITY AND AUTHENTICITY OF THE LETTER

The areas delimited by these two words are to be distinguished. By 'integrity' we mean the question whether the entire letter as we now have it belonged originally to the document sent by Paul to the Philippians. The issue is that of composition and unity, with the implication that some scholars have doubted whether the letter as we now have it is a whole. They seek grounds within the letter itself for the view that it is a compilation arranged and later published by a person other than Paul himself. Various motives for this process of piecing together Pauline fragments are then offered.

'Authenticity' tackles the issue of how much of the letter, whether seen as a unity or as a compilation, is genuinely Pauline. An extreme view is that all the epistle is non-Pauline (so F. C. Baur, *Paul, the Apostle of Jesus Christ*, ET London, 1875, ii, pp. 45–79); a more temperate view is that some of the fragments come from a hand different from that of St Paul, e.g. 2:6–11 is now largely thought to be a pre-Pauline hymn which Paul has taken over and incorporated. J. Weiss (*Earliest Christianity*, ET New York, 1959 edn, vol. 1, pp. 386f.) was a pioneer in the task of isolating 3:2–4:1 and regarding this section as different in tone from the rest of the epistle. It was reminiscent, he thought, more of Galatians and 2 C. 10–13. Therefore, he concluded, it must belong to another Pauline letter, and by accident it has become attached to the letter to the Philippians. Lastly, the work of the final editor who put the scattered fragments into a whole is seen by some scholars to have left its mark in redactional touches present in a few places in the letter, e.g., the doxology in 4:20 is followed by an additional doxology in 4:23; and the insertion of 'overseers' in 1:1b (so D. W. Riddle–H. H. Hutson, *The New Testament Life and Literature*, Chicago, 1946, p. 123).

Most interpreters, even those who find 3:1–4:1 to be an interpolated fragment, believe that the letter is Pauline. The *carmen Christi* of 2:6–11 may well be pre-Pauline, but it has been taken over, and possibly edited, by Paul for inclusion in the letter.

Attention has mainly been concentrated on the topic of the letter's integrity. The evidence may be considered under two

heads. First, the external data, by which is meant the attestation
of the letter to the Philippians in the early Church. Then, we shall
pass under review the chief arguments pro and con in the discussion over the internal witness, i.e., what the letter itself reveals
about its unity or possible fragmentary nature.

A. *The External Evidence*

(*a*) Polycarp (*c*. AD 135) comments on Paul's ministry among the
Philippians: 'He taught accurately and resolutely while he was
among you in the company of the men of that time, and also when
he was away from you he wrote letters, by which, if you study
them carefully, you will be able to edify yourselves in the faith
imparted to you' (*Phil.* 3:2). The crucial phrase is *egrapsen epistolas
eis has ean enkyptēte*: 'he wrote *letters* by which if you study *them*',
with key-words in the plural.

J. B. Lightfoot (*Epistle to the Philippians*, 1878, pp. 138–42)
interpreted the plural *epistolai* as referring to a letter of importance (cf. Latin *litterae*) as in Eusebius, *HE*. VI. 2.1; 43:3; and he
argued that Polycarp was making a specific allusion to a single
letter as in his reference to Paul's epistle (singular) in *Phil.* 11:3.
So W. Michaelis, *Einleitung*, p. 204; Kümmel, *Introduction to the
New Testament*, ET London, 1966, p. 236. W. Bauer, *Die Briefe des
Ignatius von Antiochia und der Polykarpbrief*, Tübingen, 1920, p. 287,
however, drew attention to current usage (1 *Clem.* 47:1; Ignatius,
Eph. 12:2; *Smyr.* 11:3; *Polyc.* 8:1), and to Polycarp's own distinction between a noun for the singular (*epistolē*) and one for the
plural (*grammata*, 13:1); he therefore insisted that a real plural
was intended. The evidence shows that Polycarp uses both singular (11:3) and plural (13:2) forms of *epistolē*, and that the latter
always means several letters, or a collection of correspondence.
The conclusion is that Paul had written several times to the Philippians. But this is not to be wondered at, since we know of the warm
affection Paul had for this church, and there is attestation of the
high regard he had for the Philippians in the same Polycarp (*Phil.*
11:3: 'for about you he boasts in all the churches'; an inference
from 2 C. 8:1–5?) and the Marcionite Prologue to the epistle:
'The Philippians are Macedonians. They persevered in faith after
they had accepted the word of truth and they did not receive false
prophets. The apostle praises them, writing to them from Rome in
prison by Epaphroditus.' An alternative understanding of the

meaning of *epistolai* in Polycarp is that Polycarp was referring to
a corpus of Paul's letters which was in circulation and was sent to
the churches because it was felt that each church would benefit
from the reading and study of a collection (so Harnack: see C. L.
Mitton, *The Formation of the Pauline Corpus of Letters*, London, 1955).

It then becomes possible, as Harnack thought (see his 'Patris-
tische Miscellen' in *Texte und Untersuchungen zur Geschichte der alt-
christ. Literatur* (Leipzig, 1900), 20.2, p. 91) on the basis of Polycarp's statement in 11:3, read in the light of 1 Th. 1:8, to hold
that the reference in 3:2 includes the Thessalonian letters which
were also sent to churches in Macedonia. Polycarp uses the plural
form (Gr. *epistolai*) again here and the second part of his statement,
quoted above, is similar in wording to 2 Th. 1:4. Also in Polyc.
Phil. 11:4, 'do not regard such men as enemies', there seems to
be a distinct allusion to 2 Th. 3:15. This would confirm Harnack's
theory that Polycarp knew Paul's letters as a collection, and that
he might, therefore, in referring to an assemblage of Pauline letters
addressed to Macedonia, have taken 2 Th. 1:3, 4 as a reference
to Philippians.

This assumption has been taken to what is surely an exaggerated
and unwarranted limit by E. Schweizer ('Der zweite Thessalonicherbrief ein Philipperbrief?' *ThZ* 1, 1945, pp. 90–105), who regards 2 Thessalonians as really a letter sent by Paul to the church
at Philippi. The hypothesis has been justly criticized by W.
Michaelis ('Der zweite Thessalonicherbrief kein Philipperbrief'
ThZ 1, 1945, pp. 282–6) and Gnilka (*Commentary*, p. 11). Beare
(*Commentary*, pp. 12f.) is more open to the idea. (But see the
critique in W. R. Schoedel's edition of *The Apostolic Fathers*, 5,
London, 1967, pp. 33f.)

The final way of disposing of the problem of Polycarp's plural
form is to think that he was making a guess from his reading of
the canonical epistle (at 3:1). So A. Wikenhauser, *New Testament
Introduction*, ET Dublin, 1958, p. 437.

(*b*) Another proposal is to appeal, in support of there being
several letters to the Philippians, to later extant data. The Syriac
Catalogus Sinaiticus (see J. Moffatt's documentation in his *Introduction to the Literature of the New Testament*, Edinburgh, 1918, pp. 174f.)
ascribes some apocryphal letters to Paul's hand, attributing them
to his correspondence with the Philippians. But this evidence is not
highly regarded since the *Catalogus* is dated late (*c.* AD 400), there

seems to be a textual error (A. Souter, *The Text and Canon of the New Testament*, rev. C. S. C. Williams, London, 1954, p. 209), and no such apocrypha have been preserved. The casual remark of Georgius Syncellus, a Byzantine author of *Chronologia*, to the effect that he knew of more than one letter (since he expressly refers to the 'first letter') to the Philippian church, hardly proves anything.

Both sources contribute little of historical worth (so B. S. Mackay, *NTS* 7 (1960–1), pp. 161f.). If the case for our Philippian letter being a compilation is to be proved, it must be on the internal evidence of the letter itself.

B. *The Internal Evidence*

To the question of the letter's unity we now turn, noticing that there seems to be a *prima facie* case for regarding 3:1 as marking a break in Paul's thought. Indeed, the sharp transition in the writer's movement from one subject to another is so noticeable that it has been likened to a gaping 'geological fault' (Collange, p. 22). It represents, says E. J. Goodspeed, *An Introduction to the New Testament*, Chicago, 1937, p. 90, 'a break so harsh as to defy explanation', at least on the assumption that Paul's mind was momentarily diverted to fresh topics of warning and instruction, perhaps occasioned by sudden news that false teachers were at work at the place of his imprisonment, or (more probably, since 3:2 is directed to his readers) that they were likely to invade the Philippian congregation (cf. Moffatt, op. cit., p. 173). What follows, then, in 3:1b–21 is a long digression, written in an observably different style from the foregoing and with a brisk tempo, with words repeated (3:2, 7–9) as though to suggest that Paul's spirit is agitated. He writes to express concern lest the Philippian readers should be caught off guard and become easy prey to the false teachers whom he denounces and whose doctrine and practice he answers in a detailed excursus. Paul's habit of going off at a tangent in response to pressing needs and his equally attested practice of pausing in dictation and so allowing his mind to become distracted (see E. Stange, 'Diktierpausen in den Paulusbriefen', *ZNW* 18, 1917–18, pp. 115f.) have been appealed to in defence of this view.

'Finally, my brethren, rejoice in the Lord' (3:1a), on this traditional understanding of the letter, is the intended conclusion. Paul

is interrupted by stirring, urgent news as he pauses in his dictation. He therefore turns aside to dictate a vehement warning. 'The
same things' (v. 1*b*) is a prospective term, looking ahead to the
admonitions which follow. The long exposé of the gospel's enemies
extends up to and closes on the note of 4:1 with its reiterated call
to steadfastness in the Lord against any danger emanating from
the heretical teachers.

The only other section, says Collange (p. 21), that has led to
a questioning of the letter's essential unity is 4:10–20. The problem is the placing of the section which reads as if it were a simple
acknowledgement on Paul's part of the gifts that had come from
Philippi. Already Paul has mentioned the courier, Epaphroditus,
who brought the gift (2:25). The question is why Paul delays in
the course of his letter to express his appreciation. The answer,
supplied by many scholars, including most who see 3:1–4:1 as a
fragment, is that 4:10–20 is out of place and represents a fragmentary 'Thank you' note written earlier than the main body of the
letter. But there has been some reason given for thinking that this
argument is not as compelling as it seems (see later p. 15).

The case for the letter's unity rests on the cogency of these
replies to problems raised at 3:1*a* and 4:10–20. We turn to review
the ongoing debate, with the bibliographical details supplied at
the end of the section.

C. *Opponents and Champions of the Letter's Unity. The Modern Debate*

The case for the unity of this letter has been made in recent times
largely in response to the arguments which propose a contrary
opinion. We may now review one by one these examples of attack
and counter-defence.

1. 'This most powerful argument yet advanced against the
literary unity of Philippians' is R. Jewett's description of the
assumption made in respect of the opponents of Paul and the
church in this letter. Both J. Müller-Bardorff and W. Schmithals
(see the references given later) maintain that the enemies of the
gospel referred to in 1:27–2:18 and those in 3:18ff. are identical.
However, Paul's attitude to them is different, which fact leads to
the conclusion that the earlier reference is anterior in time and is
part of a letter (B) which was written at a time when Paul's knowledge of the problems was limited. Later, in Letter C (3:2ff.), he
confronted 'a new situation in the addressees' (Müller-Bardorff),

and so responded more appropriately in a fuller warning and denunciation. Letter A is the still earlier 'Thank you' note (4:10–23).

Several writers have disputed this, insisting (a) that the invective of 3:2f. resumes the ethical admonitions of 2:12f. (Kümmel); (b) that in any case we should not overlook the way in which the attack of 3:2f. has been heralded in earlier paragraphs (1:28, 29; 2:14–16), and the violence of Paul's language in 3:2 must not be overstressed (B. S. Mackay); and, we may add, (c) that the types of dangers in the two sets of verses are hardly compatible with each other. 1:27ff. refers to persecution from a hostile world (2:15), whereas 3:2ff. more naturally relates to the inroad of a heresy within the body of the church.

2. 4:10–23 has suggested to some scholars (e.g., Schmithals, R. H. Fuller) that Paul's 'Thank you' note comes unbelievably late in the sequence of the verses and chapters as we have them in our canonical epistle. Do these verses not fall more naturally into a pattern of a letter written prior to the bulk of the canonical letter?

Kümmel replies that in his letters to the churches Paul can wait to express gratitude, though he offers no direct proof of this assertion apart from the observation that already in 1:7 and 2:25 he has alluded to the gift. But these verses contain only allusions, not thanks. A more secure foundation for the counter-proposal that Paul does not delay his thanks is the argument based on the exegesis of 1:3. As the commentary (pp. 63, 64) will maintain, this verse directly refers to the gift as Paul expresses thanks to God 'for all your remembrance of me'. We may take this 'remembrance' to express a dynamic nuance, meaning not only that the Philippians had entertained affectionate thoughts regarding the apostle, but that they had clothed these thoughts in a practical way by the material support they had sent to him repeatedly (4:16), with the latest illustration of their helpfulness just having reached him at the hand of Epaphroditus. Now, at the head of the letter, he expresses his appreciation, albeit in a 'theological' context of thanks to God for their generous thoughtfulness of him.

3. The threefold evidence presented by B. D. Rahtjen is as follows. (a) The aorist tenses of the verbs in 2:25–30 are not epistolary and they form part of a letter which must have been written later and after Epaphroditus returned home with an earlier letter

of thanks (taken to be 4:10–20; this earlier note of acknowledgement is recognized by several scholars, Schmithals, Müller-Bardorff, Beare, Bornkamm, Marxsen; Gnilka who includes 1:1–3:1a with 4:2–7, 10–23 is an exception). The isolation of this letter in 4:10–20 goes back to J. E. Symes in 1914. (b) The meaning of 'farewell' in 3:1 and 4:4 (*RSV* renders 'rejoice', but Rahtjen argues that this is not the real meaning in the context) shows that Paul did not expect to see Philippi again. This pessimistic outlook is held to be different from the confident hope of a revisit in 2:24. (c) The letter contained in chapter 3 (Letter C: 3:1–4:9 are Rahtjen's limits set to this letter) was composed 'on the classical pattern of the testament of a dying father to his children', and 3:1–4:9 is, therefore, to be regarded as Paul's last letter. In the main this division ending at 4:9 is generally agreed. But there are differences of opinion about including the whole of 3:1–4:9, e.g., Schmithals gives 3:2–4:3, 4:8, 9 to this letter; Müller-Bardorff allocates 3:2–21, 4:8f.; Beare stops at 4:1; Bornkamm has 3:2–4:3, 4:8f.; Gnilka extends the letter to include 3:1b–4:1, 4:8f. Several interpreters (e.g. Collange) want to include 4:2–7 in the letter comprising chapters 1–2 on the ground of (i) linguistic and contextual connexions between 4:6 (prayer = 1:3ff. = 2:12ff.) and 4:4 (the Lord's nearness = 1:7, 11 = 2:16), and (ii) the occurrence of the theme of joy in 4:1, 6, which is singularly absent from chapter 3. Equally, 'conflict' is a topic missing in chapter 3, but is found at 4:1, 3.

Rahtjen's arguments have been scrutinized by several scholars, with the result that this position has been virtually overthrown. B. S. Mackay remarks that the 'breaks' in Paul's thought, which Rahtjen argued must be seen in 3:1 and 4:9, are not without alternative explanation. The change in 3:1 with its 'farewell' call is only momentary, and the putative break at 4:9 is not without its precedent (e.g., Gal. 6:10, 11; and Col. 4:2–6 and 7–9). Moreover, 4:20 finds parallels in 1 Th. 5:23, 24 and 2 Th. 3:16 as a penultimate benediction not necessarily signifying the actual end of the letter.

W. Schmauch tackles Rahtjen's chief points one at a time, and argues to the contrary. This is to the effect that the tenses of the verbs in 2:25–30 must be taken as epistolary aorists, denoting the sending of Epaphroditus at the time of the letter's dispatch; that the section 3:1–4:9, which Rahtjen believed to follow a testamentary pattern, does not in fact separate itself on that account from the rest of the letter. The appeal to the testamentary pattern in Dt. 32:33 is singularly inept, since, at an earlier point and (on Rahtjen's showing) in another letter (2:15), Paul explicitly quotes from Dt. 32:5 in LXX; that Rahtjen has overlooked the fact that Paul's exhortation to become his followers or imitators (3:17) is not unique to Philippians (Letter C), but occurs also in 1 C. 4:16, 11:1; 2 Th. 3:7, 9; and that finally (with Mackay who also adopts this criticism) the verb *chairō* in Paul is never found in a formula of farewell greeting. Paul uses *charis* for this purpose. So, the verb *chairō* must be given the alternative meaning of 'rejoice' at 3:1 as at 4:4. The verse 3:1, therefore, does not herald the immediate close of a letter.

4. The enigmatic call of 3:1a, however, is only part of the problem of this verse. Even if we accept the reasoning of Schmauch and Jewett that it is a summons to glad rejoicing and not the inevitable 'farewell' formula, it still remains to clarify the sense of 3:1b. Several scholars (e.g., Bornkamm, Gnilka) see the division of two letters coming precisely at this point, and they are led to this conclusion by the lack of coherence between verse 1a and verse 1b. The issue has been fully investigated by V. P. Furnish, with the conclusion that the first part of the verse looks back to chapter 2, while at verse 1b Paul is consciously looking ahead to the warnings and directives to be given orally by Epaphroditus and Timothy when they come to Philippi (2:23, 28, 29). Paul will, however, put these warnings now in written form, which he does in chapter 3. In this way, Furnish is able to explain the Pauline reference to 'the same things', i.e., these are the matters to be discussed in chapter 3, which later his colleagues will add by their word-of-mouth teaching in his name as they arrive at Philippi. On this understanding, there is no need to separate chapters 2 and 3. Rather, 3:1a and b are the hinge on which the transition of Paul's thought swings as he commends his associates and then promises that they will supplement his instructions which follow immediately (3:2ff.).

5. The upshot of this argument is that chapter 3 (3:1b–21) could have been written at the same time as the earlier chapters (so R. Jewett), and the unity of the letter is believed to be demonstrated by the literary interconnexions which criss-cross between the chapters. T. E. Pollard endeavoured to show that there is 'a

clear terminological relationship between ch. 3 and the rest of the letter'. This upheld him in his conviction that 'there can be little doubt that chapter 3 is integral to the letter as it stands in the canon'. He mentioned several instances of words which recur in different contexts (e.g., 'gain' in 1:21 and 3:7; and the verb 'to reckon' [Gr. *hēgeisthai*] which is found in five places in this letter and only three times outside Philippians in the Pauline homologoumena). His remaining examples are also drawn from the correspondences between the language of the passage in 2:5–11 and the rest of the epistle. But this argument is precarious, since it is now generally agreed that in 2:6–11 Paul is quoting a pre-Pauline christological hymn and its language is clearly non-Pauline.

R. Jewett is on firmer ground when he draws attention to several other correspondences not found in 2:5–11, which is only one segment of the letter. These are the word for 'fruit' (1:11, 22; 4:17); the term for 'sincere' (Gr. *hagn-*) in 1:17 and 4:8; and the verb 'to strive' in 1:27 and 4:3. Perhaps the most striking correspondence (noted by Pollard and Jewett) is the Greek root *polit-* which is seen in the verb of 1:27 and the noun of 3:20, and which is found only here in the undisputed Pauline corpus (cf. Eph. 2:19). That Paul may have wished to drive home the force of his teaching by using a word which could have special meaning to men and women in a Roman colony (Ac. 16:12) is not really relevant. What counts in this discussion is that' he employs a rare word in his vocabulary in two parts of the canonical letter.

6. On a broader canvas several writers (Mackay, Kümmel) call attention to a community of ideas which pervade the entire epistle. The most striking of these are: joy on Paul's part in spite of his prison experience, his 'contentment' under trial, and his unbounded confidence in the Philippians' stand for the gospel.

To this list Jewett perceptively adds an important item. Paul is consciously setting up a link between himself as messianic apostle and the messianic community which is called to share in his sufferings (1:29, 30, 3:10, 11). These elements are seen in an apocalyptic context and they are powerful witness to the unity of Paul's understanding of himself and the Church, if not of the letter of four chapters. A common theme, however, postulates a letter of essential unity, it is claimed.

7. Those who claim that our present letter is a collection of Pauline 'fragments' have to supply the presence and work of a redactor who was sufficiently motivated to want to put the separate 'parts' together to form a semblance of unity. At this point the imagination is given ample scope, if not free rein. W. Schmithals hypothesizes the work of some 'exceedingly prudent man', who, in the interest of disseminating the Pauline epistles throughout the entire Church, so joined together the writings of one congregation that they became unified, and so as a letter it became obligatory for the whole Church in the post-Pauline world. In this way the status of 'holy scripture' is conferred on the resultant letter (Müller-Bardorff).

But W. G. Kümmel pertinently asks how this editor felt able to alter the text of the Pauline fragment, either by excision of the introductions and conclusions, or the addition of connecting sentences, such as 3:1*b*. Obviously the hypothetical sections are incomplete as we have them and form only a torso. We are driven to supply introductions and conclusions which the redactor has deleted in his task of bringing the 'fragments' together into a unified composition. How could he do this, asks Kümmel, if he regarded the text before him as sacrosanct?

This is one of the most serious roadblocks which stands in the way of accepting all redactional theories which argue that our letter is a compilation of disparate fragments. The same verdict must be rendered on W. Marxsen's elaborate reconstruction of the origin of the Philippian correspondence. He partitions the canonical epistle into three letters of epistolary fragments: A: a letter of thanks (4:10–20); B: a letter from prison (1:1–3:1, 4:4–7, 21–23); C: a letter of warning (3:2–4:3, 4:8, 9). His argument for this division is that each section meets a specific need, and that we find it hard to disentangle the three putative sections because the editor has done his work so well and expertly. He imagines that this editor played his role at a time when the Pauline letters were becoming recognized as 'canonical', and he worked to unify the Philippian fragments in order to show what Paul's legacy to the catholic Church consisted of. Further, he displayed artistic and pastoral skill and sensitivity in placing the controversial letter (C) in the middle position and softened its tone by placing after it (in Letter B) a section in 4:4–7, 21–23 which is cordial and a section in 4:10–20 (Letter A) which is less severe. But this imaginative reconstruction is to be questioned. Granted Letter C strikes a discordant warning note, it is not less true that in Letter A Paul is saying some strong words of admonition to the Philippians (4:10, 17) and addressing them on what seems to have been a very delicate pastoral issue: their support for his ministry. This is especially so if C. O. Buchanan has made out his case for believing that Paul regarded Epaphroditus' mission with the church's gift with a certain coolness and lack of enthusiasm (see commentary, p. 161), and that Paul's section in 4:10–20 betrays some irritation that the Philippians have disobeyed his orders not to send the gift.

One is left to wonder why the hypothetical editor did not place the 'acknowledgement section' in 4:10–20 (A) in the front portion of the unified letter, since many scholars, including Marxsen, profess to be amazed that Paul should postpone his 'thanks' until the final chapter in the canonical order. There is no denying the ingenuity of Marxsen's attempt to locate several 'life-settings' of the fragmented and completed epistle, part in Paul's day and part in the editor's period of church life. But so much remains speculative that it is unwise to build on it. It is more safe to admit (with W. Michaelis, C. F. D. Moule) that our knowledge of how Paul's letters were circulated, collected, and published is limited. The process may well have been slow and 'anonymous' (Moule). Even more uncertain is the answer to the question of whether they were edited as compilations of his correspondences were made.

8. Finally, we may take note of an impression which K. Grayston mentions. 'It would be worth while taking the division seriously if it solved some problems of the letter that cannot otherwise be understood. It can scarcely be said that it solves any problems of interpretation.'

Perhaps this is too severe a verdict, since the setting of chapter 3 might be taken to reflect a more serious conflict than is seen in the earlier two chapters. And conceivably the two parts belong to different phases of Paul's life. This is J. Gnilka's view. He sees two letters (a prison epistle: 1:1–3:1a; 4:2–7, 10–23; and a conflict epistle: 3:1b–4:1, 8f.), which are both addressed to Philippi and which are both concerned with rebutting Jewish-Christian propaganda. But they are different in that they emerge out of two distinct epochs of Paul's experience. The first letter belongs to the Ephesian captivity period (AD 53/54–55/56) referred to in Ac. 19. But the polemical letter in chapter 3 is set against the fierce struggle (referred to in 2 C. 7:5) which enveloped him in the following year (AD 56/57). He need not have been a literal prisoner when he actually wrote chapter 3.

But these settings are very speculative, and while they conceivably help us to a more imaginative understanding of Paul's attitude to trouble and strife, no firm conclusions can be drawn from such a tenuous reconstruction. As we shall see in the next section, it is possible to set the various parts of the letter into a set of circumstances that does not require the postulating of different epochs in Paul's missionary life.

BIBLIOGRAPHY FOR SECTION 2, IN ORDER OF MENTION

R. Jewett, 'The Epistolary Thanksgiving and the Integrity of Philippians', *NovT* 12 (1970), pp. 40–53; J. Müller-Bardorff, 'Zur Frage der literarischen Einheit des Philipperbriefes', *Wissenschaftliche Zeitschrift der Universität Jena, Gesellschafts- und sprachwiss. Reihe* 7 (1957–8), pp. 591–604; W. Schmithals, 'The False Teachers of the Epistle to the Philippians', *Paul and the Gnostics*, ET Nashville, 1972, pp. 65–122; W. G. Kümmel, *Introduction to the New Testament*, ET London, 1966, pp. 235–7; B. S. Mackay, 'Further Thoughts on Philippians', *NTS* 7 (1960–1), pp. 161–70; R. H. Fuller, *A Critical Introduction to the New Testament*, London, 1966, pp. 34–7; B. D. Rahtjen, 'The Three Letters of Paul to the Philippians', *NTS* 6 (1959–60), pp. 167–73; F. W. Beare, *The Epistle to the Philippians (Harper-Black's NT Commentaries)*, London/ New York, 1969, pp. 4f.; G. Bornkamm, 'Der Philipperbrief als paulinische Briefsammlung', in *Neotestamentica et Patristica. O. Cullmann Festschrift*, Leiden, 1962, pp. 192–202; W. Marxsen, *Introduction to the New Testament*, ET Oxford, 1968, pp. 61–3; J. E. Symes, *Interpreter*, 10.2 (1914), pp. 167–70; J.-F. Collange, *L'épître de Saint Paul aux Philippiens (CNT)*, Paris/Neuchâtel, 1973, pp. 24–30; W. Schmauch, *Anhang* to E. Lohmeyer's *Der Philipperbrief (KEK)*, Göttingen, 1933; J. Gnilka, *Der Philipperbrief (Herders theologischer-Kommentar)*, Freiburg, 1968, pp. 11–18; V. P. Furnish, 'The Place and Purpose of Phil. III', *NTS* 10 (1963–4), pp. 80–8; T. E. Pollard, 'The Integrity of Philippians', *NTS* 13 (1966–7), pp. 57–66; C. O. Buchanan, 'Epaphroditus' Sickness and the Letter to the Philippians', *EQ* 36 (1964), pp. 157–66; W. Michaelis, 'Teilungshypothesen bei Paulusbriefen', *ThZ* 14 (1958), pp. 321–6; C. F. D. Moule, *The Birth of the New Testament*, London, 1962, pp. 199–204; K. Grayston, *The Epistles to the Philippians and the Thessalonians (CBC)*, 1967, p. 4; J. Gnilka, *Der Philipperbrief*, pp. 23–5.

3. PAUL'S OPPONENTS AND THEIR INFLUENCE ON THE PHILIPPIAN CONGREGATION

A. THE PROBLEM STATED

The problem of identifying the men who form the butt of Paul's attack in chapter 3 is one fraught with special difficulty. Some of these difficulties are inherent in the fact that Paul does not specifically place an identity-label on them and is content to assume that his first readers will know just who they are. They are on the horizon as he writes, so we should not regard their presence or influence at Philippi as entrenched (3:2). But the language Paul uses suggests a very real and dangerous threat. The most we have to go on is his descriptive language in reference to their character and teaching, in such places as 3:2 and 3:18, 19.

Assuming that chapter 3 is an integral part of the Philippian letter, and not an interpolated and separate fragment from some earlier letter to the Philippians, or an independent composition that somehow has got inserted in our canonical letter (see earlier, pp. 15–21), we have still to determine whether (*a*) the enemies of Paul in chapter 3 are related to those mentioned in 1:28, and (*b*) whether the men who are categorized as 'dogs', 'evil-workers', 'mutilators of the flesh' (3:2), are the same as the 'enemies of the cross' in 3:18. It was earlier (p. 15) submitted that there is no connexion between the adversaries of 1:28 and the false teachers in chapter 3. More probably the opposition in 1:27–30 which led to the Philippians' *agōn* (1:30) came from the pagan world, and Paul's emotional reaction to the enemies of the cross (3:18) is less likely to be in regard to the world's indifference and persecution of believers than directed against misguided Christians who perverted his message. In spite, therefore, of a common link-word (Gr. *apōleia* in 1:28 and 3:19) there does not appear to be a common identity of the persons involved.

The more complicated issue is to know whether the danger which threatens from the men referred to in 3:2, and which is answered by Paul in the long debate in 3:3–16, is part of the problem which evokes the warning given at 3:17 ff. In a word, is Paul confronting a single opposition, although with several facets, i.e., Jewish nomism or gnosticizing ideas in 3:2, 6–8, a perfectionist tendency in verses 12–16, and men with libertine ways in verses 18, 19? Or does he switch the defence of his gospel from a Jewish or Jewish-Christian rival understanding of religion in the earlier part of the chapter to a defence against Gentile perversions of 'free grace' that led inevitably to antinomianism and a relaxed morality (described in vs. 18–21)? Within these broad limits of definition there are many permutations and combinations (catalogued by J. J. Gunther, *St Paul's Opponents and their Background*, Leiden, 1973, p. 2, who lists no fewer than eighteen different ways in which Paul's enemies in chapter 3 have been understood).

Two questions, therefore, press for an answer: (*i*) Are Paul's criticisms directed to the same persons throughout the chapter? (*ii*) Who are the Philippian sectarians, and what is their relation to the congregation? If it is suggested that there is a single front on which Paul is fighting—W. Schmithals' thesis for the entire Pauline engagement with opponents in all his churches—then it becomes possible to see how the composite picture, drawn from 3:2ff. and 3:17ff., can be made to fit one class of teachers. In this survey, as in an earlier section, the bibliography is given at the end.

B. THE IDENTITY OF THE AGITATORS IN CHAPTER 3

(*a*) Perhaps the simplest solution to the problem of the entire chapter is to maintain that Paul is meeting Jewish opposition throughout. This position is argued for by Klijn who endeavours to show, point by point, that the teachers reflected in the arguments of 3:2–14 are Jews. They boast of their circumcision (3:2), to which Paul replies with an assertion of the Church as the true Israel (3:3; Rom. 15:8; Gal. 2:7–9; Eph. 2:11). They glory in the 'flesh', cut in the performing of the rite; he glories in Christ alone. They are proud of their advantages (Gr. *kerdē*), especially their knowledge of God (cf. Rom. 2:19, 20); he finds true knowledge of God only in Christ. Their righteousness is based on law (cf.

Rom. 9:31; 10:5; Gal. 2:21). His confidence rests on God's gift.
The Jews pursue and hope to attain righteousness (Sir. 27:8).
Paul sets his sights on different goals and longs to win Christ.

Further pieces of evidence may be adduced. 'Dogs' (3:2) is
used ironically since it was a common Jewish designation of
Gentiles (Mt. 7:6). The claim to being 'perfect' is an equally
common Jewish one. And in 3:17–21 we are presented with two
ways of living, one of which, it is said, is clearly descriptive of
Jews. They seek to reach the true 'goal' of the law (cf. Rom. 13:10;
1 Tim. 1:5), but Paul promises that the only 'end' they attain is
destruction. Their belly-service is part of their ritualistic observance (Rom. 9:4) which centres in the food-laws (Rom. 16:17,
18). The object of their 'glory' (perhaps tantamount to 'God', as
in Ps. 106:20) should rather be a cause for 'shame'. Paul is turning
to an opposite word (Heb. *bôšet*, used as a caricature of false gods
which the Jews idolatrously worshipped, Jer. 11:13, and which
led to 'shame', Isa. 65:13, 66:5) to make a caustic comment on
Jewish worship, with a side-glance at circumcision that required
the nakedness of the human body for the surgical operation to be
performed. Nakedness and shame are placed together in Nah.
3:5 and Mic. 1:11 (cf. Rev. 3:18). Their 'mind' is devoted to
'earthly things', especially in their hopes of an earthly Jewish
community as a nationalistic, theocratic state. Above all, the
Jews deny their 'resurrection' (Rom. 11:15), for which Paul
fervently hopes in spite of their present state of unbelief. When
that period ends, it will be like 'life from the dead'.

There are some superficial ways in which these correspondences
are plausible, but the great argument against the identification is
that Paul nowhere debates with Jews as though they presented a
menace to the peace and unity of the church (Gnilka, p. 211).
Nor is there much conviction in the views put out by Lohmeyer,
supported by Dibelius, Barth, Michaelis, and Beare (who speaks
of the 'dogs' as Jewish missioners who sought to win over Gentile
converts to Judaism), that this debate in chapter 3 reflects the
struggle between church and synagogue. In the background, he
maintains, is Paul's fear that the Philippians will succumb to
pressure or be called on to suffer by martyrdom. But no such
warning against cowardice is found in chapter 3, and the only
way this view could be supported would be to carry over ideas
from 1:28–30 and 2:15 and make the prospect of suffering in

3:10, 11 refer to imminent martyrdom. Michaelis sees a threatened church in chapter 3, but this is very unlikely since 3:2
apparently begins a new warning unheralded earlier in the letter.
An alternative view is to see in these opponents hellenistic Jews
outside the Church who offered a species of false teaching akin
to the heretics in Colossians (Houlden). But this identification
fails to account for the discussion on nomistic righteousness in
chapter 3, a theme noticeably absent from Colossians.

(b) A modification of the above view comes in J. Müller-
Bardorff's essay on the literary unity of the letter. His argument
is based on the way in which Philippians was brought together
as a collection of disparate fragments with Letter C (3:2–4:3 and
4:8, 9) being written in connexion with Paul's sojourn at Corinth
(Ac. 20:2). This means that his earlier letters to Philippi (Letter
A, 4:10–23, composed during Paul's first stay at Corinth, Ac.
18:1; and Letter B, 1:1–3:1, 4:4–7, written at Ephesus during
an imprisonment there in the course of the third missionary
journey, Ac. 19) were sent when Paul had only a limited knowledge of the situation at Philippi. But by the time he comes to
address his Letter C he is better informed. This hypothesis
provides Müller-Bardorff with a guiding principle, viz., Paul
has a 'new situation' in view at 3:2 ff. The men whose lineaments
are now more clearly drawn than in 1:27–2:18 are still the same
group but their false teaching is more sharply etched. They are
both Judaizers and libertines at the same time. The link-term is
the possession of the Spirit—a claim which would fit both the true
gnostic who rejoiced in his fullness of *pneuma* and the true, elect
Israelite who professed to be a man of the Spirit. But the main
objection to this view which sees the Philippian heretics as
spiritualists concerned with both a judaizing and a libertinistic
message is that Müller-Bardorff has eliminated the central point
at issue between Paul and his opponents in 3:2 ff., viz., the law,
as Jewett observes.

(c) In a view which does not fall foul of this criticism but
which sees a connexion between the groups referred to in the
opening and closing sections of chapter 3, H. Köster argues that
the enemies maintained a 'radicalized spiritualized eschatology',
typical of early Christian gnosticism. But the opponents of Paul
were Jewish-Christians who boasted of their special spiritual
qualities and put in a claim to superiority on the ground of their

having completely fulfilled the law, especially in the matter of circumcision. They also laid claim to being 'perfect' on eschatological grounds, viz., that they already possessed the Spirit and imagined that their resurrection was already achieved. This 'transformed eschatology', by which future apocalyptic hopes are brought into the present and regarded as a spiritual possession without remainder, also accounts for Paul's insistence in 3:18ff. that these men are 'enemies of the cross'. They are not Jews nor immoral Christians, but rather misguided Christians who erred in their understanding of Christian existence. Paul's violent language is explained, says Köster, as a sign of the high tensions of the polemic against their arrogant spiritual claims rather than as an indication of their supposed shameful behaviour. The opponents were Jewish-Christian missionary apostles who were upsetting the Pauline cause by advocating a perfection attainable by law-keeping, with circumcision practised as a sign of belonging to the elect community, and a realized eschatology which brought the fullness of the Spirit into the present and led to a risen life on earth and a freedom from suffering and death. This latter feature betrays a gnostic origin.

Köster's position is vulnerable at a number of points. One issue concerns the ground of 'boasting' (3:2). Köster supposes that they boasted of their complete fulfilment of the law, especially in the matter of circumcision, but this is not shown in the text (Schmithals). Also the argument that the gnostic spiritualizing of the resurrection hope was attached to Pharisaic nomism is hard to maintain, since attainment of a spiritual state here and now belongs to a different world from legal rigorism. Finally, verses 3:18ff. are, after all, best seen as describing moral practices. When Köster and Barth interpret the phrase 'they seek their honour in their shame' (v. 19c) as a by-passing of the cross in an endeavour to reach holiness, they put an unnatural construction on what belongs to Christian conduct, and have overlooked the proud boasting of these men in their immoral ways which should rather have filled them with remorse (Jewett).

(d) W. Schmithals' reconstruction of the situation is probably the most thorough-going of all attempts to see chapter 3 as an independent unit, set in the letter. In this view, largely shared by Bornkamm and Marxsen, much is made of Paul's designation of the teachers as men who claimed the badge of circumcision as proving their membership in the Jewish-Christian-Gnostic community. It is important for this interpretation that Paul's polemic does not mention a submission to the Jewish law as such. Circumcision is being seized on by Jewish Christians to promote a gnosticizing propaganda and to conduct a missionary campaign among Paul's mission churches. This explains Paul's rebuttal in 3:3 where we can understand as a background either the heretics' demand for the Philippians to be circumcised or the heretics' boasting of their own circumcision, i.e., their Jewish origin. Schmithals prefers the latter.

The second item in the characterization of the enemies is less ambiguous. In 3:8ff. there are the tell-tale indications that Paul is meeting head-on the claims of gnostic missionaries. They parade their 'knowledge' (cf. 3:8) and profess to have achieved an already experienced resurrection from death (cf. 3:10). They are 'perfect' (3:12f. is Paul's categorical denial), and we should read verse 15 ('let those of us who are perfect') as Paul's ironical use of their self-appellation. The second half of the verse is a further ironical play on the gnostic claim to possess a full divine revelation (see commentary). 3:16 fits in well with the claims to gnostic intellectualism and sophistication. Schmithals sums up:

> It is certain that that group of Jewish Christian Gnostics with whom Paul has to debate in his Asia Minor-Greek missionary territory is boasting of its gnostically understood *apokalypseis* [revelations] (p. 104).

Schmithals' strongest arguments are seen in his exegesis of 3:18–21. The gnostics' denial of a theology of the cross on the supposed ground of their being already raised to new life is reflected in 3:18. Their 'freedom' from restrictions and controls in the twin areas of food and sex is the subject of Paul's fierce words in verse 19. Libertinism for these gnostics entails sexual promiscuity and disregard for all regulations concerning food. Both examples of behaviour are justified by the belief in a present resurrection to a celestial life on earth. With a salvation already achieved, there is no future hope—which Paul asserts in verse 20, followed by a confident statement that our present lowly body awaits the resurrection and the glorification at the *parousia* (v. 21).

The chief hesitation is with Schmithals' handling of 3:2ff. The more gnostic the single-fronted opponents are made, the less apposite is Paul's warning against their nomism and concern for legal righteousness (see Jewett, p. 48). The emphatic declarations in 3:2–6 to do with the sectarians' practices of circumcision and their boasting of the 'flesh', coupled with their claim to be true Jews who were able to trace their blood line to the elect nation, and their pursuit of a standing before God on the ground of their observances of the Torah-religion—all these signs betray a Jewish-Christian missionary movement such as Paul had to face in Galatia and at Corinth (especially 2 C. 10–13). It is true that Schmithals wants to see a common enemy in all these situations. In particular, the link with Jewish-Christian missionary propaganda is worth investigating, and especially the question of the precise issue of debate between Paul and those whom he calls 'evil-workers' (Phil. 3:2; cf. 2 C. 11:13) and who probably advocated circumcision as a necessity for Gentile converts needs a close inspection. The weakness of Schmithals' theory lies here, with an unconvincing attempt to explain the heretics' practice of circumcision. Marxsen senses this in his somewhat feeble counter-proposal that Paul has read too much into the circumcision practised by these intruders, as though he were not sure what their practice implied.

If this investigation turns out in such a way as to emphasize the Jewish character of the opposition in 3:2ff., and if the gnostic features in 3:18ff. are already demonstrated, the conclusion will follow that Paul is encountering two sets of false teaching in this one chapter, and we are forced to assume that Paul had different opponents in mind in the two sections. This is a common view, shared by a host of commentators (Lightfoot, Vincent, Kennedy, H. C. G. Moule, Michael, Michaelis, Dibelius, E. F. Scott, Beare, Friedrich, and most recently G. Baumbach). It runs into a major difficulty, however, pointed out by Schmithals, who argues that this one point favours his hypothesis of a one-front opposition. The problem is to explain the lack of transition from Judaizing nomists to gnostic libertines with a side-glance at the congregation in the middle of 3:10–16.

R. Jewett has endeavoured to meet this objection on the theory that there were three sets of enemies in view as Paul wrote the Philippian letter, viz., 'divine men' missionaries at the city of Paul's imprisonment who stressed the exalted nature of the

Christian life, especially of the apostles; the Judaizers who attacked the Philippian church from the outside; and the libertinistic heretics who had emerged from within the Philippian congregation. Using Jewett's contribution as a base, we may explore the second question.

C. THE REACTION OF THE PHILIPPIANS TO THE SECTARIAN INFLUENCES

The second issue is to inquire who these enemies may have been and what relationship they bore to the congregation.

(a) The Jewish character of the agitators whose presence Paul heralds in the warnings of 3:2ff. seems clear. Even more so, they are Jewish Christians who bear resemblances to the Pauline enemies in 2 C. 10–13. Recent studies by D. Georgi, G. Friedrich, J. Gnilka, R. Jewett and J.-F. Collange have shown the extreme plausibility that such men were charismatic figures who boasted of their spiritual prowess and lordly bearing, and claimed to exhibit the transcendent power of the exalted Christ in their lives and service. The title given to such a character is 'divine man' (Gr. *theios anēr*). Though there have been several challenges (e.g., Baumbach) to the propriety of this title (see Tiede), it seems clear that, by whatever name they were known at Corinth, their influence was felt along these lines. They placed a high value on ecstatic visions, miracle-working, rhetorical utterances that claimed to be inspired, an assertive personal demeanour, letters of commendation to validate their status and their right to the financial support of the congregations, and, above all, a transcendent life-style, in which suffering and hardship were not experienced. Their influence on the Corinthian congregation seems to have led to a practice of immoral ways (2 C. 12:20, 21) and a claim to 'perfection' (a claim denied especially in 2 C. 13:9). Most of these traits are known inferentially from Paul's apologetic defence of himself and his apostleship, but the indirect evidence for their presence and power at Corinth is almost undeniable.

It becomes possible, on the supposition that the letter to the Philippians is a unity, to believe that Paul has these people (in the church at Ephesus?) in view in 1:12–30 (see commentary) and that he returns to his defence of the Christian life as one of suffering and humiliation in 3:8–10 and 4:11–13. The link between

3:2 and 2 C. 10–13 through the common description 'evil/
deceitful workers', suggests that these are Jewish Christian
apostles, who are infected with a hellenistic spirit whose hall-
mark is assertive power and who are conducting a smear campaign
against Paul. They charge him with lacking the distinctive
features of the 'divine' apostle—eloquence, esoteric knowledge,
powerful presence, and the right to maintenance. They advocate
a circumcision-ritual on the ground that the Gentiles need to be
brought into the community of the true Israel, and especially so
since (as Jewett argues) in this way they can deflect national
Jewish hatred and persecution away from themselves. They
practise the rite of circumcision and so circumvent the charge
that they are unfaithful to Israel's covenant status. In so practising
and advocating circumcision, they avoid 'persecution'—as Paul
realized in Gal. 5:11, 12 and 6:12–16. His response in Philippians
is to deny the Jewish character of circumcision and boldly claim
its spiritual, non-literal counterpart (as in Phil. 3:3) for the new
Israel, to stress the sole sufficiency of the cross as a basis for
righteousness (as in Phil. 3:7–9), to claim no perfection in this
life in anticipation of a future resurrection (as in Phil. 3:10, 11),
and to accept the vocation of the suffering apostle (as in Phil. 3:10).

Such sectarian missionaries as he roundly condemns in 3:2–16
may well have led their followers into morally unacceptable ways,
if we follow the evidence of 2 C. 12:20, 21 and Gal. 5:13–26,
6:7–10. They did so apparently on the score that they were 'men
of the Spirit', and so unrestrained by any ethical control, since
their body and its appetites and instincts were religiously irrelevant. Paul launches into his condemnation of them on this point
in 3:18–21. But he has reason to believe that such a ready welcome
to this teaching was already in effect at Philippi, if not yet entrenched. It is the merit of some recent work on the letter to have
shown that chapter 3 does not remain in isolation but that the
lessons Paul gives belong to the entire epistle.

This line of investigation (represented in Jewett) is different
from the studies of Schmithals, Gnilka, and Collange, all of whom
see the enemies of chapter 3 belonging to a new situation, isolated
from the rest of the letter. In chapters 1–2 the threats to the church
came from the outside (Gnilka), whereas in chapter 3 the danger is
present within the community and that chapter represents a
'polemic letter' (*Kampfbrief*). Collange suggests that chapter 3

reflects a more violent opposition to the Philippian church than the first rumblings felt in chapters 1–2. Both Gnilka and Collange place the onset of the heresy later than Paul's captivity out of which he wrote chapters 1–2, and surmise that the polemical tract was written when Paul was a free man, either before his writing 1 Corinthians (Collange) or 2 Corinthians (Gnilka). See pp. 20, 21.

The merit of Jewett's study is that it avoids the necessity of finding suitable and various *Sitze im Leben* for the hypothetical fragments of the canonical letter.

(*b*) The ethos and condition of the church at Philippi are plain once we take into our view the whole letter. We should strictly regard 3:2 as a warning addressed to the church about false teachers on the horizon, and the latter are differentiated from the church members in 3:17, 18. But it is just as clear that Paul's warnings in chapter 3 take on a special poignancy and relevance if, as can be shown by studies such as Jewett's, it is the case that the congregation as a hellenistic Christian community was open to the influences that these false teachers represented. The data include the following: (*i*) the congregation's confidence in attaining its perfection in this life. They seem to have characterized themselves as 'the perfect ones' (Gr. *hoi teleioi*, 3:15), probably on the mistaken ground that they had already achieved their resurrection (Holladay). Paul counters this with his insistence on a not-yet-accomplished resurrection (3:10, 11) at a future *parousia* of Christ (1:10, 2:16), when the process of perfecting will be complete (1:6, 11) in the resurrection of the body (3:21).

Then (*ii*) the Philippian church was beset by problems of conceit (2:3) and vaunting superiority (2:3), which led to a selfishness and egocentricity (2:4) that broke the *koinōnia* spirit of goodwill for the community as a whole. The concentration on individual interests to the exclusion of concern for the 'well-being' of the entire community (called 'salvation' in 2:12; see commentary) resulted in petty squabbles (4:2) and a spirit of complaining (2:14). Paul supplies the antidote with his teaching on the corporate nature of the Christian life (2:1–4) over against a gnosticizing individualistic piety, and calls for an end to private wrangling (2:14, 4:2, 3). His teaching on the societary aspects of the Christian life (2:12) follows on a memorable exposition of what it means to be 'in Christ Jesus' (2:5), i.e., to be a member of Christ's Church. This is illustrated by a recital of the story of salvation in which the path is traced by the lowly Christ who is now exalted as Lord of the world (2:6–11). Under his rule the Philippian church is called to live out its life, by conforming to the way of life set by his selfless and sacrificial action on the church's behalf. See commentary, pp. 93, 102, 103.

(*iii*) The summons to 'obey' (2:12), and the insistence Paul gives that the Philippians should follow the pattern set by the apostle and his co-workers (3:17), as exemplified in the apostolic traditions (4:9), suggest that this church was ethically confused. They seem to be in doubt over even the elementary moral standards in their surrounding society (4:8), and were in danger of falling apart in fragmented disarray as a community (so 2:14). It is possible that the onset of opposition from their neighbours had brought these problems to the surface, especially if the teaching had been given them by infiltrating teachers that the Christian life was one of glorious triumph, to which suffering is unknown. This would explain the Pauline theodicy in 1:27–30, in which he justifies their experience of privation and persecution as a privilege accorded them by God, and calls them to stand firm (4:1). The Christ-hymn (2:6–11) is quoted to enforce the soteriological truth that the way to glory is by humiliation and obedience, even at the cost of death. They must learn this just as they see it displayed in their hymnic *credo*.

The emphasis in this letter on Paul's circumstances as a suffering apostle may also have this defensive purpose in mind. No doubt, Paul's apostleship was attacked on the score that he was no glorious figure like the hellenistic teachers (see commentary on 1:12–18, and pp. 29f). He accounts for his role as a prisoner by pleading that this is the true vocation of a servant of the Christ who came to his destiny as Lord along a path of humiliation and loss. He calls for rejoicing with himself (2:17, 18), not criticism, just as he deflects criticism away from the suffering Epaphroditus (2:25–30). He is at pains to explain his situation (1:12), and later to have Timothy amplify the details of his imprisonment (2:23). Then he hopes for his release (2:24), and for a revisit to Philippi where he can give an account of his experience, lest his credibility at Philippi should be lost (2:16). In the meanwhile, he calls for their confidence in himself as a true 'servant of Christ Jesus' (1:1) in 1:26: 'let your boasting (*sc.* not shame) overflow in Christ Jesus when you think of my situation and against the

day when I come to be present with you once more.' Several
scholars (Georgi, Müller-Bardorff, Gnilka) think that Ac. 20:3–6
reports this journey undertaken to settle accounts with the
heretics—a purpose Luke has suppressed.

(iv) Finally, the loss of eschatological hope may well have
distorted the Philippians' understanding of the gospel as Paul
expressed it. It may have cast doubt on the ethical dimension of
future judgment and have occasioned Paul's repeated insistence
on the final day (1:6, 10, 28; 2:16; 4:5). The fading from view
of a *telos* in history, after the typically Greek idea of time and
history as static or circular (see O. Cullmann, *Christ and Time*,
ET London, 1951, pp. 51ff.), possibly explains Paul's diagnosis of
the Philippians as lacking in the power of discrimination (1:10)
and as guilty of moral obfuscation (4:8). It may also throw light
on the word of judgment he reserves for false teachers whose
influence on the congregation he fears: 'their end (Gr. *telos*) is
destruction' (3:19).

CONCLUSION

It looks as if there were several influences exerted on the Philippian congregation which, contrary to first impressions (voiced by
Filson and Beare), was racked by threatening false teachings. We
can identify one such as a Judaizing inroad after the example of
the men referred to in Gal. 2:3–8. Then there was a gnosticizing
libertinism and enthusiasm. The problem is to relate the two and
to know how a single congregation could be infected with ideas
which are at first glance lacking in a common denominator.
Jewett, however, finds a common concern in the promise of
perfection held out to the Philippians:

> The Judaizers could have offered perfection through circumcision
> which made one an heir of the biblical promises, and the libertinists
> would have promised it through an exalted spiritual self-consciousness
> which released one from the imperfections of time and morality.

This is a suggestive proposal, especially since it accounts for the
single common issue on which Paul offers his response. The
attractiveness to the Philippians of the hellenistic theology underlying the 'divine men' notions would just as readily yield to Paul's
insistence on humility in 2:1–4 and 4:12, by which also all perfectionist pretensions are exposed and judged. And Paul's clear

and indivisible reply in chapter 3 accounts for the swift transition from one set of opponents to another, since Paul is offering one basic argument to clarify the issues which have made his friends vulnerable to propaganda. Jewett identifies these issues as a misguided eschatology and a lack of humility because of a failure to grasp the significance of the cross, which is both the foundation of saving experience and a pattern for Christian life.

We propose a modification of this overall thesis, which seems to be essentially correct. In addition to an offer of perfection, the Philippian intruders denied an understanding of the Christian vocation as a commitment to lowliness and suffering that Paul is championing in rebuttal of them. The root error was a presentation of the believer's life in terms of triumphalism and present glory. At all costs suffering and persecution must be avoided. Paul is being subjected to vexatious opposition in his prison life by those who believe that the 'divine' apostle, as the gnostics portrayed him (Schmithals), was an impressive figure far removed from failure. Paul enters a warning in 3:2ff. against Jewish Christians who carry through a missionary campaign among his converts to persuade them to receive circumcision in order thereby to avert persecution from the Jews, especially at a time when pressures to conform to national identity in the wake of patriotic sentiment in Palestine are strong (Jewett). Equally we may account for the hellenistic libertinism, condemned in 3:18ff., which is advocated on the ground that Christians are risen men of the Spirit who have nothing to do with suffering.

Paul's constant theme throughout this epistle is to supply a rationale for Christians in time of persecution (1:27-30), to enunciate the true motifs of Christian living under the lordship of Christ, once humbled and suffering unto death (2:1-13), and to reiterate the genius of life-in-Christ as the following of a path which is necessarily one of weakness (3:10, 11) in hope that one day the resurrection will usher believers to a new existence (3:20, 21).

But that hope is essentially future, and is known only in faith. For the present, Paul's picture of the Christian life is at odds with the sectarian viewpoints, and this explains the undertone of firm resistance to their ideas and practices which runs like a thread through this letter in all its chapters.

BIBLIOGRAPHY FOR SECTION 3, IN ORDER OF MENTION

A. F. J. Klijn, 'Paul's Opponents in Philippians iii', *NovT* 7 (1964), pp. 278–84; J. Gnilka, *Der Philipperbrief (Herders Theologischer-Kommentar)*, Freiburg, 1968; E. Lohmeyer, *Der Philipperbrief (KEK)*, 1933; M. Dibelius, *An die Philipper (HzNT)*, Tübingen, 1937; K. Barth, *The Epistle to the Philippians*, ET London, 1962; W. Michaelis, *Der Brief des Paulus an die Philipper (Theologischer Handkommentar)*, Leipzig, 1935; F. W. Beare, *The Epistle to the Philippians*, Harper-Black, New York/London; J. L. Houlden, *Paul's Letters from Prison (Pelican Commentaries)*, Harmondsworth, 1970, p. 105; J. Müller-Bardorff, as on p. 21; R. Jewett, 'Conflicting Movements in the Early Church as Reflected in Philippians', *NovT* 12 (1970), pp. 362–90; H. Köster, 'The Purpose of the Polemic of a Pauline Fragment (Phil. III), *NTS* 8 (1961–2), pp. 317–32; W. Schmithals, as on p. 21; G. Bornkamm, as on p. 21; W. Marxsen, as on p. 21; R. Jewett, 'The Epistolary Thanksgiving and the Integrity of Philippians' as on p. 21; W. Marxsen, as on p. 21; J. B. Lightfoot, *Commentary*, London, 1896, pp. 141, 153; M. R. Vincent, *Commentary on the Epistle to the Philippians, etc. (ICC)*, Edinburgh, 1897, pp. 92, 116; H. A. A. Kennedy, *The Epistle of Paul to the Philippians (EGT)*, London, 1903, pp. 448, 461; H. C. G. Moule, *The Epistle of Paul the Apostle to the Philippians*, Cambridge, 1906, pp. 57, 71; J. H. Michael, *The Epistle of Paul to the Philippians (MNTC)*, London, 1928, pp. 133, 171-6; W. Michaelis, op. cit., pp. 53, 62; E. F. Scott, *The Epistle to the Philippians (IB)*, Nashville/New York, 1955, pp. 73, 99; F. W. Beare, op. cit., pp. 109, 134; G. Friedrich, *Der Brief an die Philipper (NTD)*, Göttingen, 1961, pp. 116–21; Günther Baumbach, 'Die Frage nach den Irrlehrern in Philippi', *Kairos* 13.1–4 (1971), pp. 252–66; R. Jewett, 'Conflicting Movements', p. 389; D. Georgi, *Die Gegner des Paulus im 2. Korintherbrief*, Neukirchen, 1964; G. Friedrich, 'Die Gegner des Paulus im 2. Korintherbrief', in *Abraham Unser Vater. Festschrift für Otto Michel*, Leiden, 1963, pp. 181–215; J. Gnilka, op. cit., pp. 211–18: 'Exkurs 4: Die Philippischen Irrlehrer', and *idem*, 'Die antipaulinische Mission in Philippi', *BZ* n.s. 9 (1965), pp. 258–76; R. Jewett, 'Conflicting Movements', pp. 368–71; J.-F. Collange, as on p. 21, pp. 28–30, 33f., 120f.; G. Baumbach, loc. cit., p. 263; D. L. Tiede, *The Charismatic Figure as Miracle Worker*, Missoula, Montana,

1972; R. Jewett, 'The Agitators and the Galatian Congregation', *NTS* 17 (1970–1), pp. 198–212; Carl R. Holladay, 'Paul's Opponents in Philippians 3', *Restoration Quarterly* 12 (1969), pp. 77–90; J. Gnilka, op. cit., pp. 8–11; Collange, op. cit., pp. 33f.; Gnilka, op. cit. pp. 22–5; D. Georgi, *Die Geschichte der Kollekte des Paulus für Jerusalem*, Hamburg, 1965, p. 52; J. Müller-Bardorff, op. cit., p. 604, n. 43; Gnilka, op. cit., p. 25; F. V. Filson, *A New Testament History*, London, 1965, p. 232; F. W. Beare, op. cit., p. 15; R. Jewett, 'Conflicting Movements', p. 387; W. Schmithals, *The Office of Apostle in the Early Church*, ET Nashville, 1969; R. Jewett, 'Agitators and the Galatian Congregation', pp. 204ff.

4. THE LETTER'S DATE AND PLACE OF COMPOSITION

A Dating in Paul's Captivity at Rome

The traditional dating of the epistle is associated with the apostle's captivity at Rome (Ac. 28:16, 30). By 'traditional' is meant that the witness to this letter's origin at Rome goes back to the second-century Marcionite prologue (see p. 9) as the oldest attestation; and it is still customary to speak of Philippians as one of the Imprisonment Epistles dated when Paul was in Rome (see W. Michaelis, *Einleitung in das Neue Testament*, 2nd edn, Bern, 1954, p. 204, who remarks that no one questioned this dating until G. L. Oeder in 1731). As this imprisonment lasted for 'two whole years' the question arises: To which part of the captivity does the epistle belong? The view of Lightfoot (*Commentary*, ch. 2) is that the letter was written within the early period of that time, and that it is, in fact, the earliest of the Imprisonment Epistles. His grounds are, first, the linguistic affinity of Philippians with Romans; and, second, its marked difference, on the grounds of content and language, from Colossians and Ephesians, which are placed nearer the close of the period of Roman captivity.

Among the writers who champion the Roman dating, this relative placing of Philippians is almost universally rejected, on the following grounds: (*i*) A length of time is required for the growth of hostility to the apostle (1:15ff.), as also for the progress of the gospel in the place of his confinement (1:12ff.); (*ii*) the journeys and communications between Rome and Philippi demand a reasonable interval of time. It will be shown later that at least four (probably five) separate journeys to and from Rome are implied in the letter, and it is necessary to fit the time taken by these journeys into the period before the composition of the letter; (*iii*) the legal issue of the trial is still in the balance at the time of writing, and this points to the end of the captivity when Paul was tried and acquitted, or executed, or exiled. Or possibly the case against him went by default (cf. H. J. Cadbury's Note XXVI: 'Roman Law and the Trial of Paul' in *BC* v, pp. 297ff., and L. P. Pherigo's 'Paul's Life after the Close of Acts', in *JBL* 70 (1951), pp. 277–84. Also see G. Ogg, *The Chronology of the Life of Paul*, London, 1968, ch. 21; J. J. Gunther, *Paul: Messenger and Exile*, Valley Forge, 1972, pp. 142ff.); (*iv*) little weight of importance can be attached to the variations in the apostle's vocabulary and style. The use of different words in the other Imprisonment Epistles may be explained largely on the score of different subject-matter, and we must bear in mind that the character of Philippians is more informal and personal than that of the other letters. Affinities between Philippians and other letters in the Imprisonment Epistles group (Col., Eph.) on the one side, and other Pauline letters, do not suggest a one-sided indebtedness (J. Schmid, *Zeit und Ort der paulinischen Gefangenschaftsbriefe*, Freiburg, 1931, pp. 122ff.). The closest literary affinity is with Romans, as Lightfoot has demonstrated; but here again this close agreement betokens merely a common author whose mind is addressed to similar topics in both letters. There is no real argument based on affinities of content and style. W. Michaelis, *Die Datierung des Philipperbriefes*, Gütersloh, 1933, p. 17, maintains the view that the dating of the letter must be fixed independently of language and style.

These objections raised against the possibility of dating the writing of the letter at an early point in Paul's two-year imprisonment have been tackled by C. O. Buchanan ('Epaphroditus' Sickness and the Letter to the Philippians', *EQ* 36 (1964), pp. 157–66, especially pp. 163ff.). His counter arguments, however, fail to resolve the problem of the journeys undertaken or postulated (see later, pp. 40, 41), and the serious tone of 1:7, 20 hardly seems to fit in with the situation when Paul was a prisoner in Caesarea in the custody of Felix and Festus, as Buchanan suggests. To the contrary, he is faced with a more acute trial from which no appeal to Caesar can extricate him. His *appellatio* has brought him to Rome. All local proceedings against him have been quashed. So there is some confusion in this argument. Buchanan admits that point (*i*) is difficult to answer, and he is able to oppose it only by giving a non-precise meaning to 1:12.

The dating of the epistle at the close of the Roman captivity rests upon several grounds. All assume that Paul was a prisoner at the time of his writing the letter, at least 1:1–2:30 (ch. 3 is different, see pp. 21, 31). T. W. Manson ('The Date of the Epistle of the Philippians', *BJRL* 23 (1939), pp. 182–200 [=*Studies in the Gospels and Epistles*, ed. M. Black, Manchester, 1962, pp. 149–67]) finds indications in the letter that Paul was at liberty when he wrote it. He regards the trial as already past. The apostle is now a free man, and his 'bonds' are his continuing experiences of hardship in every place. This reading of 1:7, 12f., 16f., 30 can hardly be correct. These verses indicate that Paul's imprisonment is still going on at the time of writing.

(*i*) The writer is a prisoner (see 1:7, 13, 14, 16 *AV*) and his imprisonment is serious (1:20ff., 1:30, 2:17) because the issue of life or death is uncertain. It may result in Paul's release, which is his fervent hope for the sake of the Philippians (1:19, 24, 25), or it may be a fatal issue which will be the sentence of death (1:20–23, 2:17) and the martyr's crown (3:11).

(*ii*) From the information given in the book of Acts we know of only three imprisonments. These are Ac. 16:23–40, at the time of Paul's first visit to Philippi; Ac. 21:32–23:30, the arrest at Jerusalem, followed by a two years' detention at Caesarea (24:27); and Ac. 26–28:16, the voyage to Rome as a prisoner, followed by a further imprisonment of two years' duration (28:30). The epistle to the Philippians cannot have been written during the first; most commentators believe that the case for a Caesarean origin is weak and unconvincing; therefore it must have been written during the Roman imprisonment.

(*iii*) This is confirmed by references to the scene of Paul's captivity in 1:13: 'it has become known throughout the whole praetorian guard'. The original word *praitōrion* is taken by the *RSV*, which follows Lightfoot's conclusion here, to be the 'praetorian guard' at Rome (see the latest discussion by B. Reicke, 'Caesarea, Rome, and the Captivity Letters', in *Apostolic History and the Gospel*, ed. W. W. Gasque and R. P. Martin, Exeter, 1970,

p. 283); but for a difficulty in regard to the vast number of such praetorian soldiers, see the commentary at 1:13.

A closing greeting is conveyed to the readers from 'those of Caesar's household' (4:22). This is taken by Lightfoot and others to be an allusion to the imperial slaves or freedmen in the service of the emperor at the capital city.

(*iv*) A further argument in favour of Rome is the church situation in the place of Paul's confinement. The evidence of 1:15–17 suggests to some (see Lohmeyer, ad loc.) that Paul is not *persona grata* in this Christian community. On this basis it is argued that these hostile conditions reflect the situation at Rome where Paul is on 'strange ground' (J. Schmid, op. cit., p. 109) and where rivalry to his mission work is a feature, at least as we may learn by inference. F. W. Beare writes:

> Quite conceivable [is the theory] that when he did come to Rome, he found that his misgivings were entirely and unhappily justified, for some of the local leaders (perhaps even more, some of their followers) were jealous of his transcendent gifts and great renown, and redoubled their activities with mixed motives, with a zeal that was not wholly pure. Such a state of affairs seems unlikely at Caesarea and impossible at Ephesus (op. cit., p. 17).

If this is an inferential statement, partly based on an understanding of 1:15–17 (see commentary for some alternative explanation), O. Cullmann (*Peter: Disciple, Apostle, Martyr*, ET London, 1953, pp. 104ff.) and T. Hawthorn ('Philippians i. 12–19', *ExpT* 62 (1950–1), pp. 316f.) have tried to give it exegetical support. The former points to the evidence of 1 Clem. 5 which alludes to the animosity of the church at Rome against the apostles. But the verbal agreement is not as close as Cullmann suggests. The key term in 1 Clem. 5:5 (Gr. *zēlos*, 'jealousy') is not present in Philippians (cf. criticism brought by Michaelis, *Einleitung*, p. 206). T. Hawthorn thinks of the activity of preachers engaged in polemic against the Roman state (see commentary, p. 73). More probably, however, we should see in 1:15–17 the presence of a group of religious leaders who have a different understanding of the Christian life from that of Paul (see R. Jewett, 'Conflicting Movements in the Early Church as Reflected in Philippians', *NovT* 12 (1970), pp. 362–90, espec. pp. 371f.).

There are, however, certain reservations which have made scholars pause before regarding the above conclusion as certain and indisputable. These difficulties may be enumerated as follows:

(*i*) The menacing situation, reflected in such verses as 1:20–23, 30, 2:17 with their indication that death was an imminent possibility for Paul, hardly tallies with the comparative freedom and relaxed atmosphere described at the close of Acts. If Philippians was written at Rome it is necessary to postulate an unfavourable development in the apostle's relations with the authorities which led to a change for the worse in his conditions and prospects. His circumstances would have altered from those of the 'free custody' (*libera custodia*), as it was called in Ac. 28 (cf. Eusebius, *HE*, 2:22, 1) to those of strict confinement and impending danger of Phil. 1:20ff., 30, 2:17. But see Buchanan, loc. cit., pp. 164f., for some arguments to the contrary.

To this difference between the two situations there may be added the difference between the charge levelled at the apostle according to Philippians and that on which he was remitted to Rome. In the first case, the gravamen was the preaching of the word (1:13, 16); but in Jerusalem he was arrested because of his supposed violation of the temple (Ac. 21:28, 24:6, 25:8) and he is sent to Rome on this charge (cf. Ac. 28:17). (See Kümmel, *Introduction*, pp. 233f.)

(*ii*) Much has been made, chiefly by A. Deissmann ('Zur ephesinischen Gefangenschaft des Apostels Paulus', in *Anatolian Studies Presented to Sir W. M. Ramsay*, ed. W. H. Buckler and W. M. Calder, Manchester, 1923, pp. 121–7) who first elaborated the point, of the great distance and frequent journeys and communications between Philippi and Rome which are required by the internal evidence of the letter itself. He gives a list of no less than five journeys to and from the place of Paul's confinement, together with an extra four trips envisaged in the future plans of Paul. These are given as follows:

(*a*) The journey of Timothy to Paul's side at the place of his captivity. He is not mentioned in the journey to Rome (Ac. 26–28) and must have travelled separately from Paul's companions who were involved in the shipwreck since he was with the apostle when the letter was composed (1:1).

(*b*) A message from the scene of captivity to Philippi to say that Paul is a prisoner and is in need (4:14).

(*c*) After the collection of a love gift at Philippi it is brought by Epaphroditus, who travels from Philippi to the place of the imprisonment (2:25, 4:18).

(*d*) Epaphroditus arrives at Paul's prison, where he falls sick (but see B. S. MacKay 'Further Thoughts on Philippians', *NTS* 7 (1960–1), pp. 161–70, who suggests that Epaphroditus fell sick on his journey to Paul and not at the place of Paul's confinement. This is based, he says, on 2:30 [see commentary, pp. 120–3]. His argument is accepted and extended by C. O. Buchanan (loc. cit., pp. 158–60), and news of this somehow reaches the church at Philippi (2:26). Paul did not originate this message, otherwise he would have then mentioned the gift and said 'Thank you' for it.

(*e*) Paul now receives a message that the Philippians have heard of their messenger's sickness, and he is able to report that this news has had a painful effect upon Epaphroditus himself (2:26).

The journeys which are planned according to inferences in the letters are:

a. Ephaphroditus' journey to bring the letter to Philippi (2:25, 28).

b. Timothy's journey in the near future from the place of Paul's confinement to Philippi (2:19).

c. Journey *b* will mean that when Timothy fulfils his mission he will return to Paul so that he 'may be cheered' when he learns of their state (2:19).

d. Paul's journey in the near future (2:24).

Deissmann remarks that 'those enormous journeys', as he called them (*jene ungeheuren Strecken*, p. 126), would have taken, with intervals, longer than two years and so cannot be fitted into the period of Ac. 28:30; that the use of the adverbs 'soon' (2:19, 24) and 'immediately' (2:23) gives the impression that the distance between the place of writing and the city of Philippi is not great, and that such rapid and repeated travel is more likely to be possible in the time of the imprisonment, if the apostle is captive at a place nearer to Philippi than Rome. He names Ephesus as the most likely alternative. He sums up: 'Everything that renders the Roman hypothesis incredible, becomes quite reasonable if *x* (the place of Paul's captivity) is Ephesus' (loc. cit., p. 126).

In reply to this argument, based on distance and travel time, which is used by those who oppose the traditional dating of the epistle, it may be said that a lot depends upon the approximate calculation of the time taken to make the journey from Philippi to Rome. A distance of 730 land miles, with the addition of one or two days' sea voyage across the Adriatic, is envisaged. Lightfoot gives the required time as a month, but a period of 7–8 weeks would be more accurate. See P. N. Harrison (*Polycarp's Two Epistles to the Philippians*, Cambridge, 1936) who writes: 'in order to accomplish the whole journey in 33 days ('about a month'), they would have needed to cover those 730 land miles in 31 days at an average rate of 23½ miles a day, with no halts' (p. 113). He shows that, using the example of Ignatius' journey, a period of 49 days is more feasible (p. 116). Even on this longer reckoning it is a fact that there is evidence of the relative speed and dependability of travel in the world of Paul's day (see Lionel Casson, 'Speed under Sail of Ancient Ships', *Transactions of the American Philological Association* 82 (1951), pp. 136–48), and C. H. Dodd ('The Mind of Paul: II', *New Testament Studies*, Manchester, 1953, pp. 96ff.) and P. N. Harrison ('The Pastoral Epistles and Duncan's Ephesian Theory', *NTS* 2 (1955–6), p. 260) feel that there is no difficulty in fitting these travel times into the two years of Ac. 28:30.

C. O. Buchanan (loc. cit., pp. 160–3) has laboured to reduce the number and hardship of these journeys, and so to deflect the appeal of this counter-argument. In particular, he makes Epaphroditus' sickness occur on the journey outward to Paul's prison, and he postulates that the news of this illness travelled back before Epaphroditus reached his destination. But this reconstruction entails all manner of speculation (for instance, that Epaphroditus fell sick because of winter snows and the exertions brought on by travel through a difficult terrain) of which we know nothing certain in this case.

(*iii*) We may take note of the impression which the letter has made on several scholars (for example, W. Michaelis, *Der Brief des Paulus an die Philipper*, Leipzig, 1935, p. 3. He finds this impression strengthened by 2:12, 22 and 1:26; J. Gnilka, *Der Philipperbrief*, p. 20) that, since the foundation of the Philippian church, the apostle had not been to visit it up to the time when he wrote the epistle. References in 1:30 and 4:15f. take the reader back to the days of the first missionary journey, and appear to indicate that Paul had not renewed acquaintance with the Philippian Christians since those days. But this cannot be so, if Paul is at Rome when he writes his letter, because he *has* visited the church since the first visit of Ac. 16. Ac. 20:1–6 records such return visits. See Kümmel, op. cit., pp. 228, 231 for difficulty in denying this.

The reminiscence of 1:30 ('the same conflict which you saw . . . to be mine') suggests a shorter time than the 11–12 years which must have elapsed if Paul were writing from Rome; and a mention of the early days of their faith (1:5, 4:15) gives the impression that only a short time has intervened between Paul's first visit and preaching and the time of the letter.

(*iv*) Phil. 2:24 (cf. Phm. 22) expresses the hope and intention of the apostle to revisit the church if his release is granted. Earlier verses (1:24–7) suggest that what he had in mind was not just an isolated visit, but rather the continuation of his missionary and pastoral work among the Philippians. This is an important indication of the apostle's outlook, because we know that at the time of Romans 15:23, 24, 28 he considered his missionary work in the east to be finished, and was setting his face in the direction of the west and thinking in terms of a projected visit to Spain (see Gunther, op. cit., ch. 6). Now if, some years later than the writing of Romans 15:23, 24, 28 (on which, cf. J. Knox, 'Romans 15:14–33 and Paul's Conception of his Apostolic Mission', *JBL* 83 (1964), pp. 1–11), Paul is found expressing the intention of revisiting Philippi, we must suppose that a new situation had arisen which led him to change his missionary strategy. (Dodd, op. cit., p. 96, suggests that Paul changed his mind on the ground that, as he depended for his proposed Spanish mission on support from Rome, and as Philippians shows that a large section of the Roman church was opposed to him, he decided to postpone the projected enterprise of Rom. 15 and revisit Philippi in view of the Jewish opposition there.) While this is, of course, possible, it is also to be noted that if Philippians is brought back to a period before Ac. 20, then we have a situation in which the promised visit of Phil. 1:26, 2:24 was fulfilled in Ac. 19:21, 20:1ff., along with the pledge to send Timothy to the Philippians (2:19, 23) which was made good according to Ac. 19:22; 1 C. 4:17, 16:10f. On this view, the evidence of Rom. 15 for a mission in the west also stands (cf. 1 Clem. 5. 5–7).

This correspondence between 'the persons concerned, the objective and the sequence of events of the journeys' (as W.

Michaelis, *Einleitung in das Neue Testament*, pp. 208f., describes the close links between items found in Ac. and Phil. They suggest not a duplication, but an identity) is treated as a very impressive argument for pushing back the composition of the letter to a period into which it fits like the key piece of a jig-saw; and if the events do not correspond, it is necessary to suppose a remarkable duplication. (See, too, G. S. Duncan, *St. Paul's Ephesian Ministry*, London, 1929, pp. 77–80.) On the other hand, there is no mention of Erastus in Philippians, as there is in Ac. 19:22, and Harrison (*NTS* 2 (1955–6), pp. 258f.) finds a disparity in the reasons given for the missions of Timothy recorded in Ac. 19:22 and Phil. 2:19 (but see Duncan's reply in his article, 'Paul's Ministry in Asia—the Last Phase', *NTS* 3 (1956–7), p. 218).

If the case for the Roman origin is open to criticism on the grounds which are outlined above, what better alternative is possible? Three suggested possibilities have been offered to overcome the difficulties which are felt, by some scholars, to stand in the way of the acceptance of the time-honoured order of the Pauline letters.

An Origin of the Letter at Corinth

Recently it has been proposed by S. Dockx ('Lieu et Date de l'épître aux Philippiens', *RB* 80 (1973), pp. 230–46) that Paul wrote this letter during his time at Corinth (Ac. 18:1–18). (See Michaelis, *Einleitung*, pp. 204f., for an anticipation of this dating by G. L. Oeder in 1731.) The lines of defence for this thesis are: (*i*) there was a proconsul at Corinth (Ac. 18:12), and so, by inference, a praetorium and a body of imperial staff to correspond with the references in 1:13; 4:22; (*ii*) Corinth was nearer geographically to Philippi than other places that have been proposed, especially Rome; (*iii*) anti-Judaizing polemic which characterizes Phil. 3 makes sense if the letter was written before 1 Corinthians and at a time when Paul's mind was filled with the need to defend the gospel, as in 2 Corinthians; (*iv*) in Phil. 4:10–20 Paul concedes that the church has had no opportunity to reach him with a gift. This is true to the Acts record. And the arrival of Epaphroditus is hinted at in 2 C. 11:9 where 'brethren from Macedonia' relieve Paul's needs, which otherwise were met by his working at manual tasks (Ac. 18:3). Dockx appeals to E. Haenchen's discussion of Ac. 18:5 (*The Acts of the Apostles*, pp. 534–9), according to which the arrival of Timothy and Silas meant that they brought a money gift, possibly from Philippi; and this is related to 2 C. 11:8f. and Phil. 4:15f. Haenchen grants that this is only implied, not expressly stated. But, on Dockx's reconstruction, the situation makes good sense.

Against this interesting proposal, which puts the composition of Philippians during Paul's time in Corinth, about May–June, AD 50, and has features shared by T. W. Manson's suggestions (see later pp. 72f. *ad* 1:15–17) that Paul's struggle is with rival preachers who divided the Corinthian congregation (1 C. 1–4), there are some telling objections. First, no actual imprisonment of Paul at Corinth is recorded, though Ac. 18:10 hints at a threat on his life. This objection can be circumvented if we take into account Manson's idea that Paul was no longer a prisoner when he wrote the letter, and that the references to his 'chains' are to be construed as metaphors. But this is doubtful, and the nature of what we know of Paul's troubles at Corinth hardly tallies with his expressions in Phil. 1:20–23, 2:17.

Also, it is hard to see how Paul has been inaccessible to the Philippians' gifts during his Achaian ministry, implied in Phil. 4:10. Finally, when Paul is at Corinth, where there was a church of considerable size (Ac. 18:10), he is surrounded by faithful friends, among whom we may number Aquila and Priscilla (Ac. 18:2, 3). But his sad complaint that none but Timothy is to be trusted (2:20, 21) reads strangely in a situation where Paul could presumably call on several supporters in a time of need.

A Caesarean Origin

This was first propounded by H. E. G. Paulus of Jena in 1799 and supported later by D. Schulz, *ThStK* 2 (1829), pp. 612–17; Lohmeyer, *Kommentar*, pp. 3f., 40f; Kümmel, *Introduction*, pp. 232–235; L. Johnson, 'The Pauline Letters from Caesarea', *ExpT* 68 (1956–7), pp. 24–6; and most recently by J. J. Gunther, *Paul*, pp. 98–120. On this theory the imprisonment to which the letter refers would be located in Caesarea where Paul was detained according to Ac. 23:33. Lohmeyer dates the epistle in the year AD 58 during the time of the apostle's detention at Caesarea, advancing the evidence of 23:35 where Herod's 'palace' (lit. *praitōrion:* see *RSV*) is named as the place of confinement. This place he would equate with the *praitōrion* of Phil. 1:13. Gunther (op. cit., pp. 97f., 177) mentions that the 'palace' probably refers to the headquarters of a provincial governor (*praefectus*) who was under direct imperial control, and cites the discovery in 1961 of the Pilate inscription in Latin in which *praefectus* and *Tiberieum* are mentioned. This identification *may* be so; but it may also be true of many other provincial cities throughout the Empire. Certainly there is no necessity to trace this reference to Rome, but there is equally no necessity to place the *praitōrion* of Phil. 1:13 (see the commentary on this verse) in Caesarea.

A recent argument has been proposed by J. J. Gunther (op. cit., p. 102). This submits that Timothy's projected movements in 2:19–24 fit in with the situation of 2 Tim. 4:9–22, and that that section of the Pastorals presupposes Paul's time in Caesarea (op. cit., pp. 107–14). The setting suggested for 2 Tim. 4 is ingenious, but fraught with special problems. It would be unwise, therefore, to build on such a doubtful base. Moreover, there are some arguments against the proposed theory of dating Philippians in this period. The custody of Ac. 23:35 (cf. 24:23) does not suggest the imminent martyrdom which is one of the themes of the entire epistle (see, for instance, E. Lohmeyer, *Kommentar*, p. 3: 'Paul can count still on the possibility of release; but he seems rather to long for and await death which will bring him into eternal union with Christ'). The comparative ease of his detention contrasts sharply with the 'chains' and 'conflict' of Phil. 1 (but see Ac. 26:29), and the mention of his friends hardly corresponds with Phil. 2:20, 21. The somewhat tortuous explanation offered by Gunther (op. cit., pp. 105f.) as to why Paul makes no mention of Philip the evangelist, who was resident in Caesarea and in whose home Paul stayed *en route* to Jerusalem (Ac. 21:8), does not commend the theory. Nor does the attempt commend itself to read 'between the lines' of Paul's letter and to suggest that Paul's alternation of optimism and despair (which is thought to be reflected in chs. 1, 2) may be accounted for by the fact of Paul's hope, which was greatest during the time of his dealings with Felix and was at low ebb when Festus came to power (Gunther, op. cit., p. 107). In fact, E. F. Scott's conclusion (*Commentary*, p. 5) seems undeniable that 'in Caesarea he was not in serious danger . . . The Caesarean imprisonment was tedious and irksome, but it would not justify the tone of martyrdom which pervades the Epistle to the Philippians.' Paul's fears, expressed in 1:7, 20ff., 30, 2:17, suggest a very real threat on his life from which he was protected by Roman custody. This raises the issue of his *Caesarem appello* appeal, mentioned in Ac. 25:11, 12. (On the distinction between *provocatio* [a request to be tried by the emperor's court] and *appellatio* [a request to obtain a revision of a judgment already given] see A. N. Sherwin-White, *Roman Society and Roman Law in the New Testament*, p. 68, et passim.)

His outlook at the time of Ac. 23–24 was bound up with a visit to Rome as we know from the Acts narrative (cf. 23:11), and of this desire there is no mention in Philippians. The desperate situation which confronted him, according to 1:20ff., 2:17, could have been dispelled by an appeal to the emperor and, in fact, this is just what happened according to Ac. 25:10–12. This 'trump card', as C. H. Dodd calls it (*New Testament Studies*, p. 103), could have extricated him from danger if he were at Caesarea when his life was threatened by the authorities, and he seems to have been protected by those same authorities from Jewish 'plots' against his life (Ac. 23:12ff.). Paul's secure financial position, according to the witness of Ac. 24:26 (W. M. Ramsay, *St. Paul the Traveller and Roman Citizen*, 18th edn, London, 1935, pp. 310ff.), does not seem to be in agreement with that at the time of Philippians when his 'necessity' is relieved only by the arrival of the gift at the hands of Epaphroditus (Phil. 4:12ff.).

Finally, the size and type of a Christian community at the scene of Paul's imprisonment do not favour Caesarea. The evidence in 1:14ff. suggests a large centre where contending influences are nonetheless making a strong Christian presence felt. But, as J. Moffatt (*An Introduction to the Literature of the New Testament*, 3rd edn, 1918, p. 169) writes, Caesarea 'cannot be said to have been a centre of vigorous Christian propaganda'.

On the other hand, the bitter altercations between Jews and Gentiles at Caesarea, leading to street battles in AD 59, on the issue of the rights of citizenship (Gr. *isopoliteia*: see the discussion by B. Reicke, loc. cit., *Apostolic History and the Gospel*, pp. 281f.), may conceivably be in the background of Phil. 1:12–18, if we could accept the interpretation of these verses (see commentary, pp. 72–4) that finds in the rival preachers' messages a desire to stir up Roman opposition and to associate Paul with a politically-oriented gospel. Also the work of Jewish Christians to claim Gentile Christians as members of Israel by insisting on their circumcision may account for Paul's warnings in chapter 3:2f., especially if Zealot activity in Palestine were putting pressure on such Jewish Christians to declare their national loyalty (see pp. 30, 34). The record in Ac. 23, 25 bears witness to Zealot antipathy to Paul at this time in his life. But there are several unresolved issues in this presentation.

On balance, the case for a Caesarean origin of the letter is more suggestive and less problematical than the traditional case for Rome. But there is one further possibility which calls to be considered.

An Ephesian Origin

A final possibility of pinpointing the origin of Philippians stems from the hypothesis that Paul suffered imprisonment at Ephesus. It is during this period of his life and against the background of the troubles which befell him 'in Asia' (Ac. 20:18f.) that it is proposed to place the dating of Philippians, and to interpret many of the puzzling details of the letter.

At first glance the foundation of this theory seems very insecure inasmuch as the fact of an Ephesian imprisonment is without definite proof. Of this fact the leading exponents of the view are aware, and they freely admit that a captivity in Ephesus must remain an assumption (e.g., the admission of this obstacle by J.–F. Collange, *L'épître aux Philippiens*, p. 33). But there is, according to these scholars, cumulative evidence which makes the hypothesis very probable, if not almost certain.

We may consider the data which are offered to support such a view as a basis for a dating of the letter.

(*i*) The cryptic allusion in 1 C. 15:32 to fighting 'with beasts at Ephesus' (see A. J. Malherbe, 'The Beasts at Ephesus', *JBL* 87 (1968), pp. 71–80) may be construed either literally or metaphorically; and in either case the phrase may describe either an actual or hypothetical experience. For a figurative interpretation the statement of Ignatius (*Rom.* 5) is often cited: 'From Syria to Rome I am fighting with wild beasts (*thēriomacheō*: the same Gr. word as in Paul's verse) . . . bound to ten leopards, that is, a company of soldiers.' Ignatius quite clearly draws a distinction between the trials he endures at the hands of the soldiers who are escorting him and the expectation of his fate in the arena (5:2; cf. 4:1, 2). So here, in 1 C. 15:32, Paul may be describing, in a vivid way, the hostility of men against him rather than his fate in which he was literally condemned *ad bestias* in the arena (so Malherbe, Collange). Against the literal reading is also the fact that 2 C. 11:23–7 fails to record it in the list of his hardships. Also his privilege as a Roman citizen would exempt him from such a punishment, but we must reckon with the possibility that, if the attack upon his life were more in the spirit of mob violence than a legal sentence of death, his plea of Roman citizenship would fall on unheeding ears, as in the case of a Roman citizen who was beaten at Messina (Cicero, *in Verrem*, 5:62, 63, 66) or the Christian Attalus who escaped death in the amphitheatre one day when the governor knew he was a Roman, but the next day 'the governor, to please the crowd . . . delivered Attalus too again to the wild beasts' (Eusebius, *HE*, 5:1, 44, 50).

G. S. Duncan (*St. Paul's Ephesian Ministry*, pp. 100–7) has pointed to at least one period of contemporary history in Asia Minor when social anarchy prevailed following the assassination of the procurator Julius Silanus in AD 54, i.e., during the period of Paul's ministry in the proconsular capital during AD 52–55.

But whether this terrifying experience were an actual fact (in which case the 'beasts' must be taken metaphorically: Paul did not die in the arena) or relates to some event which seemed likely to happen but never did (as is maintained by J. Héring, *The First Epistle of Saint Paul to the Corinthians*, ET London, 1962, pp. 171f.), the term he uses implies some outstanding physical hardship endured at Ephesus in which there was a real threat upon his life (cf. 1 C. 15:31, 32*b*); and this is not the only indication there is of some danger which jeopardized the apostle's life at that time.

(*ii*) Evidence of imprisonments and severe privations prior to the Roman captivity is provided by 2 C. 11:23–7, which is confirmed by the statement of Clement of Rome (5.6) that Paul 'was seven times in bonds'. Much of the Corinthian correspondence in the first and second canonical letters to the church in that place appears to reflect a great trial or series of trials he had to endure in the vicinity of Ephesus, where 1 Corinthians was written. We may instance 1 C. 4:9–13, and especially the sombre tones of 2 C. 1:8–10 where he confesses that in (proconsular) Asia he was crushed down by some fearful burden which made him despair even of life itself. 'In fact I told myself it was the sentence of death' (2 C. 1:9, Moffatt); but in the mercy of God he was rescued from this fate, 'so terrible a death' (verse 10, Moffatt). The same anxious mood is to be detected also in 2 C. 4:8–12, 6:4–11 (cf. Ac. 20:18, 19), written while the memory of his days at Ephesus was still vivid.

With these perilous experiences Rom. 16:3ff. is thought to be in close agreement. C. R. Bowen comments ('Are Paul's Prison Letters from Ephesus?' *AJT* 24 (1920), p. 116), 'The language can scarcely mean anything else than that the apostle had been in danger of execution (cf. Rom. 16:3: 'Prisca and Aquila . . . who have risked their lives for me', Moffatt) but had somehow been saved by Prisca and her husband at the hazard of their own lives.' He connects this with the exposure to the wild beasts of 1 C. 15:32, whereas C. H. Dodd relates it to the troubles described in Ac. 19:23–40. The former crisis may be too hypothetical for a firm identification, and the latter too mild for the language of Rom. 16:3, 4 (cf. 16:7: 'Andronicus and Junia . . . my fellow-prisoners'). All we can say is that at this period of his life at Ephesus (Rom. 16 may have been written to the community there; see J. I. H. McDonald, 'Was Romans XVI a Separate Letter?' *NTS* 16 (1970), pp. 369–72) or nearby, the apostle was in mortal peril and rescued only by divine interposition and the fearless co-operation of his friends.

(*iii*) The extra-biblical witness to an Ephesian imprisonment is admittedly of limited value. It consists of the local tradition of a watch-tower in Ephesus which is known as 'Paul's prison' (Deissmann, *Anatolian Studies, etc.*, p. 127); and in the Marcionite Prologues, the prologue to Colossians reads: 'After he had been arrested he wrote to them (the Colossians) from Ephesus.' There is also the apocryphal story of Paul and the lion in the Ephesian arena (see *Acts of Paul* 7, printed in E. Hennecke, *New Testament Apocrypha*, ed. W. Schneemelcher, vol. 2, ET London, ed. R. McL. Wilson, 1965, pp. 369ff., 372f.).

√   The most obvious and cogent objection to the presupposition of an imprisonment at Ephesus is the silence of the book of Acts. At this point, G. S. Duncan's chapter which seeks to explain the lacunae in the Acts narrative may be referred to (op. cit., ch. 9, pp. 95ff.), and if his case is held to be convincing, or, at least, plausible, the Ephesian dating of Philippians may be tested. Does its origin in the Ephesian period against the background of the apostle's strained predicament of those days explain or relieve the difficulties that have been earlier noted? The following are the main attractions of this novel suggestion.

(*i*) The 'enormous journeys' between Philippi and the place of Paul's writing (which Deissmann found to be so much of an obstacle to the Roman dating) are considerably reduced. We are able to calculate with fair precision the journey time from Ephesus to Philippi. Ac. 20:13ff. gives the time for the journey from Troas to Miletus as five days; to Ephesus, then, we may estimate a time of four days. Ac. 16:11ff. gives three days from Troas to Philippi, and, with a contrary wind, five days (Ac. 20:6). Thus the entire distance between Ephesus and Philippi would be covered in seven to nine days. J. Schmid (op. cit., p. 81) reckons a journey time of eight days. And in favourable circumstances the out-going and return journeys could be done in two weeks. So the five journeys which Deissmann regards as required by the internal evidence of the letter would be covered in not more than six weeks' travelling, and the four extra journeys which are envisaged and planned in the letter in not more than four to five weeks.

This contrasts so sharply with the lengthy distances and times required by communication between Philippi and Rome that Deissmann offers this factor as strongly supporting the Ephesian provenance of the epistle.

(*ii*) There is inscriptional evidence to satisfy the requirement of Phil. 1:13, 4:22. (See these verses in the commentary and discussions on the meaning and location of 'praetorium' in the *NT* by A. Legendre, *Dictionnaire de la Bible*, v, Paris, 1912, cols. 639f.; *Dictionnaire de la Bible Supplément*, II, Paris, 1934, col. 1086; T. W. Manson, loc. cit., p. 192 [=*Studies*, p. 159]; F. F. Bruce, *Biblisch-Historisch Handwörterbuch*, ed. B. Reicke–L. Rost, Göttingen, 1966, col. 1482.) Ephesus was the site of the proconsular headquarters, and there would be a *praitōrion* there. 'Caesar's household' may well refer to the imperial fiscal staff who took charge of the imperial bank in Asia (*fiscus asiaticus*)with headquarters in that city; and there are certain advantages in this view, e.g., it reduces the number of the praetorian guard (about 9,000 in Rome), all of whom (1:13) had heard that the apostle was a prisoner for Christ's sake.

(*iii*) At the time of Ac. 19 Paul had been to Philippi only once, and references to 'the beginning of the gospel' read more naturally if the period between the founding of the church and the time of the letter were a short one than if it were a longer one (see Gnilka,

Der Philipperbrief, p. 101, who argues, on the basis of 1:30, that 'it is unlikely that Paul had seen the church in the interval since its foundation'). The plans of Phil. 2 also relate with precision to the missionary itinerary of the Acts narrative; Phil. 2:19 (the mission of Timothy) will be that of Ac. 19:22 (cf. 1 C. 4:17, 16:10), and Paul's hoped-for visit of 2:24 (and 1:26) will have been fulfilled in Ac. 20:1 (cf. 19:21).

On the other hand, this neat identification has been challenged by P. N. Harrison (*NTS* 2 (1955–6), pp. 250–61), who says that the movements of Paul following his experience of Ac. 19 betray such a lack of urgency to leave Ephesus (cf. 1 C. 16:5–9) that they cannot reflect the outlook of the man who wrote of hoping 'shortly' (Phil. 2:24) to revisit Philippi. But we do not know the reason for Paul's delay at Ephesus (1 C. 16:8, 9), which may have been a situation which developed subsequent to his release from the imprisonment in that city and, therefore, later than the writing of Philippians. One suggestion is that Paul wanted to exploit fully the opportunities presented by an increased population who came to the Artemesia festival in honour of the city's patron goddess (so Duncan, op. cit., pp. 139f., 288f.). Duncan dates Philippians in the period when a crisis occasioned by the charge of temple robbery (Ac. 19:37) put Paul's life in jeopardy. As the crisis subsided, the Ephesian authorities deemed it wise to place Paul under protective custody at the time of the Artemesia in the spring of AD 54, when anti-Christian feelings would run high. Paul wrote Colossians then (see *New Century Bible* on that epistle, 1974, pp. 26–30) and expressed some restiveness at being in (mild) restraint and so prevented from engaging in mission work; so Col. 4:3, 4.

(*iv*) Other items of an incidental character fall into place on the assumption of an earlier dating. Ac. 19:22 confirms the presence of Timothy with Paul at Ephesus, whereas there is no sure knowledge from Acts that Timothy came to Rome. Yet he was with the apostle according to Phil. 1:1.

Phil. 4:10 refers to the Philippians' desire to send help to Paul, but they had not been able to do so because they 'had no opportunity'. This can hardly have been the case if the date is sometime in the years of the Roman captivity, because 4:16 will then refer to a period twelve years earlier and in that interval Paul had revisited Macedonia (Ac. 20:3) and Philippi (20:6). That it must have been the first gift to the apostle that is mentioned in 4:15, 16 is shown by the historical allusion to 'the beginning of the gospel' in 4:15. And yet Paul harks back to that time in spite of at least two visits to Philippi and recalls the lack of opportunity for further gifts! As T. W. Manson says, 'If Philippians was written from Rome, Paul's remarks on the subject of the gift sent from Philippi cannot be construed except as a rebuke, and a sarcastic rebuke at that' (*BJRL* 23 (1939), p. 190 [=*Studies*, p. 157]).

If, however, only three or four years have elapsed since the first gift, it will be quite true that the Philippians have had no opportunity to send a further contribution, for in that time Paul had been in the east or in the 'upper' country of Ac. 19:1.

To this argument C. H. Dodd (loc. cit., p. 98) raises the objection that, at the time of the Ephesian ministry, the Philippians lacked opportunity to help because they were in the grip of financial depression (2 C. 8:1–6). Also he remarks upon the necessity which Paul felt, at a time when he was engaged in the task of collecting money for the Jewish 'poor' at Jerusalem, of not receiving personal gifts which may have laid him open to the charge of underhand dealings in financial matters. But the apostle never alludes to their past economic stringency to explain their tardiness to come to his help, and 4:10 suggests that they had the money in spite of their poverty but could not get it to the apostle. 2 C. 8:3 records how that, even in their extreme necessity, they supported the collection 'beyond their means'. The care with which Paul avoids the charge of covetousness (2 C. 12:14–19) can hardly be used as an objection to Paul's receiving the Philippians' gift in view of 4:17, and it overlooks the special bond of affection which made the church at Philippi something of a favourite in his eyes (see 4:15: 'no church . . . except you only').

The criterion of an affinity of language and ideas with other epistles is one which we have regarded as secondary, but many scholars buttress their advocacy of an earlier dating of Philippians by a demonstration of its literary connexion and theological associations with 1 and 2 Corinthians and Romans. In this way Lightfoot's linguistic parallels with Romans are justified by another route as Duncan places the two epistles to the Corinthians in close juxtaposition with Philippians immediately *before* Romans and not *vice versa*, as does Lightfoot (see G. S. Duncan, 'Were St. Paul's Imprisonment Epistles written from Ephesus?' *ExpT* 67 (1955–6), pp. 163–6).

There are, nevertheless, at least two factors which militate against the proposed reconstruction of a crisis at or near Ephesus leading to Paul's arrest and mortal peril and forming the background of the hopes and fears expressed in Philippians.

(*i*) The singular absence of any mention of the collection for the poverty-stricken Jerusalem churches is an objection which J. Schmid calls 'a chief argument' against the suggested origin of the letter (op. cit., p. 114). We know that this matter filled his thoughts and controlled many of his movements at this time (cf. 1 and 2 Corinthians and Romans), and yet in a letter putatively set in the context of the third missionary journey there is not a word about it.

Against this omission it is said that Timothy's mission (in Ac. 19:22), which is promised in 2:19, may have been for this purpose (cf. Harrison's discussion, loc. cit., pp. 258, 259), and Paul was hopeful that he would himself soon be with them. J. H. Michael (*Commentary*, pp. xx–xxii) proffers the suggestion that instructions concerning the collection may have been given orally through Epaphroditus. Or, it has been proposed by Gnilka (op. cit., p. 24) that Timothy was charged to deliver oral instructions from Paul (cf. V. P. Furnish, 'The Place and Purpose of Philippians III', *NTS* 10 (1963), pp. 80–8), and that, along with warnings and directives, Paul's instructions about the collection would be sent in order to cement relations between Paul's Gentile converts and the Jewish-Christian homebase and to validate his apostleship (see K. F. Nickle, *The Collection*, London, 1966, ch. iv).

(*ii*) The second objection which has been launched against the Ephesian hypothesis is one which Schmid calls 'the decisive argument against any other dating but the Roman' (op. cit., p. 107). In brief, the question is this: If Paul found himself in the hands of the authorities at Ephesus or elsewhere, why did he not exercise the right and privilege of his citizenship and appeal to Caesar against any sentence of condemnation which may have been brought against him? Phil. 1:20, 2:17 reckons with an unfavourable issue of his trial (1:17) and the grim prospect of death looms large before him. If Paul were in such a desperate situation and threatened by the death sentence, why did he not do what he did at Caesarea and insist that all local proceedings be quashed and the case transferred to Rome? There are three explanations possible in answer to this question.

First, the language of 1:23 and 2:17 may be taken to describe a situation of less peril and gravity than one which would have arisen if Paul feared judicial condemnation and death. This is Michaelis' interpretation, which holds that, at the time of his writing, the apostle was *not* seriously in danger because he can contemplate the possibility of both life and death in 1:20ff.; and he interprets 2:17 in a general way as referring to Paul's apostolic service in which he was daily spending his life for the gospel's sake. But a more definite danger than the hourly peril of his apostolic ministry (1 C. 15:31; 2 C. 4:10, 11) seems in view in the light of such verses as 1:20, 30, 2:27, 28, and 3:11; and 2 Tim. 4:6, which repeats the metaphor of sacrifice and offering, is a later confession of a specific, serious danger to his life. C. H. Dodd (op. cit., p. 103, note 2) observes with justification, 'That it is a "life and death" matter is clear from Phil. i. 20, and Paul's confidence that his life will be spared (i. 25) is not based on a calculation of probabilities, but on a conviction that his life is so important to his churches that he must escape, even though by a miracle.' This observation needs to be borne in mind when it comes to understanding the fluctuation in Paul's mind between despair and optimism. His despair is real, since he is faced with a very real possibility of death. Yet his hope of release is secure since it is grounded in God's answering the prayer of the Philippians in setting him free, if it is his will. But, from a human point of view, he has no such hope.

Secondly, Paul may have been in danger, not from the result of formal legal procedure, but from an unofficial attempt upon his life. If the peril were from Jewish opponents (Ac. 20:19) or mob violence, a protest of his Roman citizenship would be of no value, and this possibility is strengthened if the language of 1:30 is taken literally. His present conflict (Gr. *agōn*) is the 'same' as that which he endured at Philippi (Ac. 16), viz., a lawless outburst in which his citizenship did not save him from the lash, the stocks, and the indignity of the prison.

Rom. 16:7 speaks of Andronicus and Junia as his 'fellow-prisoners', and it has been suggested that their imprisonment with the apostle was the result of anti-Christian riots promoted by unbelieving Jews (cf. Ac. 20:19) and that Paul did not claim his rights as a citizen because, as they were not Roman citizens, he would not leave them in the lurch. Or else, it may be that in a time of social confusion his appeals to his status went unheeded (see earlier, p. 49).

We are here in the realm of conjecture. If Paul were in danger of his life at Ephesus and for some reason refused to use his privilege to extricate himself from that peril, we can only say with Michaelis(*Die Datierung des Philipperbriefes*, p. 40; idem, *Einleitung*, p. 209) that his circumstances there are unknown to us and that, as we know too little about the courts in Ephesus, we cannot say what weight his Roman citizenship would have carried there.

Thirdly, we come back to the 'traditional' reading of the situation underlying the letter. The reason why he does not mention an appeal to Caesar is that just such an appeal has brought him before his judges at Rome. His grave danger is before the imperial court, and there is no more, humanly, that he can do. The threat upon his life is a very real one, but he knows that he is in God's hands; and amid the oscillation of feelings, hopes, and fears reflected in the epistle (e.g., 2:23, 24), he awaits his destiny, which will be a divine opportunity for Christ to be magnified, whether by life or death (1:20).

Recent discussion of the date and origin of the letter has run into an impasse. This frustration is evidenced in Dibelius' conclusion (p. 98) when he writes: 'therefore a definite solution of this problem can hardly be reached because, even if we consider it difficult to imagine its having been composed at Rome, the Ephesian hypothesis still rests on mere supposition.' All possible identifications can present arguments that have strengths and weaknesses. The relative cogency of the traditional view is not very strong in the view of contemporary scholars. Those who accept it do so with caution (e.g., Houlden, p. 42) and in default of the rival theories being persuasive. Interestingly, Houlden suspects G. S. Duncan's case because of its apparent dependence on the Acts narrative (including the attempt to 'rescue' the historical data given in the Pastorals), whereas continental scholars champion the Ephesian origin because it fits in with their theories of (*a*) Philippians being a composite document, made up of several 'letters' which come out of Paul's debates during his Ephesian ministry (Schmithals, Bornkamm, Gnilka; see earlier, pp. 19–21); (*b*) the letter's affinities with 2 Corinthians in two ways: first, its literary history is one of being the result of the addition of fragments, and, then, its presentation of Paul's

case against sectarian opponents seems identical with, or at
least similar to, the arguments found in 2 C. 10–13 (Schmithals;
R. H. Fuller, *A Critical Introduction*, p. 35; and J.-F. Collange);
and (*c*) the identity of the rival preachers in Phil. 1:12–18, who
are thought to be 'divine men' itinerant propagandists located
in Ephesus (Jewett).

5. ANALYSIS OF PHILIPPIANS

PAUL'S GREETING   1:1, 2

PAUL'S PRAYER FOR THE CHURCH   1:3–11

PAUL'S AMBITION FOR THE GOSPEL   1:12–26

EXHORTATIONS TO THE COMMUNITY   1:27–2:18

   (a) 1:27–30
      The need for unity and courage in the face of persecution
   (b) 2:1–4
      The need for harmony in the church
   (c) 2:5–11
      The basis of the Christian life laid in the story of salva-
      tion
   (d) 2:12–18
      Appeals to good relationships

[APPENDED NOTE ON PHIL. 2:6–11]

PAUL'S FUTURE PLANS   2:19–30

PAUL'S WARNING AND SELF-DEFENCE   3:1–14

   (a) An introduction and severe warning (3:1*b*, 2)
   (b) Paul's life—past and present (3:3–6)
   (c) The benefits of his new life (3:7–14)

AN APPEAL FOR UNITY IN
  CONVICTION AND CONDUCT   3:15–17

SECTARIAN TEACHERS TO BE
  SHUNNED   3:18–19

THE LETTER OF PAUL
TO THE
PHILIPPIANS

1:1 The opening lines of the letter introduce the names of the sender(s) and the addressees according to ancient conventions of letter-writing practice. But there is a fullness of description embodying the divine names of the Christian faith which is unique in this letter. The simplest way of salutation would be: *Paul to the Philippian church, greetings.* Instead there is a rich theological significance given to a formal statement by the inclusion of the divine names.

Timothy is included in view of his association with Paul in his imprisonment; it is also clear from 2:19–24 that Timothy had a special attachment to the Philippians and was Paul's trusted envoy shortly to be sent to Philippi. His name is introduced in the prescript to prepare for the later mention of Paul's plans in chapter 2.

Both the apostle and his colleague are given the title **servants of Christ Jesus** to mark out their sense of responsibility under God. The term 'servant' (Gr. *doulos*) probably reflects a dependence on the *OT* picture of Israel's prophetic figures who are described as 'servants of Yahweh'. This title denotes their God-given authority to speak and act in his name, as his accredited representatives. 'To be a servant, in the religious language of Judaism, meant to be one chosen by God' (Lohmeyer, on 2:7). So, while Paul does not make explicit claim to apostleship in this opening part of his letter, his use of a self-appellation such as 'servant of Christ Jesus' is a token of his sense of apostolic authority (cf. 2 C. 10:8), which runs through the letter. **Timothy** shares the dignity of the title since Paul intends to send him to Philippi as his personal representative (2:23). There is no hint that Timothy's name appears because he was the amanuensis at Paul's side when the letter was written, as some commentators surmise. Nor is his presence at the head of the letter intended to give a corporate character to the contents, as though Paul were disclaiming the authority of a private revelation known only to him (so K. Barth). Just as speculative is the idea which lies behind E. Haenchen's proposal (*The Acts of the Apostles*, ET

Oxford, 1971, pp. 489f.) that Timothy may have been Paul's travel-companion who confirmed the Macedonian call and supported the plan to evangelize Philippi (Ac. 16:10). A simpler explanation has to be sought (as above).

The Christian community which came into existence following Paul's 'initial evangelism' at Philippi (Ac. 16:12ff.) is described as **all the saints in Christ Jesus who are at Philippi.** It is interesting that just as the term 'apostle' is not found in reference to Paul's ministry, the word 'church' is missing. In its place there is the comprehensive title **all the saints** (Gr. *hagioi*, holy ones) **in Christ Jesus.** The plural is intentional, since the adjective as applied to Christian believers is found only in reference to a group in the *NT* literature. 4:21 in our epistle is no real exception. The corporate character of the title is clear, and is a pointer to its origin.

In the *OT* Israel was God's holy people, separated from the other nations by its calling as Yahweh's possession (Num. 23:9; Ps. 147:20) and dedicated to the worship and service of the one God (Exod. 19:5, 6; Lev. 19:1, 2; Dt. 7:6, 14:2). The Church of the *NT* was self-consciously aware of its place as successor to this sacred community of Israel (1 Pet. 2:9, 10) and boldly appropriated the title 'God's holy ones' as a mark of this destiny. But 'holiness' is not a self-enclosed piety, nor is it a badge of merit. Christians are holy **in Christ Jesus,** i.e., by union with him who claimed them as his people and who becomes the ground of their new life (so Gnilka). ' "Holy" people are unholy people, who nevertheless as such have been singled out, claimed, and requisitioned by God for his control, for his use, for himself who is holy' (Barth).

Paul singles out for special mention **the bishops** (*RSV* margin, 'overseers') **and deacons.** They are leaders of the Philippian congregation, and the most likely guess which explains this specific mention at the head of the letter is that in some way these men played a responsible part in the collecting of the money-gift sent to Paul. But we should note that there is no allusion to them in 4:10ff. where Paul expresses his thanks for the gifts. W. Marxsen (*Introduction to the New Testament*, ET Oxford, 1968, p. 62) suggests that if 4:10–20 formed an earlier letter of gratitude, the reference to the 'officials' of the church concerned with the collection may have been included in 1:1 from this source.

On the more problematic question of the precise status and functions of these church leaders at Philippi, it is difficult to decide whether the titles they bore describe their work or determine their ecclesiastical office. Is it that they were known as 'overseers and attendants' because they performed this type of service within the community? Or were they church officers in the (later) technical sense, found in the Pastorals (1 Tim. 3), 1 Clem. 42 (*c.* AD 96) and Ignatius, *Magnes.* 6.1, 13.1; *Trall.* 3.1, 7.2 (early second century)? Evidence for the functional meaning of their title comes from other Pauline epistles, e.g., 1 Th. 5:12f.; 1 C. 12:28-31; Rom. 12:6-8, and recently it has been maintained that the work of the Philippian leaders finds a parallel in the duties of the Essene 'guardian' (*The Damascus Rule* 13.7ff.; Vermes, p. 115) and the Qumran leader who is called 'the Guardian (Heb. $m^e baqq\bar{e}r$) of the Congregation' (1QS 6.11ff; Vermes, pp. 81f.), who is apparently the same as the 'Bursar of the Congregation' (6.14). See Gnilka (p. 37) for a critical discussion of this supposed link between the sectarian leader and the Philippian *episkopos* and *diakonos*. He concludes, with H. F. von Campenhausen (*Ecclesiastical Authority and Spiritual Power in the Church of the First Three Centuries*, ET London, 1968, p. 9) that we should see in the letter the dawning of churchly positions to which select men were appointed. On this verse, see E. Best, 'Bishops and Deacons: Phil 1:1', in *SE* iv (ed. F. L. Cross), Berlin, 1968, pp. 371-6.

2. The invocation of **grace . . . and peace** joins in a single phrase the two words from Greek and Hebrew prayer speech which came to play a central role in liturgical practice. In place of the customary greeting (Gr. *chairein*) Paul goes to the Greek equivalent of the *OT* word for God's mercy (Heb. *ḥesedh*) and couples with it the rich Hebraic wish for peace (Heb. *šālôm*). The latter is 'the salvation of the whole man both body and soul', not just 'spiritual prosperity' (W. Foerster, *TDNT* ii, pp. 414f.). God's gift of 'wholeness' comes from his grace made known in Jesus Christ the Lord, whose name is frequent in this opening section and gives a weighty emphasis to Paul's pastoral letter.

PAUL'S PRAYER FOR THE CHURCH 1:3-11

3. Paul's prayers are worthy of study at several levels. Their *formal* characteristics borrow some features from the contemporary world of antiquity in which letter-writing habits included prayers of thanksgiving to the gods and a supplication for divine protection. Paul takes over this trait, but christianizes it in his own way by relating his prayers to his pastoral concern for the churches and a desire to see his readers attain to their maturity in Christ.

On the overall structure of the letter, which includes, after the salutation (1:1, 2), the elements of (1) thanksgiving (1:3–11), (2) the body of the letter, which incorporates a formal opening (1:12–18), theological argument, both theoretical (e.g., 1:23*b*–26) and practical (e.g., 1:27ff.), leading to the promise of an apostolic *parousia* (2:24), and the 'travelogue' sections (2:19–30), (3) *paraenesis* (or exhortation) in chapters 3, 4, and (4) closing items of greetings, doxology, and benedictions, see J. L. White, *The Form and Function of the Body of the Greek Letter: A Study of the Letter-Body in the Non-Literary Papyri and in Paul the Apostle*, Missoula, Montana, 1972.

Recent study has shown that his prayers, while giving the appearance of spontaneous outbursts of warm affection and devotion, conform to a pattern set by 'the liturgical form of the prayers of the Christian community' (J. T. Sanders, 'The Transition from Opening Epistolary Thanksgiving to Body in the Letters of the Pauline Corpus', *JBL* 81 (1962), pp. 348ff. See, too, W. G. Doty, *Letters in Primitive Christianity*, Philadelphia, 1973, ch. 2). Important features of this structure are the opening thanksgiving (modelled on the Jewish *hôdāyôt*, a title taken from the phrase 'I thank thee', which is current in Jewish prayers and is especially evident in the scroll 1QH at Qumran) and a doxological tribute at the close of the Pauline period. Verse 11 has the form, 'to the glory and praise of God'.

One further factor needs to be mentioned since it has considerable bearing on the task of exegesis, particularly at verse 3. A conclusion demonstrated by Paul Schubert (*Form and Function of the Pauline Thanksgivings*, Berlin, 1939, pp. 71–82) is that (a) in the other Pauline letters apart from Philippians the construction *epi* (for) with the dative case (which is found at verse 3) invariably introduces the cause for which thanks are offered; and that (b) as in other epistles, the thanksgiving introduces 'the vital theme of the letter', or what he calls 'the epistolary situation' (pp. 71, 78).

If this conclusion is a sound one, it throws light on the problematic way in which verse 3 is written, and it helps to indicate a solution. **I thank my God in all my remembrance of you.** The usual way in which Paul's thought of thankfulness is taken is as follows: I thank my God upon every occasion when I remember you. The Greek, however, is capable of a different sense, represented in Moffatt's translation: I thank my God for all your remembrance of me. The occasion of Paul's thankful spirit is the generosity of the Philippian church who have remembered (i.e., supported) him in a practical way with their repeated gifts (4:15, 16, 17). Verse 5 is the complement of this thought since verse 4 is a parenthesis (so Lightfoot, Gnilka); and the total picture is an impressive one. Paul expresses his gratitude to God for the Philippians' support of him, which is then described as their partnership in the gospel from their first meeting with Paul up to the present. There is everything to commend this interpretation, not least the fact that it shows how Paul expresses his thanks for the church's love-gift right at the head of the letter. He does not (which would be a strange feature) leave his 'thank you' until a final section (in ch. 4).

4. always in every prayer of mine for you all. The Philippians have remembered Paul in his need. For this active interest, most recently seen in the coming of Epaphroditus as their messenger (4:18), he praises God and reciprocates with an assurance of *his* supplication on their behalf. Moreover, he prays for them **with joy.** Paul's unbounded joy in the midst of his sufferings as a prisoner is a theme of this letter.

5. The second ground of his gratitude is now given. He is **thankful for your partnership in the gospel.** This phrase introduces a favourite Pauline term *koinōnia*, **partnership.** There are several possible nuances of meaning, each to be decided by its context. One suggestion, proposed and argued for by H. Seesemann (*Der Begriff KOINŌNIA im Neuen Testament*, Giessen, 1933, pp. 73–83), is that the special meaning of 'fellowship' in this verse is 'sharing in the faith'. Seesemann sees no reference to the Philippians' gift to Paul here, and takes *koinōnia* to be equivalent to their faith in Christ which the preaching of the gospel evoked on 'the first day', i.e., the time of Paul's initial evangelism. He insists that *koinōnia* with the prepositional phrase *eis to euangelion* must have this meaning and refer to an objective and divine work in which the Philippians had come to have a share (*Teilnahme, Anteilhaben* are Seesemann's terms to describe *koinōnia*). This agrees with Lohmeyer's view (*Kommentar*, p. 17) when he argues that *koinōnia* in Paul never refers to a bond joining Christians, but relates to the participation in an object outside of subjective experience, an 'objective reality', as he calls it.

Alternatively, we may submit that it is hard to avoid seeing some subjective element in Paul's praise of the Philippians' *koinōnia* not only at the first but up to the present. This seems to match exactly the sentiment of 4:15. They had repeatedly showed their interest in the gospel by their continued help to Paul; and it is their 'generosity', i.e., Seesemann's category of *Mitteilsamkeit*, which is in view.

The parallels are then to be sought in Rom. 15:26; 2 C. 9:13, and the specific application of their generous attitude is seen in their practical expression of what they sent to Paul repeatedly to assist the work of the gospel, i.e., the apostolic mission. 2 C. 8:7 speaks of the Macedonians' sacrifice in their gifts, and not the least feature of their giving was its constancy and its faithfulness to Paul and his work. But this interpretation is not the same as that offered by L.-M. Dewailly ('La Part Prise a l'Evangile. Phil. 1.5', *RB* 80 (1973), pp. 247–60) for whom Paul's use of the *koinōn*-term in 1:5 and 4:15 implies a sharing in the gospel and a sharing in Paul's grace of apostleship. Paul, it seems, never so speaks of apostleship in this corporate way, but regards his calling as unique, although aided by the help Christians gave him to fulfil it.

6. from the first day recalls the founding of the church in Ac. 16. Paul is thereby reminded that the origin of the church, though brought about through his preaching and pastoral labours, must be traced back to God **who began a good work** in their midst. Some commentators prefer to take the allusion to **a good work** to refer to the church's participation in the apostolic ministry by their gifts, 'their co-operation with and affection for the apostle', as Lightfoot puts it, and 2 C. 8:6 uses almost identical verbs, 'begin, finish' for Titus' administration of the relief fund for the Jerusalem church. But much more likely is the view that Paul is supplying a theological undergirding to his confidence that the Philippian church will be preserved to the end-time, **the day of Jesus Christ.** He is led to this consideration by reflecting on how the church began on **the first day**

and this work of God is described in a way which recalls Yahweh's creation (Gen. 2:2, 3, LXX; 2 Esd. 6.38: O Lord, thou didst say on the first day, 'Let heaven and earth be made', and thy word accomplished the work; 6.43: For thy word went forth and at once the work was done). Moreover, Yahweh's work was pronounced 'very good' (Gen. 1:31). Paul knows the *OT* teaching which unites God's work in the beginning with his purpose to bring it to consummation (e.g., Isa. 48:12f.); and he applies this to a community which needs reassurance in the face of threats and fears (1:28, 29).

7. **It is right for me to feel thus about you all.** It is appropriate for Paul to express this conviction as a settled issue in his mind (the verb rendered **to feel,** Gr. *phronein*, is a key verb in this epistle; it signifies a combination of intellectual and affective activity which touches both head and heart, and leads to a positive course of action). The object of his strong sense of concern and confidence is the security of the church in spite of the assaults levelled against it by hostile forces. It is the recognition of this opposition which provided E. Lohmeyer with what he regarded as the central theme of the letter: Paul the prisoner writes a tract of consolation to a beleaguered and persecuted Christian community which undergoes a trial similar to his (1:30). As a thesis offered to explain the letter's main purpose, Lohmeyer's view cannot stand, but there is no denying some measure of truth in it in the light of the present verse.

because I hold you in my heart. Paul's relationship to his readers is warm and tender. He clasps them close in his affection (see v. 8). **you are all partakers with me of grace.** More importantly, as a factor in a total situation which inspires him with confidence for their future, he knows that both he and they are sharers in a common reality, the **grace** of God. This affirmation is unexpected, and is rightly called 'a genuinely Pauline paradox' (Dibelius). It is clear that both apostle and church are sharers in suffering and conflict; what is unusual is the awareness now expressed by Paul that they are together as partners in divine grace. By this they are sustained and encouraged to endure. **grace** here carries the meaning of God's strength made available to his people in their weakness and need (see 2 C. 12:9).

Paul's **imprisonment** was not a punishment he had brought upon himself. He was a prisoner on account of his calling as a

Christian apostle. As such he was required constantly to engage
in a **defence and confirmation of the gospel.** The two
nouns may well suggest the two sides of his apostolic work.
'Defending the gospel' may mean his responsibility to disarm
prejudice and overcome objections to the message (cf. 2 C. 7:11).
Positively he was called upon to 'confirm' the preaching by a
forthright declaration of it. However, both Greek terms (*apologia,
bebaiōsis*) are part of a legal vocabulary attested in the papyri,
and it is highly probable that we should give a technical sense
to the use of the words here. Paul's sure hope is that he and his
readers are secure in God's keeping and may draw on his resources, even though he is in bonds and will shortly be called to
testify in the arraignment of his trial. See H. Schlier, *TDNT* i,
p. 603.

**8. For God is my witness, how I yearn for you all with
the affection of Christ Jesus.** A window into Paul's deep
relationship with his converts opens as we read this verse. He
departs in a striking way from the rabbinic custom of avoiding
the name of **God** in such a solemn asseveration, and he calls
God to **witness** that he has a profound longing to be re-united
with his friends at Philippi. The Greek verb *epipothein*, rendered
here **yearn**, is often used by him to denote his desire to see
Christian friends (Rom. 1:11; 1 Th. 3:6; 2 Tim. 1:4). See
C. Spicq, '*Epipothein*, Désirer ou chérir?' *RB* 64.2 (1957), pp. 184-
195; and the comment on 2:26. This intense yearning to be
reunited with the church fellowship which evidently meant so
much to him (see 4:1 for a similar sentiment) is now described
as nothing less than Christ's love expressing itself through Paul.
So Lightfoot who comments: 'his pulse beats with the pulse of
Christ; his heart throbs with the heart of Christ.' This is one of
the most moving, if indirect, examples of Paul's 'mysticism',
which is another name for the closeness of union he knew with
the risen Lord in the spirit (cf. 2 C. 3:17, 18). See J. D. G. Dunn,
'2 Corinthians iii. 17—"The Lord is the Spirit," ' *JTS* 21 n.s.
(1970), pp. 309-20. Here he confesses that his union with Christ
is no private affair, but extends to embrace fellow-Christians
also. Notice the frequent repetition of **all** in these verses (4, 7
twice, 8) to underscore the inclusiveness of Paul's attitude, in contrast perhaps to the cliquish spirit of the Philippian congregation.

9. The desire which he felt to see the Philippians must, how-

ever, remain unfulfilled, at least for the present. He hopes that
shortly it may be realized (2:24). But his prison confinement will
prevent its immediate realization. So Paul at a distance discharges
a pastoral ministry by his prayers.

The following verses embody the substance of his prayer,
already spoken of at verse 4. The words used are slightly different.
Verse 4 has the Greek *deēsis*; now he uses a verb (*RSV*, **it is my
prayer**) from which the noun *proseuchē* derives. But the distinction is slight. 'Only with great reserve we may distinguish and
say that *proseuchē* denotes prayer comprehensively while *deēsis* can
also have the specific sense of petitionary prayer' (H. Greeven,
TDNT ii, p. 807).

It is more important to note the function of Paul's prayers for
the churches. They are embodied in his letter not only to give
specimen examples of his prayer; they have a hortatory purpose
by encouraging his readers to act upon the counsel which the
prayers contain. They are thus a type of *paraklēsis* (so Gnilka).

love in this context is apparently the Christians' love for one
another (cf. 1 Th. 3:12; cf. 4:10). But it is a gift of God and a
sign of his grace in the Messianic age, thus replacing the Torah-
religion (cf. Collange). Paul asks that this quality in human life
may increase and develop in **knowledge and all discernment.**
These terms, and also Paul's later expression, **what is excellent**
(v. 10), are common in hellenistic moral philosophers such as
Epictetus and Plutarch, who use this vocabulary in the twofold
sense of an intellectual apprehension of the good in life and a moral
choice which determines a man's course of action. For the
Christian, the mainspring of both his knowledge of what is moral
excellence and his desire to translate approval into action is
love. Paul's prayer is that the Philippians' love may be expressed
in their mutual relationships as they recognize what needs to be
done in a given situation and then apply that understanding.
Perhaps his eye was already on a community where there was a
tendency to selfishness, disunity, and fault-finding (2:2; 2:14;
4:1ff.). One of the saddest features of this church was a confusion
of moral issues which made them easy prey to the sectarian
teachers who are condemned in chapter 3. See Introduction,
p. 32.

10. Two results follow from the cultivating of these virtues.
One is that the Philippians **may approve what is excellent,**

and then, on the level of Christian character, that they **may be pure and blameless** in preparation for the day of eschatological testing (Rom. 2:16).

The verb **approve** (Gr. *dokimazein*) means to 'put to the test' (1 Th. 5:21) and then to 'accept as tested', to 'approve'. As a commercial term it was used to denote the testing of coins. The coins which are 'approved' are genuine currency, not counterfeit. The thought of testing was evidently a familiar and favourite one with Paul (see Rom. 12:2; 1 C. 3:13, 11:28; 2 C. 8:22, 13:5; Gal. 6:4; 1 Th. 2:4).

The object of the verb in this context may be translated 'the things which differ' as well as in the *RSV*. However, the parallel reference in Rom. 2:18 suggests that the expression should be derived from current hellenistic philosophy (see A. Bonhöffer, *Epiktet und das Neue Testament*, Berlin, 1964 edn, pp. 298ff., referring to Epictetus, *Diss.* I. 20, 7, 'the greatest task of the philosopher is to test the impressions and discriminate between them') and be rendered, 'the things that really matter' (*AG*). Cf. Moffatt's translation, 'a sense of what is vital'. The idea is that Paul's readers may have the ability to discern, and then to practise in their corporate life as believers, the really important matters of community living. The Jewish background which shows that a Jew was to choose what was essential in life on the basis of the Torah is appealed to by Lohmeyer as important here. For the Christian, Torah is replaced by love (v. 9) as the all-important criterion for moral judgment. (See D. Bonhoeffer, *Ethics*, ET London, 1955; in 1965 edn, pp. 49–54.)

The Philippians' calling is to be both **pure** and **blameless**. Probably these adjectives are to be taken in a complementary way, one suggesting a positive element of genuineness, the other assuring them negatively that there is no fault to be found in their character. The adjectives are brought together in 1 Clem. 2:5.

pure (Gr. *eilikrinēs*) denotes moral not ritual purity (see F. Büchsel, *TDNT* ii, pp. 397ff.). It is found in the *NT* only here and in 2 Pet. 3:1. Moffatt renders 'transparent', on the basis of a derivation which sees the word as coming from *heilē* ('sunlight'), i.e., 'tested by sunlight' (Müller, *Commentary*, p. 46). **blameless** may carry a transitive sense, 'not causing offence' to another person (cf. 1 C. 10:32; Ac. 24:16).

11. fruits of righteousness is a phrase which may be understood in two ways, depending on the force of the genitive. It means in the first view, 'fruit which consists of being rightly related to God'. **righteousness** is seen to belong 'within the framework of Paul's common forensic metaphor—it is the condition of acquittal which God graciously gives through Christ' (Houlden; cf. Collange). Most commentators prefer another view, which is to see in the phrase an ethical sense. Paul is praying that his readers' lives may produce a crop of moral qualities in right living, which are the 'fruit of the Spirit' (Gal. 5:22) and made possible in union with Jesus Christ (see J. A. Ziesler, *The Meaning of Righteousness in Paul*, Cambridge, 1972, pp. 151, 203). Either way, both a forensic acquittal and a life worthy of the Christian's profession are important in view of the 'day of Christ' when all secrets are known and men's lives brought to the final test of the great assize. This allusion to the day of judgment looks back to the reference to the *parousia* in verse 6.

Paul's prayer closes on a note which is characteristic in the prayer-speech of both Jews and early Christians. **to the glory and praise of God** are not part of the apostolic prayer, but a liturgical borrowing added to conclude the period of thanksgiving.

For a recent study of verses 3–11, see G. P. Wiles, *Paul's Intercessory Prayers*, Cambridge, 1974, pp. 202–15, and P. T. O'Brien, *Pauline Thanksgivings*, Leiden, forthcoming.

PAUL'S AMBITION FOR THE GOSPEL I:12–26

This long section forms a unity and is dominated by a central theme. Commentators are generally agreed that the centre of gravity is to be found at verse 18 in Paul's overriding concern to see Christ proclaimed. He has this ambition not simply as a private individual but as an apostle whose present circumstances of confinement are bound up with the destiny of the gospel message which he is charged to deliver (so Gnilka). For that reason he devotes so much of his writing to an insistence that the gospel is not jeopardized by his imprisonment and to an explanation of why he suffers—as though to rebut the innuendo that he is no true apostle since he is suffering. He by-passes many questions to do with his personal circumstances on which we would be interested to have light. There is a tantalizing obscurity about these verses, and we can only guess at the solution to some problems of identification and background. But the leading issue (for Paul) is not in doubt: Christ is being proclaimed, and his message will be advanced whatever the outcome of Paul's fate as a prisoner.

12. The language of the verse reads as though Paul wanted to assure the Philippians that all was well with him. Perhaps they have expressed a concern for him through Epaphroditus' visit (2:25). **I want you to know, brethren** is Paul's reassurance expressed in a disclosure formula (J. L. White, *The Body of the Greek Letter*, pp. 121f.); but he does not turn aside to mention his personal needs. His interest focuses on giving a statement of personal vindication of his apostleship and on announcing the progress of the gospel. The Greek term rendered **to advance** (Gr. *prokopē*) is more specifically 'advancement in spite of obstructions and dangers which would block the traveller's path'. As a term of moral philosophy, it has a long history (see *TDNT* vi, pp. 704–7, 710f.), and 'Paul seems to have coined the statements' at this verse and 1:25 for his own purpose (loc. cit., p. 712). Certainly they are expressive.

13. He amplifies how the mission work has made headway in the teeth of opposition from outside. His captivity has become plain for all around him to see, and they recognize that he is a prisoner because of his commitment to Christ's cause, i.e., he is not a political or civil wrong-doer. Nor is his apostolic service placed in doubt because he is a suffering apostle. Quite the opposite.

The sphere in which Paul's witness has been effective is **throughout the whole praetorian guard and to all the rest.** The second part of the phrase clearly refers to individuals, and so fixes the meaning of *praitōrion* (a Greek loan-word from the Latin *praetorium*). It refers then not to the imperial or governor's residence but to either the emperor's bodyguard or praetorian cohorts stationed in the metropolis (so, most recently, B. Reicke, 'Caesarea, Rome, and the Captivity Epistles', in *Apostolic History and the Gospel*, ed. W. W. Gasque and R. P. Martin, Exeter, 1970, p. 283), or to the senatorial guard on duty at the provincial capital of Ephesus (see Dibelius, p. 55), or Caesarea or even Corinth. See earlier in the Introduction, pp. 38, 51.

The *RSV* rendering follows Lightfoot's discussion and conclusion (*Commentary*, pp. 99–104) which maintains that the guard was at Rome. They would be brought into touch with Paul in the course of their supervisory duties, although as there were 9,000 *praetoriani* it is difficult, if not impossible, to imagine that the case of one prisoner should be known to all. Perhaps then in this setting, we are not meant to take the reference to the whole praetorian guard in a literal way (cf. McNeile-Williams, *Introduction*, 2nd edn, Oxford, 1953, p. 181); or perhaps it is not the praetorian guard at Rome which is envisaged, as supporters of the view that Paul's captivity was in the provinces argue.

all the rest takes in a wider circle, probably of pagans, who heard of Paul's imprisonment and the reason for it.

14. As a second consequence of the news of his captivity others within the Christian fellowship are being given fresh stimulus to the work of evangelization. The Greek behind the phrase **most of the brethren** points to a contrast with the groups of persons mentioned in the previous verse (see BDF, sec. 244.3). Christians have found a new accession of strength (becoming **confident in the Lord**) and are encouraged, by Paul's example, **to speak** out more boldly in witness to **the word of God**, i.e., the apostolic message.

On a different reading of this verse another view is possible. This is to take Paul's Greek phrase (*hoi pleiones*) to mean 'the majority' (but not all), in reference to the Christian preachers in the place of Paul's captivity. This would mean that not everyone was so positively stirred by Paul's presence as an imprisoned apostle, and this paves the way for a division mentioned in verses 15–17. In either case, they are Christian preachers (**brethren**), and this title gives support to the first view, viz., that Paul's presence and his deportment in his confinement have had a salutary effect on the Christian community around him in general.

15–17. This is an important section of the letter, giving rise to diverse interpretations. It appears to stand in some tension with the foregoing verse 14. There Paul had written approvingly and enthusiastically of preachers who were strengthened by his witness in prison and who were launching out on active missionizing work. Now he has sadly to comment that not all are motivated by the highest intentions. **Some indeed preach Christ from envy and rivalry**, moved by motives of **partisanship, not sincerely but thinking to afflict me in my imprisonment.**

The issue is whether we can identify this group alongside the others who are Paul's supporters and concerned to carry on his work **out of love** for him.

The small section of verses 15–17 is artistically formed; it is made up of antithetical parallel statements after the fashion of the Greek rhetorical device of *chiasmus*. It is obviously a self-contained unit. But it cannot be detached from the surrounding context and treated as an excursus as some German commentators propose. Nor is there much to favour E. Lohmeyer's description of the rival preachers as heretics. Paul does not condemn the substance of their preaching. His sad observation touches their motives in preaching Christ.

T. Hawthorn ('Phil. 1:12–19 with special reference to vv. 15, 16, 17', *ExpT* 62 (1950–1), pp. 316f.) tries to detach this preaching from religious controversy and to see it as aimed at the civil authorities in the place of Paul's confinement (presumably Rome). These men are proclaiming an anti-imperial message (perhaps couched in a revolutionary-style similar to the allegation of Ac. 17:7, 8), and so they are stirring up strife with the Roman civil order. They are provoking persecution and inviting martyrdom, inspired by the belief that suffering must be endured before the end-time which they are concerned to hasten. Thereby they are making life difficult for Paul in his dealings with the authorities.

This reading of the text makes a lot of the terms **envy** and **rivalry** as anti-social vices. More likely the terms belong to the world of Christians who are basely motivated *against Paul*, not against the Roman imperium or against their fellow-believers (so T. W. Manson, *Studies in the Gospels and Epistles*, ed. M. Black, Manchester, 1962, pp. 161ff., who locates the scene of this contentious preaching in Corinth where Paul is a prisoner at the time of the letter. 1 C. 1–4 speaks of their factiousness and strife), or against the Jews (as F. C. Synge, *Commentary*, pp. 24f. who thinks that these men are deliberately antagonizing the Jews and denouncing them as a reprisal for what they have done to Paul). Paul, however, will have none of this kind of preaching, verse 17.

What seems intended is a group of Christian preachers who disdain Paul because he is an apostle in prison, who are inspired by thoughts of envy and animosity towards him because he seems to have placed the Christian message in doubt by his weakness as

a prisoner and to have imperilled its progress in the world. Their
rivalry is, however, not directed against him personally; rather
they have a rival missionary strategy which excels in power,
proves its claim by a triumphalism over all opposition, and
glories in success. In effect, they see themselves as 'divine men',
similar to the itinerant religious teachers and preachers who were
familiar figures in the ancient Graeco-Roman world. This understanding of Paul's enemies is proposed by R. Jewett ('Conflicting
Movements in the Early Church as Reflected in Philippians',
NovT 12 (1970), pp. 362–90). The merit of this interpretation is
that it illuminates other references to Paul's situation in the place
of his detention.

Paul's retort is many-pronged. He is grateful for the loyalty of
those who see the true meaning of his imprisonment. He is still
active in witness, and it is his faithfulness to the apostolic gospel
which has brought about his sufferings (v. 16). He is **put here** by
God (the Greek *keimai* is a theological term, emphasizing that his
appointment is a divine commission [cf. Lk. 2:34; 1 Th. 3:3;
possibly 1 Jn 5:19]), and not (as an allegation against him may
well have run) because of some foolhardy action, or because he
has no exemption from suffering as 'true apostles' may claim. If
the rival preachers were making inordinate claims for their
ministry (perhaps, as Jewett suggests, venturing to adopt for
themselves the title of 'God-manifest' as divinely appointed
messengers), then Paul would counter this claim by remarking
that his badge of office and his credentials are seen in the chain he
wears (v. 13: his bonds are manifest [Gr. *phanerous*] as worn by a
Christian).

18. So he sums up his reaction to the situation created by a
hostile segment of the surrounding church. **What then?** or
better, 'what does it matter?' (BDF, sec. 299.1). He is indifferent
to these attacks on him as a man of no reputation or as a false
apostle. His sole concern is to see Christ promoted; and this fact
fills him with joy both in the present and for the future.

19. Yes, and I shall rejoice. That expectation of future gladness is renewed. Paul now returns to the matter of his fate as a
prisoner, or at least to his desire to be a witness in his confinement. His rejoicing is grounded not on any human calculation
but on his confidence in God's help. In that sphere he can count
upon two kinds of assistance: one is human (**your prayers**), the

other comes directly from God (**the help of the Spirit of Jesus Christ**). Both parts of the aid he is glad to be able to summon are expressed in touching detail. The Philippians' prayer (Gr. *deēsis*) answers to his supplication for them (v. 4). The **help** of the Holy Spirit suggests an undergirding and strengthening of his life so that his courage will not fail nor his witness be impaired (v. 20), whatever the outcome of the trial may bring to him. The noun *epichorēgia* belongs to several worlds: in marriage contracts evidenced by the papyri it means 'to provide for a spouse'; in medical terminology the verb can be used of 'the ligament which acts as a support' (Eph. 4:16; Col. 2:19); and in Athenian drama festivals it is used of the furnishing of the chorus. The Spirit's help is nothing less than Christ's power available to his people (E. Schweizer, *TDNT* vi, p. 417).

By this combined assistance Paul expects to gain a **deliverance** (Gr. *sōtēria*). A few commentators see this hope as centring in Paul's confidence regarding his 'eternal deliverance or salvation' (G. Friedrich, ad loc.; J. L. Houlden, p. 64). Alternatively, the word is equivalent to his vindication at court. He hopes that his trust in God will be honoured and his witness to divine faithfulness will be attested by the turn of events. But this is not the same as the hope of release from prison since in the next verse he envisages the possibility of death.

J. H. Michael (*Commentary*, ad loc.) argues for this second meaning, remarking that Paul's sentence is a quotation from Job 13:16: 'This will be my salvation' (LXX is exactly the same as Paul's Greek). He is confident that whether he is acquitted or not his stand for Christ will be vindicated; and Job expressed a similar confidence that his trust would be validated by God (13:18). See Gnilka and Collange, ad loc.

Paul's presence in court and arraignment before his judges (see verse 7) will be an occasion for the gospel's vindication also. Then he will be sustained by the Spirit whom Jesus promised to the disciples when they stand before their accusers (Mk 13:11; Lk. 12:11, 12).

20. as it is my eager expectation and hope. He has his eye still on the future when the time of testing will come. A prospect which would have filled most men with foreboding and alarm is in fact eagerly awaited by Paul. *apokaradokia* (**eager expectation**) is a picturesque word, denoting a state of keen anticipation of the future, the craning of the neck to catch a glimpse of what lies ahead, 'the concentrated intense hope which ignores other interests (*apo*), and strains forward as with outstretched head (*kara, dokein*)', as H. A. A. Kennedy well describes it (*Commentary*, ad loc.). It is thus a positive attitude to whatever the future may bring, a meaning attested in the secular use of the Greek verb. See G. Bertram's study, '*APOKARADOKIA* (Phil. 1, 20)', *ZNW* 49 (1958), pp. 264-70.

His buoyant outlook is governed by several considerations. He trusts that his courage will not succumb to fear; rather he wants his ordeal to be matched by new courage (Gr. *parrhēsia*, literally, 'boldness in public speaking'). Above all, he longs that **Christ may be honoured**. The contrast **not . . . ashamed . . .** the Lord glorified (Gr. *megalynthēsetai*) is a familiar one in the *OT* Psalter, and in the Qumran Hymn scroll, e.g., 1QH 4.23f.:

> They have no esteem for me
> [that Thou mayest] manifest Thy might (i.e., make
>   Thyself great) through me.
> Thou hast revealed Thyself to me in Thy power as
>   perfect Light,
> and Thou hast not covered my face with shame

(cf. Vermes, p. 162).

The honour of Christ will be achieved, Paul goes on, in a sublime indifference to what appear to us today as momentous issues, either **by life or by death**. Both destinies touch his bodily existence but it is quite likely that Paul's use of **in my body** includes his total life as a responsible human being and servant of God (cf. Rom. 12:1 for this inclusive sense of *sōma*, denoting 'the whole man and not just a part . . . [and also] the sphere in which man serves': see E. Schweizer's important discussion, *TDNT* vii, pp. 1065f.).

21-24. Now, in a series of contrasting statements which may be arranged in parallelism, he sets down the alternatives facing him. The schema is carefully drawn up in the form of headings, but the syntax which would make the section fully intelligible as a piece of connected writing is broken. The outline of what was in Paul's mind is clear, however:

a. Life:	for me it is Christ	(v. 21*a*)
b. Death:	it is gain	(v. 21*b*)

c. Life: if I am to live on . . .   (v. 22)
d. Death: my desire is to go to be with Christ   (v. 23)
e. Life: my pastoral responsibility demands my con-
                  tinuing presence   (v. 24)

Each of these statements fits together into a progressive chain of
thought as Paul's mind turns over the possibilities. In a sense he is
balancing only theoretical issues, because his life is still at risk and
at the mercy of his captors. Yet he knows, as a Christian and an
apostle, that his life stands in the field of God's providential
ordering and control, where no evil force can touch him except
by divine permission. The real issue resolves itself into a decision
as to what kind of 'deliverance' (v. 19) he can best contemplate.
If the Philippians' prayers for his survival are heard, he can expect
a prolongation of his missionary service (**fruitful labour**) and
an eventual return to Philippi for a resuming of his pastoral relations with the church there (v. 26). If, on the other hand, the
verdict goes against him, it will mean a death sentence and an end
to his life here. But this thought holds no terror for Paul since
many desirable 'ends' are served by this eventuality: his martyrdom will be **gain** as Christ is honoured in that act and his message proclaimed (v. 21), and his own personal desire will be
fulfilled as he enters into deeper fellowship with his Lord beyond
death (v. 23).

The choice is a genuine dilemma like the pressure of opposing
forces. He is 'hemmed in on both sides' (Lightfoot's translation
in v. 23). The verb *synechomai* suggests the idea of total control,
submission to claims which in this case are so evenly balanced in
their competition that Paul is under equal pressure from two sides
(see H. Köster, *TDNT* vii, pp. 883f.) and cannot break free. If it
were left to his own natural inclination, the option would be clear:
he would choose **to die** (as a martyr; the aorist infinitive *to
apothanein* has that fate in view) and so go to **be with Christ**.

to depart (Gr. *analysai*) is not to be construed as a yearning for
immortality which the Greeks sought to achieve by shedding the
physical body and thus permitting the spirit to escape its tram-
mels. The metaphor of the verb may be drawn from the military
terminology for striking camp, such as Antiochus' army did in its
retreat from Persia (2 Mac. 9:1, which uses the verb), or from
the nautical language of releasing a ship from its moorings to sail
away. But the more immediate general background is not the

Greek philosophical debate on the immortality of the soul which
seeks for release from the body at death (cf. the Jewish version in
Tob. 3:6) but the hope of a closer union with Christ for which
there is no adequate parallel in antiquity (so Gnilka). **to be with
Christ** expresses his hope of 'his personal "being with Christ"
. . . consisting of the personal fellowship between Christ and the
apostle' (W. Grundmann, *TDNT* vii, p. 784). The closest parallel
is 2 C. 5:1–10, on which see M. J. Harris, 'Paul's View of Death
in 2 Corinthians 5:1–10', in *New Dimensions in New Testament
Study*, ed. R. N. Longenecker and M. C. Tenney, Grand Rapids,
1974, pp. 317–28.

The exact phrase **to be with Christ** has given rise to some
discussion. What precisely does Paul mean by it? Are there
parallels sufficiently close that it could be suggested that he derived it from outside sources? The latter question is more easily
answered. W. Grundmann (loc. cit., pp. 781ff.) takes a starting
point by referring to a parallel expression ('to be with God') in the
Psalms of the *OT* which express the hope that (cultic) fellowship
with Yahweh will continue beyond death. Later Judaism believed
that fellowship between God and man vanquished death, and
'this is probably the theological basis of Paul's statements'
(Grundmann, p. 782). This supposition is far more likely than
alternative proposals, e.g., that Paul borrowed the idea of re-
union with Christ beyond death from the hellenistic mystery cults.
However, in its precise formulation, there seems to be no exact
parallel, and Paul's use of the term is his own, without borrowing.
The closest analogies are with Jewish ideas, as discussed by
P. Hoffmann, *Die Toten in Christus. Eine religionsgeschichtliche und
exegetische Untersuchung zur paulinischen Eschatologie*, Münster, 1966,
pp. 286–320; and J.-F. Collange, *Excursus 2*: 'L'expression
"être avec Christ", et l'eschatologie paulinienne,' pp. 62–5.

The background to the formula 'to be with Christ' is problematical, with the most probable idea that Paul's thought is best
understood as an expression of his teaching on dying-and-rising
with Christ. (See the discussion in A. R. George, *Communion with
God in the New Testament*, London, 1953, pp. 150–5, and R. C.
Tannehill, *Dying and Rising with Christ*, Berlin, 1967.) By his death
Christ overcame man's enemy, death; in his resurrection he inaugurated a new age. But he was not alone in this triumph. He
represented his people who share in the benefits of his victory over

death (Rom. 6:1–11). In human experience that union with
Christ by faith is begun by a response to his call, expressed in
faith and exemplified in the baptismal confession. So intimate, in
Paul's teaching, is the bond between the believer and his Lord
(see, e.g., 1 C. 6:17), that death cannot break it. Rather, death
ushers him into an even deeper communion, so that Paul can
actually say, in a reinforced comparative, that this union beyond
death is **far better** as a consummation devoutly to be wished.
The triple adverb in the Greek (literally, 'much rather better')
means 'by far the best', a most emphatic superlative.

However, Paul is guided by other than personal desires. His
'cross-centric' thought is related not so much to personal immortality or interest in the after-life, as to a concern for Christ's work
and fidelity to his word (Collange). Paul's pastoral altruism
shines through as he returns to the situation of his 'care for all the
churches' (2 C. 11:28, *AV*). It is **more necessary on your
account** (a thought including but not restricted to the Philippian
congregation) that his life should be spared and should continue.

**25, 26. Convinced of this, I know that I shall remain and
continue with you all.** These verses open with a note which has
suggested to some commentators that Paul is expressing a new
confidence regarding his future. Earlier verses in the chapter (vs.
20, 23) were heavy with the thought of imminent martyrdom, and
it seemed that death was just around the corner. 'Paul . . . in his
inmost heart anticipated for himself no other fate than death'
(J. H. Michael). The question is whether his outlook changed at
verse 25 and he goes on to contemplate the prospect of survival of
his ordeal and a return to Philippi (v. 26).

Many guesses have been offered to account for this hypothetical
change in his prospect. Was it a prophetic illumination that God
gave him that the issue of his trial would be favourable to him (so
Lohmeyer)? Or that news came to him that his judges' decision
had been made in his favour (so Michaelis)? Or possibly Paul's
conviction grew out of a meditation on God's purpose in the events
of his recent exposure to risk (so Bonnard)? We cannot answer
these questions with any degree of certainty. Perhaps after all
Paul's confidence was strictly related to his sense of pastoral responsibility, and he is considering his own conviction 'based
on his sense of the Philippians' need of him' (J. H. Michael). To
support the last idea we need to recall that in 2:17 he returns to

the distinct possibility that he will not escape from the fate of martyrdom.

What is more certain is that Paul's return to Philippi and the resumption of his ministry as long as the future lasted would help the Philippians. The second verb **continue** is a tautology which repeats the first verb **remain.** If it has a separate function in the sentence, it may well suggest Paul's hope to survive until the *parousia* of Christ: so Lohmeyer, Bonnard.

For one thing, it would ensure his assistance on the road of their **progress** (the same word as in 1:12) and **joy in the faith.** The latter is a human touch which illustrates the closeness of the tie which united apostle and community. His presence with them would enhance their **joy,** as their common life was a source of gladness and satisfaction to him (1:4; 4:1). Then, they would have ample ground for exultation by the fact that their prayers for his deliverance had been answered (v. 19) and his witness had been maintained (v. 20). His restoration to the Philippians would be a token of divine mercy evoking their praise. Such a positive outcome of his trials would be an encouragement to them, as well as making good Paul's hope to see them once more (2:24).

If the letter comes out of Paul's Ephesian imprisonment, he did live to see his hope realized (Ac. 20:1–6, which suggests two probable visits to Philippi). On a Roman dating, we cannot be sure; and the question is a broader one involving the reliability of the tradition that he was released at the close of the period in Ac. 28:30 and the authenticity of the Pastoral epistles (1 Tim. 1:3). (See G. Ogg, *The Chronology of the Life of Paul*, London, 1968, chs. 21, 22; and J. J. Gunther, *Paul: Messenger and Exile*, Valley Forge, Pa., 1972, ch. 6.)

EXHORTATIONS TO THE COMMUNITY 1:27–2:18

Paul's mind has just been directed to the possibility of seeing the Philippian community once again. This animadversion now suggests to him that he should give direct counsels even in his enforced absence. He frequently expresses the thought of his personal presence with the churches even though he cannot be with them in person (1 C. 5:3; Col. 2:5). In the case of the Philippians he has in mind the need to caution them against a spirit of divisiveness and self-seeking as well as to offer them encouragement in the conflict which they were apparently facing. These are the twin

motifs of this long section. The Pauline emphases fall on the need
for unity, humility, and a closing of the ranks in the face of
threatened danger from the outside. That much is clear. But if
we press our enquiry further to ask about the reason for the disunity and quarrelsomeness within the fellowship, and the nature
of the hostility from the world outside the church, we are at a loss
to find precise details. We can only conjecture.

It is reasonable to think that part of the trouble inside the church
was a loss of confidence arising out of unexpected suffering. 2:14
warns against 'complaining' and 'disputing'. Both terms suggest
a querulousness and perplexity at what had just happened to the
church. Why should they have to suffer for their faith and endure
a bitter conflict? Paul's reply is to offer a theodicy, i.e., a justify-
ing of these events in the light of the purpose of God and the nature
of the Christian life which does not exempt Christians from mis-
fortune and trials (so in 1:29, 30). Part of that theodicy is to
summon the example of his own experience of suffering, both past
and present, and to implore the Philippians not to disappoint
his expectation of them (2:16). His self-description, as a martyr-
figure on behalf of the churches, adds poignancy to the appeal
(2:17).

The chief thrust of Paul's answer is to show how God's plan includes the suffering of the churches (1:29) and how the nature of
the Christian calling gets its model from the incarnate Lord himself (2:6–11). He came to his exaltation along a road of self-
humbling, rejection, and obedience unto death. The life of the
church is thus cruciform since it derives from him who exemplified
the 'dying to live' pattern; and the appeal of 2:5 is to exhort the
Philippians to let their life together take its shape from the recognition that this is what their destiny is as members of Christ's body
'in Christ Jesus'.

The suffering Lord and the suffering apostle together (see E.
Güttgemanns, *Der leidende Apostel und sein Herr*, Göttingen, 1966)
prove that there is nothing incoherent or inconsistent in the Christians' 'fate' as a persecuted community set in a hostile world
(2:15); and this should be an effective antidote to the distraught
and rebellious spirit which was evidently present at Philippi.
Paul's tone in reply is similar to his appeal in 1 Th. 3:3, 4: 'No
one [should] be moved by these afflictions. You yourselves know
that this is to be our lot. For when we were with you, we told you

beforehand that we were to suffer affliction; just as it has come
to pass, and as you know.'

(a) **1:27–30.** *The need for unity and courage in the face of persecution*
27. Only. 'Just one thing' is how Barth's translation of Paul's
single Greek word (*monon*) runs; it is an admonition 'lifted like a
warning finger'. He desires for them as church members at Philippi
the highest quality of corporate life set by the standard of their
allegiance to **the gospel of Christ.** The life of the community is
likened to the citizenship (Gr. *politeia*) which the citizens at Rome
enjoyed in the ancient world. So Paul's verb (Gr. *politeuesthe*)
should be rendered to bring out this flavour. True, an exclusively
political meaning has been sometimes suggested, e.g., by R. R.
Brewer ('The Meaning of *Politeuesthe* in Phil. 1.27', *JBL* 73 (1954),
pp. 76–83), who translates 'discharge your obligations as citizens'.
But it is more likely that Paul is using the technical verb to call
the Philippians to their double responsibility: they were proud of
being treated under the *ius Italicum* (see A. N. Sherwin-White,
Roman Society and Roman Law in the New Testament, Oxford, 1963,
pp. 78f., 175–7) as citizens of the empire with privileges to enjoy
and responsibilities to fulfil. They must also remember that they
are citizens of a heavenly kingdom (3:20), and by this membership of Christ's kingdom on earth their conduct within the Church
and in the world is to be determined. The same thought is picked
up by Polycarp in his later letter to the *Philippians*: 'If we are his
worthy citizens (Gr. *politeusōmetha axiōs*), we shall also reign with
him' (5.2).

The notion of a worthy standard is frequent in the Pauline
corpus as part of his ethical mandate directed to the churches
(1 Th. 2:12; Rom. 16:2; Col. 1:10; Eph. 4:1). Here it is **the
gospel** which sets the ethical norm. **gospel** is not the written
record, but the proclaimed message, and the essence of Paul's
appeal is, as Gnilka says, 'Live as converted people', both in
church fellowship and in the outside world. This is the apostle's
earnest wish for them, even if he cannot be personally at their side.

Paul is realistic in his understanding of the church's struggle
against hostile powers. The section comprising verses 27–30 is rich
in military terms: **stand firm** (as resolute as soldiers set at their
post; Lohmeyer, p. 75, n. 2, prints the evidence for this sense of
the verb); **striving** (which carries the association of a military
contest, either in battle or in the arena where the gladiators

struggled in a life and death combat; cf. 2 Tim. 2:5); **your opponents** (or, better, 'adversaries'), whether human or demonic; and **conflict** (Gr. *agōn*), such as Paul had known at the time of his first visit to their city (1 Th. 2:2, which uses the same noun) and possibly had also recently endured at the time of his writing (Col. 2:1, if this letter belongs to the same general period of his life; see *New Century Bible Commentary*, 1974, pp. 23–32).

The call to the Philippians is to **stand firm in one spirit, with one mind striving side by side for the faith of the gospel.** The summons is notable for the interplay of the human and the divine. Certainly this is a stirring call to action and to present a unified front against a hostile world. But equally Paul is promising the help of God (as in 4:1), who by his Spirit (**one spirit** is better taken as referring to the Holy Spirit than to the human spirit, though Lohmeyer and E. Schweizer, *TDNT* vi, p. 435, prefer the latter) will assist his people to defend **the faith of the gospel.** Not by their faith but by their faithfulness to the apostolic teaching, which was evidently under fire at Philippi, would they be able to win through in their conflict, even if Paul's presence with them is not possible. See on 2:12, 13 for a similar encouragement drawn from the pledge of God's help. On this verse, see V. C. Pfitzner, *Paul and the Agon Motif*, Leiden, 1967, pp. 116–18.

28. not frightened in anything by your opponents. Exactly who these enemies of the church were Paul does not say. Clearly they were non-Christians since they are on the road to destruction (cf. 1 C. 1:18 which uses the same Greek term in its verbal form to denote the eschatological judgment reserved for the Church's enemies in the world). This consideration argues against the view (taken by J.-F. Collange; and also G. P. Wiles, *Paul's Intercessory Prayers*, p. 210) that 1:27f. looks forward to the warnings of chapter 3 and is set within the framework of the church's struggle against Jewish-Christian preachers who tried to introduce a perfectionist teaching on the ground of legalistic obedience to the law. On the contrary, Paul's call to steadfastness in this section has in mind a conflict (v. 30) which the Philippians associated with Paul's lot at the time when he was with them ('you saw') and which he is presently enduring ('and now hear to be mine'). This description can only fit the case of opposition coming from the pagan world.

Paul's outlook is optimistic. Although the church is feeling the pressure of persecution, he is confident that its final salvation is assured provided the believers maintain 'the faith' (v. 27), which seems to be referred to as **this** in Paul's statement **this is a clear omen** (the relative is attracted into the case of the noun 'faith'). Alternatively, the referent is the Philippians' constancy under trial, their fidelity which stands firm. (See the discussion in Hermann Binder, *Der Glaube bei Paulus*, Berlin, 1968, p. 78.) This confidence comes from Paul's conviction that even the persecution of the church is **from God.** The antecedent of this phrase is neuter (Gr. *touto*), and refers back to the whole episode of opposition in its double effect, i.e., leading the enemies to destruction and the Church to eschatological salvation. Either way, Paul says, it is God's purpose which is served. This seems to be the meaning of Paul's writing, though the Greek is elliptical. Westcott and Hort solve the problem of the difficult Greek by suggesting that verses 28b–29 are a parenthesis, and they attach verse 30 directly to verse 28a. This certainly helps the sense, and explains the intervening verses as a Pauline 'aside', added to give a theological commentary on the Philippians' sufferings.

not frightened uses an expressive verb, suggesting the stampede of startled horses. Paul is sure his friends will not break loose in disarray under this pressure. It is possible that the firmness of their faith is the sign of both the persecutors' doom and their own deliverance (so Dibelius, Gnilka, Michael); but this is less preferable than the above view, especially in view of the following verse.

29. For it has been granted to you [from God] **that for the sake of Christ you should not only believe in him but also suffer for his sake.** This magnificent statement is offered as a theodicy to help the Philippians to understand their sufferings at least in part. The passive voice **has been granted** is Paul's way of ascribing the activity to the will of God. The 'divine passive', as J. Jeremias calls it (*New Testament Theology*, vol. i, London, 1971, p. 9), is an *OT* manner of speech to emphasize that God is in control of all events. Therefore, the Philippians should not be upset by their bitter experience as if God had forgotten them or were angry with them. On the contrary, the verb (Gr. *echaristhē*) would remind them that even this trial comes to them as a gift of his grace (Gr. *charis*). Only in faith which comes from grace can suffering be regarded as a privilege (Gnilka).

But the chief weight of the verse lies in the teaching to Paul's readers that fellowship with a suffering Christ (**for the sake of Christ,** twice repeated here) necessarily entails a sharing of his destiny, and that Paul's understanding of the Christian life insists that there is no way to know that life in its truest expression, except along a road of personal identity with a Christ who was exposed to all the risks and hazards of a cruel world. This will be elaborated in 3:7–10. Already Paul is tacitly opposing the false teaching that regards apostolic and Christian sufferings as an unnecessary intrusion and believes that Christians are already advanced to a blissful state of a divine life on earth (see on 1:15ff. and 3:12ff.) and exempt from life's stresses and humiliations. These men may have claimed that 'glory' was the badge of the Christian. Paul insists that the distinctive mark is the cross.

30. The readers would well recall the circumstances of Paul's **conflict** which they had seen at the time their church was founded (Ac. 16:22ff.; 1 Th. 2:2). Later reports of his experiences 'when [he] left Macedonia' (4:15f.) would also be known to them. So he appeals to what they **hear to be mine.** Nor should we exclude his present trial, which for him is even more serious since it has brought him face to face with death's reality (1:20; 2:17). The Philippians were doubtless wondering how he was faring in captivity (1:12). His letter will set their minds at rest on that score, at least. Even if his **conflict** (Gr. *agōn*) is fierce and he is faced with momentous issues of life and death, he knows that his apostolic ministry is in God's hands and that the outcome will be 'deliverance' (1:19) because his hope is set on God (cf. 2 C. 1:8–10). This is precisely the hope he offers to the Philippians, since they are engaged in the same conflict and may know the same confidence as he does.

On **conflict** here, see V. C. Pfitzner, *Paul and the Agon Motif,* pp. 114–29.

(*b*) **2:1–4.** *The need for harmony in the church*
2:1. Up to this point Paul has been concerned to fortify the church in its struggle with 'enemies' on the outside (1:28). Now he turns his attention to the state of the church as a family of believers. He bids the Christians to examine the life they share inside the church (so Bonnard, Gnilka). This transition, expressed by **so** (Gr. *oun,* 'therefore'), assumes that he is turning from the menace of a hostile world to deal with the equally threatening problem of a divided

community. J.-F. Collange objects that this is not so, since 2:1–4, in his view, continues the warning against false preachers and calls the church to close its ranks. But Paul might just as well have felt that a disunited church would be easy prey to the frontal attack from the outside society. By a studied repetition of terms ('spirit', 'soul', 'present or absent') Paul moves from his exhortation to be firm and resolute to issue a call to a church in danger of falling apart through internal divisions.

There is a fourfold ground of his appeal. To Paul's mind there is nothing more certain than the realities to which he appeals, and for that reason any translation which suggests that the Philippians may not have known these bases on which their church life was built is to be deplored. Cf. W. Hendriksen's 'If then to any extent you have all these experiences and share in these benefits, then . . .' Paul's introductory word is 'since' rather than 'if', which expresses contingency. 'If, as is the case' would accurately convey his mind, as Hendriksen earlier conceded (p. 99).

any encouragement in Christ. If this is the best rendering of the Greek *paraklēsis* (it is accepted by Beare, Gnilka, Houlden), it suggests that, arising directly out of their common life 'in Christ', there is an obligation laid upon them to act together in harmony. The alternative translation is 'consolation' (championed by Bonnard, Collange, and W. Barclay, 'Great Themes of the New Testament. I: Phil. ii, 1–11', *ExpT* 70 (1958–9), p. 40) on the ground that Paul is making allusion to Christ's concern for the Church and that his tone is gentle, not domineering or dictatorial. Moreover, he is inviting the Philippians to recall their status as a community loved by Christ.

any incentive of love. Here again it is Christ's love for the Church which is in view (Barth quotes 2 C. 5:14 where Christ's love 'constrains' and moves the apostle). Less probable is the thought of their love for Paul or for the Lord, and even further removed is the idea of Paul's love for them. In calling them to live together in harmony Paul is appealing to the highest motive: the love which the head of the Church has for his people which should impel them to live worthily.

any participation in the Spirit. This is a much controverted phrase, raising several issues of interpretation. Almost certainly we should interpret the word for 'spirit' to refer to the Holy Spirit and not the human spirit. Then, the large question is whether the

genitive 'of the Spirit' is subjective or objective, that is, whether it
is to be rendered 'fellowship created by the Holy Spirit, which
only the Holy Spirit can give' (so W. Barclay, *ExpT* 70 (1958–9),
p. 40), or 'fellowship in the Holy Spirit', which comes about
through his indwelling presence in the Church and the Christian's
personal communion with him. The latter view is strongly argued
for by H. Seesemann, *Der Begriff KOINŌNIA im Neuen Testament*,
pp. 56–62, and accepted by many interpreters since then.

Seesemann observes that Paul takes the possession of the Holy
Spirit by the believer as a truth readily acknowledged and experienced by his readers (Gal. 3:2; 1 C. 12:13; contrast Ac. 19:1–7).
Then there is a parallel in 1 C. 1:9, where the meaning is 'participation in Christ' (see A. R. George, *Communion with God in the
New Testament*, London, 1953, pp. 175–7). Also, there is evidence
from early Christian writers that the Greek phrase used here,
koinōnia pneumatos, was understood to mean **participation in the
Spirit.** Finally, Seesemann argues from the form of Paul's wording in the verse. This appeal, he says, falls into two sets of pairs.
The 'fellowship of the Spirit' and 'affection and sympathy' go together as realities which are internal to the Christian, over against
'exhortation' and 'incentive' which are exterior to him. To take
the genitive *pneumatos*, 'of the Spirit', as subjective here would ruin
the parallelism because it would imply an action outside the believer's experience rather than in subjective experience, his 'share
in the Spirit' which, like 'heartfelt sympathy', is an internal quality
of his life.

The case for the rendering **participation in the Spirit** given
by Seesemann seems convincing, and even later writers who challenge it—such as E. Schweizer (*TDNT* vi, p. 434)—conclude that
even by taking the genitive as subjective ('fellowship given by the
Spirit'), since what he gives is a share in himself, the net result is
the same as Seesemann's conclusion leads to. (See also *TDNT* iii,
p. 807 (Hauck). For the stylistic features in v. 1, see Lohmeyer,
pp. 138f., and Gnilka, pp. 102f.)

The force of the appeal is: your common sharing in the Spirit
by whom you were baptized into one body should sound the
death-knell to all factiousness and party-spirit.

any affection and sympathy is sometimes taken to be a
hendiadys, as though Paul were saying no more than 'heartfelt
sympathy' (so Dibelius and R. Bultmann, *TDNT* v, p. 161). But

H. Köster (*TDNT* vii, pp. 555f.), has maintained that the two terms should be kept separate. The first word is *splanchna* and means literally the human entrails, thought of as the seat of the emotional life (as in 1:8). In these two verses in our epistle it is really a synonym for love of an intensely personal kind. In 1:8 it is Paul's love in Christ for the Philippians; here it is Christ's 'love from the heart' reaching out to the church members in their estrangement from one another. *oiktirmoi* are the human emotions of tender pity or sympathy. But whose sympathies is Paul invoking? Parallelism with the first word would suggest that it is Christ's personal concern for his people which is in mind, and this is to be preferred to the common view (cf. Bultmann, *TDNT* v, p. 161) that Paul is appealing to the Philippians' sympathy. The latter might be the case if there were an element of doubt in the apostle's mind. But, as we have seen, his opening words convey a certainty: 'as sure as there are' (Dibelius) these realities which stem from the head of the Church and which are the ground and basis of the apostle's appeal for harmony in the body of Christ.

On the grammatical question of Paul's use of *tis*, see BDF, sec. 137. 2; 145; and in reference to the last member of the quartet, see Moulton, *Grammar*, p. 59.

2. complete my joy. Paul will go on to pay tribute to this church as 'his joy and crown' (4:1). Now he asks that by responding to his call in verse 1 they will enhance that regard he has for them. They will answer his call **by being of the same mind,** a phrase which translates the Greek verb *phronein* (cf. 1:7). This is an important verb in the epistle, being found, as Lohmeyer points out, some ten times out of the 23 occurrences of the verb in Paul's other writings. See p. 66 for a comment on its meaning.

Paul builds up an impressive collection of ideas to emphasize the need for the church's unity. **having the same love** for one another (as I have for you, or better, as Christ has for you, referring back to v. 1). **being in full accord** may be an independent statement (so Lohmeyer, Gnilka), or an extension of the following phrase: 'as you are one in heart with other people so you will be of one mind with them' (so Collange). The last statement repeats the verb *phronein* and stresses the need for the believers to have a common purpose and action in their community life (cf. Rom. 12:16; 15:5; 2 C. 13:11). This admonition will be applied to a special case in 4:2.

3. The ethical terms used expose the spiritual malaise at the heart of the church and point to the remedy. **selfishness** (Gr. *eritheia*) is, more properly, 'faction' caused by 'base self-seeking' (Büchsel *TDNT* ii, pp. 660–1, who describes it as 'the nature of those who cannot lift their gaze to higher things'; cf. 3:19). Paul has already used the word in a different context (1:17) and it belongs to his vocabulary of social evils (2 C. 12:20; Gal. 5:20).

conceit goes to the root cause. 'Factiousness and vanity— these were the evils that menaced the Christian community at Philippi' (Michael). But the second term is deeper in meaning than 'vanity'. It is more like its literal translation 'vain, empty glory' (Gr. *kenodoxia*). If we recall the frequent mention of 'glory' (Gr. *doxa*) in this letter, usually with reference to God (1:11, 2:11, 4:19, 20), and once (3:21) with regard to Christ's resurrection body, we shall see that *kenodoxia* is a proud bid to rival God and to establish a self-assertive status which quickly leads to a despising of others (as in Gal. 5:26). It is destructive of true community life. Paul has put a probing finger on the exposed nerve of the Philippians' problem.

The remedy lies **in humility count others better than yourselves.** J.-F. Collange perceptively draws attention to the assonance between Paul's frequent verb (*phronein*, to reckon, to regard) and the word for humility (Gr. *tapeinophrosynē*). The message would be clear to the readers: let your attitude to and regard for others (*phronein*) be humble (*tapeinos*), and that means a total lifestyle of *tapeinophrosynē*. **humility** was a term of opprobrium in classical Greek thought, connoting 'servility' as the attitude of a base-born man and a slave (W. Grundmann, *TDNT* viii, p. 2). In the *OT* it takes on a different complexion as man is seen before God. Therefore, 'to cast oneself down' is a proper attitude of a servant of God in his presence, and at Qumran this idea receives an application to the community which is composed of men who are under obligation to 'practise truth and humility in common' (1QS 5:3f.: cf. 1QS 2:24, 4:3f., 5:25; Vermes, pp. 74, 76, 78, 80). Paul's thought has similar reference to the community of the saints. He goes on to show that the practice of humility consists in giving to other people a dignity and respect which Christians expect of themselves, especially as both parties are seen in God's sight (cf. Rom. 12:3, 10). **count others better than yourselves** is a summons to see ourselves in our rightful condition as creatures of God yet with a nobility given to us as his vice-regents upon earth (Gen. 1:26, 27). In that light we can see our fellow men as equally deserving of respect and honour.

4. The train of Paul's thought moves on to amplify what he has just written. **Let each of you look not** [**only;** this should be omitted as not in the Gr. text] **to his own interests, but** [**also;** some MSS omit this word *kai*] **to the interests of others.** If this shorter version of the text is accepted (cf. Houlden), it supports the interpretation that Paul is not making a general statement to do with Christians' responsibility to live 'each with an eye to the interests of others as well as to his own' (Moffatt's translation). Rather the verb *skopein* always has a definite object in its sights and means 'regard as your aim' (Lightfoot). Then, Paul is advocating that his readers fix their gaze on the good points and qualities in other Christians; and, when recognized, these good points should be an incentive to our way of life. The negative side to this admonition is that Christians at Philippi should not be so preoccupied with their own concerns and the cultivation of their own 'spiritual experience' that they fail to see what plainly should be evident for emulation in the lives of their fellow believers. Paul may well be gently correcting the self-centred preoccupations of a perfectionist group at Philippi (cf. 3:12-16). (See earlier, pp. 31f.)

On a positive level, this verse is a 'curtain-raiser' to a statement of what the Christian life should be. On one understanding of the next verse, he will direct attention to the mind or disposition which is exemplified 'in Christ Jesus' whose incarnate existence was that of humble obedience (2:8). A more recent view of 2:6-11 sees it as a story of salvation explaining how Christians came to be 'in Christ Jesus' as members of his Church. Paul in verse 5 is telling them to adopt in their communal life a disposition which is in character with their profession as Christians. Either way, he is setting a pattern of living before their eyes, and bidding them to conform to it.

(*c*) **2:5-11.** *The basis of the Christian life laid in the story of salvation*
5. **Have this mind among yourselves.** Once more Paul employs the verb (Gr. *phronein*) which more than any other in the epistle focuses attention on what he expects his readers to do. The verb is both a summons to adopt an attitude and an exhortation to carry that attitude into practice. It suggests a combination of

mental disposition and practical outworking. **among yourselves** shows that Paul has the church family in view and not the individual Christian as such, though the Greek *en hymin* could mean that. But he is talking to Christians as a community with social problems, not inculcating personal virtues based on a moral example.

which is yours in Christ Jesus is a *crux*. The Greek does not have a verb and it is an open question which verb is to be supplied as most suitable. The full range of possibilities should be displayed, since this question is fundamental to an understanding of the next six verses.

A. We begin with a summary that includes all ideas of ethical example, i.e., Christ is presented as a model to be followed.

(*i*) *Imitative.* What is perhaps the traditional view (see *AV*) wishes to add a part of the verb 'to be'. It reads: 'Let this mind be in/among you which was the mind that was in Christ Jesus'. E. Larsson (*Christus als Vorbild*, Uppsala, 1962, pp. 231ff.) gives a clear statement of this position: 'Paul has reached the point where he can introduce the great example for such a way of life (of humility) in his exhortation. It is Christ himself and his freely-willed renunciation of the heavenly power and glory which he possessed before the incarnation . . . the Philippians must have among themselves the same disposition (and so the same manner of life) which was in Christ Jesus . . . *en Christō Iēsou* . . . refers to Christ as an individual person. . . . In this view verses 1–5 are joined to the "hymn" by the introductory *hos* ["who"] which finds a natural correlative in the "individual" sense of *en Christō Iēsou*. Our interpretation has tried to show that Christ in verse 5 is presented as an example for the conduct of the Philippians. In verses 6–11 this is worked out fully.'

(*ii*) *Paradigmatic.* We may use this descriptive term to denote the view which supplies a part of the verb 'to be' but understands the meaning as 'which (mind or attitude) was also found in the case of Christ Jesus'. E. Lohmeyer has proposed this, also suggesting that a verb 'you see' (Gr. *blepete*) or 'you know' (Gr. *oidate*) would be suitable. C. F. D. Moule ('Further Reflexions on Philippians 2:5–11', in *Apostolic History and the Gospel*, ed. Gasque and Martin, Exeter, 1970, p. 265) has more recently followed this line (cf. I. H. Marshall, 'The Christ-Hymn in Philippians 2:5–11', *TynB* 19 (1968), pp. 104–27 [p. 118]).

(*iii*) *Mystical*. If we supply the verb 'to have' or 'to regard', it becomes possible to give a mystical turn to Paul's thought. Earlier suggested by C. H. Dodd (*The Apostolic Preaching and its Developments*, London, 1944, pp. 64f.) and A. Deissmann (*Paul*, London, 1925, p. 170), this translation has been picked up by *NEB*: 'Let your bearing towards one another arise out of your life in Christ Jesus'. This is taken by Dodd to be an illustration of 'ethics developing directly out of "Christ-mysticism" '.

B. Quite distinct is the interpretation which gives an ecclesiological dimension to the key-phrase 'in Christ Jesus'. R. Bultmann (*Theology of the New Testament*, ET London, 1952, vol. 1, p. 311) has clearly expressed the view that ' "in Christ", far from being a formula for mystic union, is primarily an *ecclesiological* formula'. When this conclusion is applied to our text, the latter yields the sense: Let this disposition be yours which it is necessary [or 'as it is fitting': so Gnilka, who suggests the Gr. *prepei* as the verb to be understood] to have as those who are 'in Christ Jesus'. So in K. Grayston's rendering (*Commentary*, p. 91): ' "Think this way among yourselves, which also you think in Christ Jesus", i.e., as members of His Church.'

C. Perhaps the most ingenious interpretation is that offered by E. Käsemann ('A Critical Analysis of Philippians 2.5–11', ET in *God and Christ*, ed. R. W. Funk, *JThC* 5 (1968) Tübingen/New York, pp. 83f.), who builds on the view given as *B* and adds another storey to the edifice. The essence of verses 6–11 is a drama of salvation, and verse 5 introduces a soteriological setting by calling upon Christians to live in their community relations as those who belong to Christ's rule. 'In Christ Jesus' means the sphere of salvation-history in which they were 'inserted' at their conversion-baptism, when the saving events of the story of Christ took on personal meaning and they passed from the domain of the old order to the 'new world' inaugurated by Christ's victory over all spirit-powers. So, 'Paul did not understand the hymn as though Christ were held up to the community as an ethical example. The technical formula "in Christ" . . . unquestionably points to the salvation-event; it has soteriological character, just as, according to Paul, one comes to be "in Christ" only through the sacrament' (p. 84).

Several reasons are forthcoming to support the case stated by Käsemann. They are: (*a*) 'in Christ Jesus' does have a technical sense in Paul, referring to membership of his body, the Church. (b) Paul does not habitually point to the earthly life of Jesus as an ethical example. Closest parallels to this idea are 2 C. 8:9; Rom. 15:7. But these are short statements, not comparable with an extended passage such as verses 6–11 in our letter. (c) On any interpretation other than Käsemann's, verses 9–11 are left 'in the air' and must be treated as an excursus, because Christ's elevation to world rulership cannot be the theme of the Christian's imitation. (d) Käsemann's view has the merit of connecting verse 5 with verse 11, and thereby of showing that the centre of gravity in the hymn is Christ's lordship over the cosmos, not a piece of teaching on his moral example, or even a discussion of his relationship to God. (e) The origin of verses 6–11 as a pre-Pauline hymnic composition now takes on new meaning as a 'song of salvation', describing the 'way of Christ'—Klaus Wengst (Christologische Formeln und Lieder des Urchristentums, Gütersloh, 1972, p. 149) calls 2:6–11 a 'hymn of the way', and finds an entire literary Gattung in this description, based on an ancient story of the redeemer—from his place with God through his incarnate life and death in humiliation and shame to his enthronement as Lord of the universe. Thereby the hymn celebrates the drama of redemption and tells the Philippians how they came to be 'in Christ'. (f) If the hymn has a baptismal setting (see J. Jervell, Imago Dei, Göttingen, 1960, pp. 206–9), the implied exhortation in verse 5 is 'become what you already are', risen with Christ to new life, and work out in your church difficulties the new life you received at your baptism into Christ (Rom. 6:1–14). This thought admirably links on to the sequel to the hymn in 2:12: 'work out your own salvation' as those who are 'in Christ' and heirs of salvation.

Accepting this conclusion about the meaning of verse 5 and the origin of the hymn in the following verses, we proceed to deal with the text from this vantage-point. A fuller treatment of these exegetical matters is offered by R. P. Martin, Carmen Christi: Philippians ii. 5–11 in Recent Interpretation and in the Setting of Early Christian Worship, Cambridge, 1967. The following pages are concerned (a) to isolate the significant issues, and (b) to take note of recent discussions since 1967. See the Appended Note on the literature concerning the more technical and background matters to do with 2:6–11.

6. who, though he was in the form of God. The relative
pronoun is one indication out of many that we are dealing with
a liturgical piece of composition (as in Col. 1:15; 1 Tim. 3:16;
Heb. 1:3), though, as Lohmeyer was first to identify, it is a
complete, self-contained poem or hymn, not a fragment (*Kyrios
Jesus*, 2nd edn, Heidelberg, 1961, p. 7).

the form of God (Gr. *morphē theou*) has been interpreted in
several ways. (*i*) Older writers equate our Lord's pre-existent
'form' with his metaphysical status within the Godhead. In this
view, the term *morphē* (taken to be equivalent to the Aristotelian
ousia) is 'used in a sense substantially the same which it bears in
Greek philosophy' (Lightfoot). (For the evidence, see H. Schum-
acher, *Christus in seiner Präexistenz und Kenose*, vol. i, Rome, 1914,
p. 160). The meaning is 'essential nature' as opposed to 'exterior
form' or shape (*schēma* in v. 8).

(*ii*) E. Käsemann ('A Critical Analysis', pp. 61f.) draws attention to the precise wording in verse 6. Paul's hymn does not say
that the pre-incarnate Christ *was* the 'form of God' but that he
was 'in' it. This must carry a technical sense and designate 'the
realm in which one stands and by which one is determined, as in
a field of force'. The best rendering of the term is 'mode of being'
(*Daseinsweise*), and is to be understood on the background of
hellenistic thought as a tribute to Christ's rank as 'equal with
God' as a heavenly man (in gnostic thought). But reliance on the
'heavenly man' myth to interpret the passage has been severely
criticized by D. Georgi ('Der vorpaulinische Hymnus, Phil.
2.6–11', in *Zeit und Geschichte*, Tübingen, 1964, pp. 263–6) and
J. T. Sanders (*The New Testament Christological Hymns*, Cambridge,
1971, pp. 66–9). Georgi's recital of seven points on which the
Philippians hymn moves in a world different from the gnostic
redemption saga is part of his rebuttal. Especially noteworthy
are (1) the absence of any incarnational motif in the gnostic
myth; (2) the omission of any thought of elevation by God in
sovereign power, as in 2:9; (3) the passing over of the idea of
universal dominion, such as Isa. 45:23 proclaims. Nor are the
recipients of the gnostic redemption explicitly mentioned. K.
Wengst, *Christologische Formeln*, pp. 154ff., attempts to answer
these objections by drawing on the 'Hymn of the Pearl' in the
Acts of Thomas (ET in *Gnosticism. An Anthology*, ed. R. M. Grant,
London, 1961, pp. 116–22). But the value of this document as a

witness to a pre-Christian gnostic redemption myth is disputed
(see E. M. Yamauchi, *Pre-Christian Gnosticism*, London, 1973,
pp. 95–8).

(*iii*) On the assumption that the more likely background is in
the world of the *OT* and hellenistic Judaism, it has been proposed
that *morphē* finds an equivalent in Greek words for 'glory' (*doxa*:
cf. J. Behm, *TDNT* iv, p. 759) or 'image' (*eikōn*). First argued for
by J. Héring (*Le Royaume de Dieu*, Paris, 1936, pp. 162ff.), this
theory of linguistic and conceptual equivalence has more recently
been supported by A. Feuillet (*RB* 72 (1965), pp. 365–80; and
idem, *Christologie paulinienne et tradition biblique*, Paris, 1972, pp.
101–10). It offers the attractive picture of the pre-existing Lord
as reflecting the divine splendour as the image of God (cf. Col.
1:15), and matches exactly the thought of Jn 17:5: 'the glory
which I had with thee before the world was'. But there are some
difficulties voiced by D. H. Wallace (*ThZ* 22 (1966), pp. 19–25),
and J.-F. Collange has criticized this view on the ground that it
fails to account for the parallel use of *morphē* in verse 7b. He opposes
any idea of a contrast between the biblical 'first Adam' of Gen.
1:26 made in the divine image and Christ as the second Adam
who also reflected the glory of God. But E. Schweizer (*Erniedrigung und Erhöhung*, 2nd edn, Zürich, 1962, p. 96 n. 383) has
introduced important evidence to show how *morphē* was used in
this description of Adam in speculative Judaism, and M. D.
Hooker ('Philippians 2:6–11' in *Jesus und Paulus*, Festschrift
W. G. Kümmel, ed. E. E. Ellis and E. Grässer, Göttingen, 1975,
pp. 160–4) has offered some fresh arguments in support of the
thesis that 'being in the form of God' means 'being-like-God' (as
the first Adam was, yet he failed to understand it and, in contrast, the second Adam understood that this likeness was already
his, by virtue of his relationship to God). The idea of 'God-likeness'
which links the first and second Adam is supported too by
P. Grelot ('Deux expressions difficiles de Philippiens 2, 6–7', *Biblica*
53, 1972, pp. 495–507). On the linguistic problem of *morphē*, see
now S. G. Wilson, 'Image of God', *ExpT* 85, 12, 1973–74, pp.
356–61.

(*iv*) E. Schweizer's discussion leads to the idea of *morphē* as 'condition' or 'status' in referring to Christ's 'original' position vis-à-
vis God. He was the 'first man', holding a unique place within the
divine life and one with God. This sense of 'condition' would fit

the meaning required in verse 7*b*. He who was in the beginning (that seems to be implied by the participle *hyparchōn* in the Greek, and recent attempts [e.g., by C. H. Talbert, *JBL* 86 (1967), pp. 141–53] to deny pre-existence in the hymn have not been favourably regarded) at God's side—like wisdom in Prov. 8 and Sir. 24—chose to identify himself with men and to accept the human condition, 'in the form of a servant'. On balance, this last-named view has most in its favour, especially in view of the close tie-up between the 'righteous one' and a personalized figure of wisdom in Jewish sapiential literature (Georgi, loc. cit., pp. 276ff.; Sanders, op. cit., pp. 70–4).

did not count equality with God a thing to be grasped. The older discussion focused on the precise lexical significance of the Greek term *harpagmos*: is it 'an act of plundering', or 'what is plundered and seized', and so 'a spoil' or 'prize of war'? Most recent writers incline to the second meaning, but C. F. D. Moule ('Further Reflexions', p. 271) has re-opened the question with his proposal to understand the term as an 'act of snatching (*raptus*)'. See, too, the lexical support for this translation in L. L. Hammerich, *An Ancient Misunderstanding (Phil. 2.6 'robbery')*, Copenhagen, 1966 [on which see *ExpT* 78 (1966–7), pp. 193f.]; cf. P. Trudinger, *ExpT* 79 (1967–8), pp. 279; D. W. B. Robinson, *ExpT* 80 (1968–9), pp. 253f. Paul's line then runs: 'he did not regard equality with God as *consisting in* snatching' (p. 266, italics in the quotation). Moule elaborates his meaning (p. 272) by saying that for the pre-incarnate Christ, 'instead of imagining that equality with God meant *getting*, Jesus, on the contrary, *gave*—gave until he was "empty" '. This certainly accords with the train of thought in verse 7, but it runs into the difficulty that Paul's hymn does not flow from verse 6 to verse 7 by a simple conjunction or connective. Verse 6 sets up the first member of a contrast, and we must give full weight to 'but' (Gr. *alla*) in verse 7. Verse 6*b*, on the contrary, states what Christ might have done, i.e., seized equality with God; only in verse 7 does it say what he chose to do, i.e., give himself. Moule's interpretation, we submit, runs the two verses together, whereas they should be kept separate and their mutual tension should not be lost.

So *harpagmos* is what Christ refused to seize. To ask what it was precisely that lay in his power as an advantage (*harpagmos* means just that, according to R. W. Hoover's philological discussion,

HTR 64 (1971), pp. 95–119), the answer must be: the enjoyment and use of 'equality with God' in its characteristic expression, namely, the title to lordship as a springboard from which he might, had he so decided, have aspired to be the universe's ruler. He had the opportunity to grasp what lay within his reach— since he shared God's throne as his 'form' (so T. F. Glasson, 'Two Notes on the Philippians Hymn (II. 6–11)', *NTS* 21 (1974–5), pp. 133–9, interpreting Lightfoot) – and by an act of self-assertiveness and pride he might have striven to be Lord in his own right. But 'equality with God' in this way was an intolerable thought, since in the Jewish tradition (cf. Jn 5:17, 18: see W. F. Howard, *Christianity according to St. John*, London, 1943, p. 71; C. H. Dodd, *The Interpretation of the Fourth Gospel*, Cambridge, 1953, pp. 325–8) to claim such equality is tantamount to aspiring to a false independence and to setting up a rebellion against the divine government. What, then, is the other side of his choice?

7. but emptied himself. This is the other part of the scenario in the drama of the heavenly court. Strictly the 'decision' refers to the incarnation, though to read the whole verse in the light of Isaiah's suffering servant chapter (Isa. 53) is clearly possible (see J. Jeremias, *NovT* 6 (1963), pp. 182–8). Then, he **emptied himself** (Gr. *heauton ekenōsen*) is a plausible equivalent to Isa. 53:12 (LXX): 'his soul is delivered up to death', and **taking the form of a servant** means exactly 'playing the part of the *'ebed Yahweh'* in Isaiah's servant poems. Critical opinion, however, has raised some formidable objections to this reconstruction (e.g., R. Deichgräber, *Gotteshymnus und Christushymnus in der frühen Christenheit*, Göttingen, 1967, pp. 123f.), not least on the score that (*i*) the verb is an incarnational one, and does not refer to the death of the cross at this point in the hymn; and (*ii*) the phrase **form of a servant** (Gr. *morphē doulou*) is capable of wider reference than being related specifically to Isaiah's suffering servant. Most probably it fits in to the general pattern of righteous sufferers in late Judaism who are consistently called 'servants of God' (E. Schweizer, *Erniedrigung und Erhöhung*, pp. 21–33). A commonly accepted view, shared by several continental interpreters, is that *doulos* here means 'slave' to the cosmic powers which tyrannize over man and make him the plaything of fate (so E. Käsemann, loc. cit., p. 67). The hymn's line says that Christ identified himself with unredeemed humanity in its

bondage to evil forces, since he was born in the likeness of men.
But that expression in verse 7 is so worded that he is marked out
as distinct from men (**likeness**, Gr. *homoiōma*, suggesting a mys-
terious appearance of one who, since he came from God, still
retains a secret relationship with him, and is, to that extent, removed from men); O. Michel ('Zur Exegese von Phil. 2.5–11,' in
Theologie als Glaubenswagnis, Hamburg, 1954, pp. 77–95) is one
of the few writers to have observed this sense of **likeness**: 'the
author is conscious of portraying something transcendent in the
face of which any earthly method of expression can only be employed with a special hesitancy' (p. 91), and it is this reluctance
to say that Christ became fully man *in this verse* which explains
the paraphrastic style and the caution contained in the term
likeness which does not imply identity or equivalence. The statement of a real incarnation will come in verse 8.

The incarnate Lord chose to step on to the stage of history in an
epiphany-like appearance. But it was a self-emptying because he
accepted the condition of a **servant**, a slave with no rights or
privileges in contemporary society (Moule, loc. cit., p. 268). He
aligned himself with Israel's righteous men who, as 'servants of
God', trod a road of obedience in suffering. In either case, *doulos*
is used in direct antithesis to *kyrios* (Lord). What he might have
seized, he relinquished—and accepted the direct opposite, a life
of utter dependence on his God as an obedient son.

8. in human form marks out his earthly life. Some interpreters read into this line a Son of man christology on the ground
that the Greek *hōs anthrōpos* veils an allusion to Dan. 7:13 (so
Lohmeyer, *Kyrios Jesus*, p. 42), but this seems exaggerated. However, see M. Black, 'The Son of Man Problem in Recent Research
and Debate', *BJRL* 45 (1963), p. 315, who suggests a link with Dan.
7:13 in the preceding phrase. Again, a developed *'ebed Yahweh*
christology drawn from the picture in Isa. 53 is sometimes traced to
the verbs **he humbled himself and became obedient unto
death.** There are some echoes of this sentence in Isa. 53:8 (LXX)
and the *'ebed* does pour out his soul unto death (Isa. 53:12). But
there can be no final certainty that the hymn is consciously using
the model of Isaiah's servant, since (*i*) it is strange that no soteriological value is attributed to the Lord's obedience and death in
the Philippians passage; and (*ii*), while obedience is a theme in
the hymn, it is left an open question as to *how* he was obedient.

We naturally assume that it was the Father's will he accepted, but the hymn does not say so explicitly, whereas in Isa. 53 (cf. Isa. 50:4-7), the *'ebed* acts in direct response to Yahweh's command.

Obedience and humiliation to death are not depicted as ethical qualities. Those who regard the passage as offering an 'imitation of Christ' in his earthly life, however, appeal to these twin features for support, as Käsemann is quick to point out: 'It is here that the attempt at an ethical interpretation seems to find its strongest support' (loc. cit., p. 70). But Käsemann is opposed to this use of the verbs ('he was obedient', 'he humbled himself') on the ground that the heavenly man, though he moves through time and space, does no more than 'reveal obedience, but he does not demonstrate it as something to be imitated' (loc. cit., p. 74). This conclusion seems to push the ideas of the text too far into an abstraction. We may concede the point that verse 8 says simply that his incarnate life was marked by obedience and suffering to the point of death. We accept at this juncture G. N. Stanton's argument (*Jesus of Nazareth in New Testament Preaching*, Cambridge, 1974, pp. 104-6), but continue to doubt that the hymn is being used as an 'ethical exhortation' (p. 103), since the relevance of the second part (vs. 9-11) is related to the lordship of Christ not the exaltation of Christians—a theme singularly inappropriate in Paul's debate with his enemies (see earlier pp. 29-34). The way in which verses 9-11 are regarded as 'less relevant' (p. 103) to Paul's total thought remains as an unsolved issue in any view which maintains that the hymn portrays Christ as *exemplum ad imitandum*. If we are pressed to ask, why are these features of his earthly existence in verses 7 and 8 singled out for mention? the answer will be that these are precisely the lot of the slave. He has no choice but to obey his master, often take unjust punishment, and sometimes suffer death. At all points, he stands in contrast to the master, the *kyrios* (so Collange).

even death on a cross. The ultimate limit of Christ's life of obedience and self-giving is now reached. If this phrase is a Pauline addition to an already existing hymn, it will serve as his emphatic comment addressed to his Philippian readers. In a Roman city and in the ears of church members who no doubt were proud of their connexions with a Roman colony (Ac. 16; see pp. 3-5), this mention of the cross would sound a note of horror and disgust. Only the lowest order of society—the slave-class—died

by crucifixion (Cicero, *Pro Rabirio* 5.10: cf. *in Verrem* 5.64 for
well-known texts abhorring crucifixion in Roman eyes); and yet
the Church's Lord consented to end his life on a Roman gibbet,
and (from a Jewish angle) to die under divine condemnation
(Dt. 21:23: cf. Qumran *Commentary on Nahum*, Vermes pp. 231,
232). Yet no soteriology (as in Gal. 3:13) is implied. The hymn's
line simply and starkly makes the observation: he yielded himself to the furthest limit of submission, to a death reserved for
those who have no claims on society. At this juncture the first
part of the hymn is reached. 'These three stanzas [vs. 6–8] lead,
in one great sweep, from the highest height to the deepest depth,
from the light of God to the darkness of death' (Lohmeyer,
Kommentar, p. 86).

9. In Greek drama the term *peripeteia* is used to denote the
change of fortune in the hero's life. After a succession of mis-
fortunes and sufferings, he now begins to climb upwards and to
win his way back. The obvious difference in the Christian epic
is that Christ's reversal of fortune is directly attributed to the
intervention of God. So it is not accidental that, whereas in
verses 6–8 the emphasis has been on what Christ did, now the
accent falls on what is done to and for him by God. **Therefore
God has highly exalted him.** The connecting **therefore** (Gr.
dio) seems clearly to show an element of 'reward' (*pace* Barth, pp.
66ff., followed by Collange) and the opening of a new chapter
in Christ's existence as the exalted one. Possibly in the background
is once more the Jewish-rabbinic idea that the righteous sufferer
will be vindicated by God (E. Schweizer, op. cit.). But Christ's
elevation is not the outworking of a 'divine law' of recompense
(Lohmeyer), nor is it a question of a new 'worthiness' he has
acquired. The following verb is **bestowed on him** which suggests
a gift by grace (Gr. *charizesthai*) and that excludes any notion of
merit. (See Gnilka, p. 125.)

The exaltation is to the highest possible station. Paul's verb
hyperhypsoun could mean that God lifted him to a rank higher
(comparative) than the one he had before (as being then in God's
form), and a concise statement of a 'two Adams' theology based
on this meaning is given by O. Cullmann (*The Christology of the
New Testament*, ET London, 1959, pp. 174–81, but see for a
denial of any allusion to Adam, T. F. Glasson, loc. cit., pp. 137–9).
In his pre-existence he was Son of God; now, after his exaltation,

he is entitled to the rank of Lord. But no such comparative sense seems intended (so Moule, loc. cit., p. 269), and G. Delling (*NovT* 11 (1969), pp. 127-53) has shown that Paul's verbs with *hyper* (e.g., Rom. 8:37) are usually elative in force.

the name above every name is a descriptive phrase patterned on the Jewish-rabbinic designation of 'Yahweh' as the 'all-excelling' name of God. There seems no other way of interpreting the gift of a new name (but cf. Moule, p. 270) than to regard it as God's bestowal of his own lordship on the exalted Christ. But recent writers (Moule, Collange) who note how quickly Paul's hymn passes on to the name of 'Jesus' (v. 10), are saying something fundamental to the hymn's message. Lordly power is to be seen as committed to the hands of the historical person of Jesus of Nazareth, who is not some cosmic cipher or despotic ruler but a figure to whom Christians could give a face and a name.

10. So at the sound of this **name**—perhaps the invoking of his name at worship or in baptism is the cultic setting of the occasion —**every knee should bow** (Isa. 45:23) in total surrender. Even denizens of the underworld as well as inhabitants of heaven are included along with dwellers upon earth. That is, the entire cosmos is brought under the lordship of Christ, as in a vision the poet sees the fulfilment of God's purpose in the end-time. But the vision is born out of the reality of the Church at worship, since the final acclamation of the universe is at the same time the confessional slogan of the present-day Church, 'Jesus Christ is Lord'. Both cosmos and Church join in a common acknowledgement and a consentient tribute (see J. G. Gibbs, *Creation and Redemption*, Leiden, 1971, p. 76).

11. The confession **Jesus Christ is Lord** stands as the climax of the drama of salvation portrayed in these poetic verses. Now at length the sovereignty over the world, which was held up before the pre-incarnate Lord as a prize to be snatched, is freely accorded to him. He receives the new name which is none other than God's own name, and with it, the title to lordship. Believers who sing this hymn pay tribute to his present rule in their lives and their communities (Rom. 10:9; 1 C. 8:5, 6; 12.3; Col. 2:6) and recall their baptismal pledge by which they were introduced to a new age of eschatological fulfilment and a new world of cosmic reconciliation. This is the outstanding importance of E. Käsemann's discussion, which shows, following Lohmeyer, that the hymn's climax is no utterance of personal piety but the sign of a new aeon already begun in the Church and the world. 'He puts an end to the history of the old world. And only the obedient one is able to do that. He is the new man and therefore the Lord of the new world' (loc. cit., p. 87).

Yet his lordship is not in competition with God's, nor does his enthronement threaten the sole monarchy of the Father. Hence, it is **to the glory of God the Father** that he rules. The sovereignty he has is the Father's gift (v. 9). That which he refused to grasp selfishly in a senseless act of aggrandizement is now bestowed on him at the Father's pleasure. The last word is **Father**, as though to emphasize that now in Christ, pre-existing, incarnate and humiliated, and exalted, God and the world are united and a new segment of humanity, a microcosm of God's new order for the universe (Eph. 1:10), is born.

On the basis of this declaration Paul will launch into his ethical admonition (verses 12, 13). But in effect he has already made his point in verse 5: Let your relationships in the Christian community be such as show that they are conducted in the sphere of this new humanity of which Christ Jesus is the Lord and in which we are members who, in allegiance and confession, proclaim that lordship.

(d) **2:12–18.** *Appeals to good relationships*
12. Following the recital of the soteriological hymn (2:6–11), Paul proceeds to make a pointed application. **Therefore** looks back to the conclusion of the quoted section (v. 11): he does not begin again, as Barth suggests.

The call is to obedience. **as you have always obeyed** my instruction, given in the apostolic preaching and *didachē* when I was with you (**in my presence**) at Philippi, **much more in my absence,** since I am in prison and kept away from you, **work out your own salvation.** The way of salvation has been depicted in the hymn. What remains for the Philippians to do is to apply it to their corporate life and learn to live 'in Christ'. There cannot be an individualistic sense attached to salvation here since Paul has the entire Church in view. They are encouraged to work at their salvation, by which we should understand (following J. H. Michael, 'Work out Your own Salvation', *Expositor* 9th ser., 12, (1924), pp. 439–50) the health of the church which was sorely distressed by rivalries and petty squabbles. Several reasons support this conclusion: (*i*) salvation (Gr. *sōtēria*) can mean 'wholeness' as well as deliverance both in the spiritual sense and in the physical (see 1:19); 1:28 shows a corporate application; (*ii*) after the passage in 2:5–11 it would be inappropriate to stress personal salvation; (*iii*) **your own** salvation cannot mean that each church member is to concentrate on his own soul's salvation, since Paul has bidden them to do the opposite in 2:4; (*iv*) the state of the Philippian church needed just this call; and an exhortation to live together in harmony and peace flanks these verses (2:1–4 and 2:14). (But see I. H. Marshall, *Kept by the Power of God*, London, 1969, p. 113.) (*v*) How the Philippians are to accomplish this restoration of their church relationships to good health is conveyed in the words **with fear and trembling.** In the traditional view, their wholesome attitude is directed to God and this reference has naturally raised problems; so much so that O. Glombitza ('Mit Furcht und Zittern. Zum Verständnis von Phil. 2.12', *NovT* 3 (1959), pp. 100–6) thinks that a negative has dropped out in transmission, and that Paul really wrote '*not* with fear and trembling', as though the Philippians were afraid of divine retribution. But this hypothesis is unnecessary once we admit that the 'fear and trembling' are manward attitudes (as in 1 C. 2:3; 2 C. 7:15; and Eph. 6:5). Let the Philippians have a healthy respect for one another in the resolving of their differences.

13. They are not, however, left to themselves in this enterprise. **God is at work in you** (or, better, 'among you'), **both to will and to work for his good pleasure.** At first glance it seems to remove all responsibility from the Philippians, except perhaps the passive consent to let God work in their midst. This is why G. Bornkamm ('Der Lohngedanke im Neuen Testament', *Studien zu Antike und Urchristentum*, Munich, 1959, p. 91) can call the verse 'an oddly paradoxical sentence', raising all manner of dogmatic issues to do with justification *sola gratia* and synergism. But such matters seem remote from this Pauline situation, even if later generations of Christian thinkers have to wrestle with the mutual relations of human accountability and divine initiative and grace (see Barth, pp. 71–5). In the context Paul probably introduces the promise of divine help to reassure his friends that, since he cannot be with them ('in my absence'), they should not despair but remember that God's gracious assistance (his 'active good will', Gr. *eudokia*; the Heb. equivalent is *rāṣôn*, meaning

God's declared purpose of good in electing and blessing his people; cf. Lk. 2:14 and E. Vogt's discussion *ad rem* in *The Scrolls and the New Testament*, ed. K. Stendahl, ET London, 1958, pp. 114–17) is available **both to will** (i.e., promote the desire) and **to work** (Gr. *energein*, effectual action in bringing human aspiration to good effect is implied). The Greek phrase rendered **for his good pleasure** is a little unusual. *hyper tēs eudokias* is 'in the interests of, for the sake of, his good pleasure', and this wording suggests to BDF (Sec. 231.2) that it should be detached from verse 13, and made the opening of the next verse: 'for the sake of [human] goodwill (as in 1:15; cf. Rom. 10:1; 2 Th. 1:11) do everything without complaining, etc.' But G. Schrenk (*TDNT* ii, p. 746, n. 32) is critical of this expedient.

14. Troubles within the Philippian church are now brought to the surface for the first time. **Do all things without grumbling or questioning.** There is reason to believe that Paul is drawing upon some personal knowledge he has of strained relationships at Philippi, even if he does formulate his advice in *OT* language. The two social ills mentioned are sins which stained the shield of the Jewish people in their wilderness wanderings (Exod. 16:7; Num. 11:1). The correspondence of terms perhaps points to Paul's typological understanding of the *OT* and his concept of the Church as a pilgrim people of God. See 1 C. 10:1–11 (Gnilka).

grumbling (*NEB* 'complaint') has reference to the people's discontent in the *OT*, and the Hebrew word (*lûn*) is found mainly in Exod. 15–17 and Num. 14–17 where they murmur against God and Moses (see K. H. Rengstorf, *TDNT* i, pp. 729f.). In our verse it is more likely that the grumblings of the Philippians were directed against one another, so breaking the harmonious spirit, though it is just possible that the rank and file of the members were being critical of their leaders (1:1), as Bonnard suggests, or that their disgruntled attitudes were levelled against God himself (Beare, Gnilka), especially if persecution and suffering were posing an unexplained difficulty for faith. (See Introduction p. 32.)

questioning (Gr. *dialogismoi*) might also suggest the latter. But the word has a legal connotation of 'dissensions', 'litigation' (the evidence is given in Moulton-Milligan and AG) and this would indicate that the Philippian Christians were resorting to pagan courts (cf. 1 C. 6:1–11) to settle their differences.

15. The good relationships between Christians at Philippi are not only desirable to promote a Christian spirit inside the church. The effect of a disunited church on the surrounding world is an additional factor in Paul's appeal. **be blameless** (Gr. *amemptoi*, a term used elsewhere of Paul's own character, 1 Th. 2:10, as well as forming part of his admonition, 1 Th. 5:23) **and innocent** (Gr. *akeraioi*: see Rom. 16:19 for this and the preceding moral term) suggest a life of exemplary behaviour. But the motivation is the important thing. The Church is called to be true to its Christian character, because it is set in the world of hostile men who will be only too ready to deal harshly with any lapses on the part of Christians. Paul's preposition **in the midst of** is interesting. It represents an addition to the LXX of Dt. 32:5 in which the song of Moses laments the state of Israel: 'They have dealt corruptly with him (sc. Yahweh), they are no longer his children (Gr. *tekna*) because of their blemish (Gr. *mōmēta*); they are a perverse and crooked generation' (Gr. *genea skolia kai diestrammenē*). The repetition of words in Paul's text: *tekna, mōmēta* (which he quotes as *amōma*) *genea skolia kai diestrammenē* is proof that he is alluding to the *OT*. But the application is different. In Deuteronomy the reference is to apostate Israel; Paul applies the description to the pagan world among whom the Philippians as God's true **children** are summoned to live and witness. Cf. Mt. 17:17; Ac. 2.40 for other uses made of this description of a wayward generation.

The life of the Church in the world is likened to the influence of light in a dark place. The reference is sometimes taken to be that of stars which shine in a dark sky (so Moffatt's translation). But Lohmeyer has raised cogent objections to this. The verb is *phainesthai*, 'to appear', not *phainein*, 'to shine'. **lights** (Gr. *phōstēres*) may mean any object which bears light (e.g., torch, lantern, even harbour beacons to guide ships in the Mediterranean: S. K. Finlayson, *ExpT* 77 (1965–6), p. 181; in Rev. 21:11, the only other *NT* use of the word, it describes the holy city which reflects God's glory like the light of a jewel). A more suggestive line of thought in this verse is that the Philippians are to play the role of light-bearers in their environment just as Adam, Israel, the Torah, and certain rabbis were 'light-bearers' in the world (SB i, p. 237; ii, p. 357; *TDNT* ix, pp. 324, 327 [H. Conzelmann]). The last-named accepts an eschatological meaning for *phōstēr* and thinks of Paul's designation of Christians as that of an elect community illuminated by God (loc. cit., pp. 345f.). The title 'children of light' was claimed by the covenanters at Qumran, also in an eschatological sense (1QS 1:9; 2.16; 1QM 13:5, 9, 24f., passim; Vermes, pp. 72, 74, 141).

16. holding fast (Gr. *epechontes*) **the word of life.** An alternative meaning 'hold forth' (*AV*) seems preferable, if the imagery of light-bearer is continued into this verse. But if the weight of the verse comes at the end, then Paul's admonition is to 'hold firm' the apostolic message (perhaps lest the torch be dropped and extinguished), so that he will have no cause for shame or regret that his work at Philippi has failed. Rather, he is confident that at the last day when his work is tested (**the day of Christ**; 1 C. 3:13, 4:1–5) it will be shown by the Philippians' obedience to his exhortation (v. 12) and by their consistency of living that **I did not run in vain.** For the metaphor, see Gal. 2:2, which suggests that, in the different circumstances contemplated in both verses, this was a favourite idea in Paul's mind, perhaps suggested by the use of Hab. 2:2 at Qumran (1QpHab 7:3–5; Vermes, p. 236), that a man divinely commissioned runs to bring others out of confusion and error. For Paul to reach the end alone would be to run in vain, i.e., his mission to others would be a failure. (See O. Bauernfeind, *TDNT* viii, p. 231.)

or labour in vain. A. Deissmann connects this hypothetical loss with Paul's knowledge of weaving. A piece of cloth, if badly woven, would be rejected and useless (Gr. *eis kenon*). (See his book, *Light from the Ancient East*, ET London, 1927, p. 317.) But Paul's use of 'labour' (Gr. *kopian*) is much wider. (See A. von Harnack's study, '*kopos* (*kopian, hoi kopiōntes*) im frühchristlichen Sprachgebrauch', *ZNW* 27 (1928), pp. 1–10.)

Both possibilities are mentioned only to emphasize Paul's confidence that he will be **proud** (lit. 'glory': see on 3:2) of his converts' stability.

17. Why does Paul revert to the theme of his martyrdom in the words **Even if I am to be poured as a libation upon the sacrificial offering of your faith**? Two points of connexion with the foregoing paragraph are suggested by Gnilka: Paul's apostolic labours will be crowned by his death as a martyr (1:21), and a previous mention of 'the day of Christ' (v. 16) suggests that the alternative to his reaching the parousia will be a homecall through a martyr's death. Paul's terminology for such a death is heavy with sacrificial tones. In a reference which is the most solemn and personal in the entire letter, he contemplates the prospect of a martyr's crown as something very real; 'the possi- ⌐ bility of his execution is vividly present to his own mind' (Michael).

The key verb is **if I am to be poured as a libation** (Gr. *spendomai*). It means to offer a libation or drink-offering or, as here, it is used of the apostle who is about to be offered up 'to shed his blood as a sacrifice' (cf. 2 Tim. 4:6; AG). But if the drink-offering is the accompaniment of the ritual, what is the sacrifice? The answer is that the Philippians are offering their faith— perhaps by their gifts to the apostolic mission as part of his 'labour' (v. 16) or their own willingness to suffer as he is doing (1:29, 30) — and the apostle is offering his life in his allegiance to the gospel, and so both church and apostle are united in one sacrifice (Bonnard). This is then a cause for great celebration. Death, which is very real before his eyes (as in Ignatius, *Rom.* 2.2, which has the same verb, *spendisthēnai* 'to be poured out to God'), is greeted with solemn joy because the gospel work is advanced, whether by Paul's own self-sacrifice or by the Philippians' *koinōnia* (1:5; 4:14ff.) with him in that work. **sacrificial offering** is a combination of two words, one of which is *leitourgia*. The two terms form a single idea by hendiadys. *leitourgia* is a cultic word in association with *thysia* (sacrifice) and together the term speaks of the sacrificial service performed by the Philippians' faith in actively supporting Paul, even when they were poor (2 C. 8:2; see on 4:18, 19). Their gifts were like a fragrant offering to God.

But it is just as possible to take the entire verse in a non-cultic way (as Michaelis does), with the offering of Paul's missionary activity being the chief point. Rom. 15:16 is quoted as support; and *leitourgia* (cf. H. Strathmann, *TDNT* iv, pp. 216f.) can refer to public services rendered to the body politic. Then, the phrase would more specifically relate to the Philippians' material gifts to aid Paul's mission work. (See *TDNT* iv, p. 227.)

Paul's amazing spirit of equanimity in the face of death may, however, be contrasted with what he writes in 1:19–26. There his mind's perturbation was reflected in his broken syntax and oscillating hopes between life and death. This shift in 2:17 has given rise to an alternative exegesis, first stated by Michaelis, ad loc., developed by T. W. Manson, *BJRL* 23 (1939), pp. 184f., and made a central issue in A. M. Denis' article, 'La fonction apostolique et la liturgie nouvelle en Esprit', *RSPhTh* 42 (1958), pp. 401-36. The latter maintains that the verb *spendomai* means 'to offer' in sacrifice; in the passive it says no more than that some liquid is poured out as an accompaniment of the sacrificial ritual, whether pagan or Jewish. 'Neither in the Greek Bible (LXX) nor in the hellenistic world is the term ever used to denote offerings of blood (for which the Greek is *haimassein*)' (J.-F. Collange). This leads to the conclusion that Paul does *not* have his death in view here, but is referring to his apostolic labours. There is no sudden onset of pessimism in verse 17. As the previous verse ended with the thought that he would be proud of the Philippians in the end, so he continues: 'but if (= 'even though', in a restrictive sense) it is on the sacrifice of your faith that I suffer in my labours, none the less I do it with joy'. His joy, in other words, is occasioned not so much by the mystique of the martyr as by the evidence of a community which is concerned to promote the gospel. But this exegesis fails (*i*) to account for the use of a rare verb *spendomai* in a context which *does* suggest an offering in death (cf. 2 Tim. 4:6, and Ignatius' use of the term), (*ii*) to explain the adversative *alla* ('but', not in *RSV*), and (*iii*) to have regard to the gravity of Paul's predicament, even in 1:19–26, where, if he survives, it will be only by a special dispensation of God's providence (1:19).

18. Paul repeats the call to **be glad and rejoice with me** from verse 17. The reason for this renewed invitation is either Paul's sense of his impending martyrdom (Gnilka) or his confidence that his work as an apostle will not be fruitless by any defection at Philippi. The piling up of terms for 'joy' and association (Gr. prefix *syn-* before the verbs) are characteristic of this letter as a whole. They underline Paul's indomitable spirit under trial and express the confidence that his readers will catch the spirit too. The words equally demonstrate the close bond of union between the apostle and the congregation even in Paul's absence (1:27; 2:12), and they are his way of emphasizing the need for the Philippians, in face of threats to their community from both the outside world and the danger of divisiveness inside the church, to stand together with him.

APPENDED NOTE ON PHIL. **2:6–11**

The purpose of this section is to supply some bibliographical guidelines regarding the progress of understanding the passage in 2:6–11. The present writer's survey of the history of interpretation up to 1963, for which omniscience was not claimed, appeared in 1967 as *Carmen Christi* (Cambridge), and the following note is intended to draw attention to chief lines of recent development.

(*a*) *Literary Form*. The debate continues as to the best method of arranging the verses in poetic or hymnic form. A consensus has decided that the passage is a piece of poetry or hymnody, and that its unusual language, rhythmical pattern and elevated, solemn style are all features which betray the presence of a lyrical composition. The centre of discussion is (*a*) how to set down the lines so as best to reproduce the hymnic structure, and this procedure entails paying respect to literary or rhetorical devices, whether based on Old Testament (e.g. parallelisms) or Greek (e.g. assonance, rhythm) patterns; and (*b*) to enquire how far we can detect an original pattern of the hymn which was edited or altered (by Paul's additions) at the time when Paul decided to use it in enforcement of his pastoral appeal to the Philippians. In other words, the major area of scholarly interest in all the christological hymns (which J. T. Sanders' book, *The New Testament Christological Hymns*, Cambridge, 1971, only partly reflects) is that of 'tradition and redaction' (see *New Century Bible: Colossians*, 1974, pp. 56f., 62f., and G. Strecker, 'Redaktion und Tradition im Christus-Hymnus', *ZNW* 55 (1964), pp. 63–78). But M. D. Hooker's article ('Philippians 2:6–11') resolutely opposes any idea of a hypothetical 'original version' of the hymn which Paul has 'edited', and produces a compact two stanza (each with ten lines) versification that includes the entire passage without any excisions. Certain ideas, however, are sacrificed in this attempt including (*a*) the neglect of several rhetorical devices (*Carmen Christi*, pp. 37, 39); (*b*) the cogency of the argument that the proposed additions to a *Vorlage* are 'typically Pauline' terms set into a *Vorlage* that is full of non-Pauline *hapax legomena;* and (*c*) the tearing asunder of lines that seem to be closely linked in thought (e.g. 7b, 8a). See P. Grelot, 'Deux notes critiques sur Philippiens 2, 6–11', *Biblica* 54, 1973, pp. 169–86, expressing agreement with *Carmen Christi*, p. 198.

On the other hand, the analysis offered by H.-W. Bartsch, *Die konkrete Wahrheit und die Lüge der Spekulation*, Bern, 1974, is open to the criticism that it is too bold in its attempt to reconstruct the pre-Pauline tradition underlying the hymn. Bartsch is concerned to relate Paul's teaching to the social background of early Christianity and to see its message in terms of the messiahship question. While his denial of the relevance of the gnostic redeemer myth and his championing of an Adam-Christ typology (pp. 65–79) are legitimate canons of interpretation, it is not so clear how he can justify recasting the wording of the hymn and arranging it into strophes (p. 129) that are not found in the text. When this procedure excludes lines (such as v. 6a, that seems clearly to imply Christ's pre-existence) and adds lines that import ideas (e.g. adoption of Jesus as God's son in v. 11) that are alien to the hymn, we may suspect that his analysis is not a true understanding of what Paul intended.

Starting with E. Lohmeyer's division (*Kyrios Jesus*, Heidelberg, 1928, 2nd edn 1961, pp. 5f.) of the passage into six stanzas each of three lines and with three stresses to a line, form analysis has proceeded to arrange the verses into three stanzas of four lines apiece (*i*. 6, 7a; *ii*. 7b–8; *iii*. 9–11, with certain lines omitted as Pauline amplifications: this is J. Jeremias' attempt, in *Studia Paulina*, Haarlem, 1953, pp. 146–54), and into a series of couplets capable of antiphonal recitation (*A*. 6a, 6b; *B*. 7a, 7b; *C*. 7c, 7d; *D*. 8a, 8b; *E*. 9a, 9b; *F*. 10b–11). See R. P. Martin, *Carmen Christi*, pp. 36–8. Later suggestions revert to a two-part division: Stanza I (6–8); Stanza II (9–11). This is adopted by G. Strecker, *ZNW* 55 (1964), p. 70; R. Deichgräber, *Gotteshymnus und Christushymnus*, p. 124; and J.-F. Collange, *Commentary*, 1973, pp. 79, 87. But the reversion to a pre-Lohmeyer pattern destroys the arrangement of vs. 6–8 into parallel lines, which Jeremias detected (see R. P. Martin, 'A Formal Analysis of Phil. 2:6–11', *SE* ii, Berlin, 1964, pp. 611–20), and makes unlikely the inclusion of the thought of pre-existence in verses 6a–7. Indeed, C. H. Talbert's argument and strophic arrangement (in 'Pre-existence in Philippians 2:6–11', *JBL* 86 (1967), pp. 141–53) in proposing an analysis of four stanzas, each with three lines, effectively eliminates any

teaching on Christ's pre-incarnate 'state' and makes vs. 6–8 refer
to his earthly existence. While there has been some positive
response to this idea (e.g., G. Strecker, loc. cit., on the ground
that pre-existence serves no paraenetic purpose, is inserted only
to show the qualifications of Christ's capacity as revealer ('Der
vorpaul. Hymnus', p. 278), and is contained only in a participial
phrase; R. H. Fuller, *CBQ* 30 (1968), pp. 274f.; and F. Stagg,
Broadman Commentary Nashville/London, vol. 11, 1971, pp. 194,
196), most writers are persuaded that one cannot eliminate this
element of pre-existence in v. 6a. (See J. A. Sanders, 'Dissenting
Deities and Philippians 2:1–11', *JBL* 88 (1969), pp. 279–90;
J. G. Gibbs, *Creation and Redemption*, Leiden, 1971, pp. 80–3; cf.
F. B. Craddock, *The Pre-existence of Christ in the New Testament*,
New York, 1968, pp. 108f. and P. Grelot, *Biblica* 53, 1972,
pp. 503–7.)

The firm resolve to see the hymn as built up of couplets
(Jeremias' original insight, loc. cit.; Martin, op. cit., p. 32) has
been taken seriously by J. Gnilka (*Commentary*, pp. 136–8) and
J.-F. Collange (*Commentary*, pp. 78f.). Klaus Wengst (*Christologische
Formeln*, p. 148) tries to combine Lohmeyer's strophic arrangement in verses 6–8 and a division into couplets in verses 9–11.
But this is confusing. There is less unanimity over Jeremias' other
proposal to omit several phrases and lines as Pauline additions
(with the exception of v. 8b, 'even the death of the cross', which is
generally acceded to be by Paul's hand and to break whatever
metrical symmetry the various patterns yield). One of the latest
attempts at form analysis (by C.-H. Hunzinger, 'Zur Struktur
der Christus-Hymnen in Phil 2 und 1 Petr 3', in *Der Ruf Jesu und
die Antwort der Gemeinde* (*J. Jeremias Festschrift*), ed. E. Lohse *et al.*,
Göttingen, 1970, pp. 145–56) strikes out also the conclusion 'to
the glory of God the Father' (v. 11), and wishes to make the
acclamation-confession 'Jesus Christ is Lord' the climax of a
eulogistic *Urschrift* that, with these deletions, conforms to the
pattern of three 4-line strophes. But opposing any idea of a general
revision of an existing hymn by Paul, and utilizing the idea of a
'dialogue' pattern, Collange produces a two-fold division: stanza I,
made up of *A*. 6–7a; *B*. 7b–8 (climaxing in v. 8c); and stanza II,
A. 9–10a; *B*. 10b–11 (with the climax 'to the glory of God the
Father'). The antiphonal character is recognized in the two main
stanzas with the cries, 'even the death of the cross' and 'to the

glory of God the Father', seen as a choral response from the community at the close of each stanza (p. 79).

Recognition of the hymnic, or at least poetic, features of 2:6–11 is important as a double warning against (*i*) treating the verses as a piece of exact dogmatic writing concerned with Trinitarian relationships or intended to fix the precise meaning of cosmological ideas (e.g., v. 10); and (*ii*) regarding the order of words as an indispensable clue to their meaning. On the second point, however, J. Carmignac ('L'importance de la place d'une négation: *OUK HARPAGMON HEGESATO* (Philippiens 11.6)', *NTS* 18 (1971–2), pp. 131–66) argues that the position of the negative before the *noun* and not the verb in the sentence, 'he did not count equality with God a thing to be grasped', has to be recognized. Paul's customary usage (204 times against 4 in other instances, p. 141) is to place the negative with the *verb* when he wants to call attention to the precise sense of the negation. By placing the negative in front of the complementary object (without the definite article), Paul is emphasizing this part of the sentence in a way subordinate to the main verb. The sense is then: 'he thought that it was not a usurpation to be equal with God' (p. 142). This leads to Carmignac's conclusion (now accepted by M. D. Hooker, art. cit., pp. 151f.) that *harpagmos* refers to Christ's pre-incarnate divinity which he possessed without any sense that it was wrong for him so to have it—an interpretation similar to the older view stated by E. H. Gifford (*The Incarnation*, London, 1897, pp. 30ff., in 1911 edn). But this erudite study seems to overlook (a) the poetic nature of the passage, and (b) the fact that after all the line in verse 6 may be by a hand other than Paul's. See too the critique, on the ground of Greek syntax, brought by A. Feuillet, *Christologie paulinienne*, pp. 120ff. Carmignac's interpretation is opposed by P. Grelot ('La valeur de *OUK* ... *ALLA* ... dans Philippiens 2, 6–7', *Biblica* 54, 1973, pp. 25–42), who argues that the unusual meaning attached to the negative is not required to give excellent sense to the adversative *alla*-clause which follows.

(*b*) *The Identity of the Author.* The traditional view sees the passage in verses 6–11 as composed by Paul either as an earlier tribute to Christ and now utilized in his pastoral letter or as written *currente calamo* at the time of his letter-writing. Of these two possibilities the former is more likely when we have regard to the careful composition and well-constructed turns of phrase.

Arguments for this are presented in R. P. Martin, *An Early Christian Confession*, London, 1960, pp. 14–16, and J.-F. Collange, *Commentary*, pp. 84f. But the special emphases in verses 6–11, with a passing over of the soteriological significance of the cross, the presence of the servant idea, and the de-emphasis on the resurrection in favour of the exaltation of Christ, have placed a serious doubt over Pauline authorship. The vocabulary test is impressive in reinforcement of these doubts, since so many words are non-Pauline, and *NT hapax legomena*.

The Old Testament-synagogue background has been appealed to in L. Ligier's study, 'L'hymne christologique de Phil. 2.6–11, la liturgie eucharistique et la bénédiction synagogale *nishmat kol hay*, in *Studiorum Paulinorum Congressus Internationalis Catholicus 1961* (1963), pp. 65–74. This has suggested a Jewish author, as Lohmeyer originally proposed (*Kyrios Jesus*, p. 9). But R. Deichgräber has spotlighted some eight literary expressions which he regards as decisively non-Semitic, and this argues against an original Hebrew/Aramaic version (op. cit., p. 129), the case for which is recently re-opened by P. Grelot ('Deux notes', *Biblica* 54 (1973), pp. 176–86).

The Semitic influence cannot be entirely ignored, whether it is seen in the formal style of verses 7–8 or in the use of the *OT* categories in verses 9–11. E. Käsemann ('A Critical Analysis', e.g., pp. 66f.) virtually eliminates all Jewish influence on the author and sees him at home in the hellenistic world of the gnostic myth. But this is an extreme position, just as unlikely as the view of a thoroughgoing Jewish background (see Georgi, loc. cit., and J. T. Sanders, op. cit., p. 69). Indeed, an integration of Semitic and hellenistic ideas is the thesis of J. A. Sanders' paper (loc. cit., p. 282). A mediating view of the author's *locus* has been suggested by Georgi (loc. cit., pp. 292f.) and R. P. Martin (*Carmen Christi*, pp. 304f., 318f.,) who thought that this hymn could be traced to a school of the hellenistic Jewish mission, represented by Stephen who glimpsed the cosmic dimensions of Christ's coming and victory and sought to explain it in categories drawn from the Judaeo-hellenistic wisdom literature. (So too R. H. Fuller, *The Foundations of New Testament Christology*, London, 1965, pp. 205f.; J. G. Gibbs, *Creation and Redemption*, pp. 90f.)

(c) *The Interpretation of 2:6–11*. It is here that the chief interest lies, and in this area the three special concerns are with (i) the sources on which the passage is dependent; (*ii*) the categories of thought and expression used by the author to convey the message of Christ's 'modes of existence' (in J. Jeremias' phrase); and (*iii*) the 'life-setting' of verses 6–11 in early Christianity and their place in the structure of the letter.

(*i*) Against the polarities of the *OT simpliciter*, on the one side, and the religious thought of Hellenism in general (Beare) and Gnosticism (Käsemann, Friedrich, Bornkamm, Wengst) in particular, on the other, more recent discussion of the indebtedness of the author is veering to the belief that, as a hellenistic Jewish Christian, his chief authority lies in the wisdom literature of inter-testamental diaspora Judaism (e.g., *The Wisdom of Solomon*). So Georgi, A. Feuillet (*Le Christ, Sagesse de Dieu*, Paris, 1966, pp. 340–69), Gibbs, J. T. Sanders. Georgi has proposed the notion of a 'developing myth' centred on wisdom and her desire to dwell with men (Sir. 24; Wis. 1–5) and embodied in the figure of the 'righteous one'. He suffers a bitter fate and is promised an exaltation by God. There are some problems with this recon-struction when it is made the *sole* background out of which the author has fashioned his presentation of the Christ-story (see Martin, *Carmen Christi*, pp. 318f.; J. T. Sanders, op. cit., pp. 72–74; Wengst, op. cit., p. 152, who remarks that 'pre-existent wisdom is essentially a mediator in creation', a feature singularly absent from our passage). But it seems to be a growing consensus that if we are to talk meaningfully about 'myth', it must be in Jewish rather than hellenistic categories (clearly, E. Schweizer, *Erniedrigung und Erhöhung*, 2nd edn., pp. 100f.). And for a general discussion of the legitimacy of the term 'myth', see E. M. Yamauchi, *Pre-Christian Gnosticism*, London, 1973.

(*ii*) Since the hymn stands at the meeting-place of *OT* inter-pretation (seen through hellenistic Jewish-Christian eyes) and some form of Jewish-hellenistic missionary concern to relate the wisdom idea to the larger world of Hellenism, it remains only to emphasize (with Collange) that the hymn is above all a Christian composition. Whatever sources or background ideas may be traced in the author's writing, his chief interest is to set forth the kerygmatic message of humiliation and exaltation as they are seen uniquely in the Church's Lord. For that reason, the key-verse is verse 5, which has the phrase 'in Christ Jesus'. The hymn which follows is intended to explicate that phrase and to show that Christ's way from God to man involved a self-humbling to the lowest levels and that, now vindicated and enthroned, the incarnate Christ is given the name of Lord.

It is a still-debated question how far the putative first draft of the hymn was expressed in a mythical or docetic form and to what extent Paul's editing of the *Urschrift* may be seen in his additional lines. This is a speculative exercise, and probably the most we can say is that by the line 'the death of the cross' Paul has accentuated the special significance of his death for his Philippian readers, and possibly by inserting 'all things [or beings] in the heavenly world, on earth and under the earth' he has enlarged the scope of Christ's lordship to ward off any delimiting in his present rule and rebut any idea of a dualism in the universe. Equally he has met an objection that Christ's lordship is a threat to monotheism by clarifying the point (in v. 11) that he is Lord only 'to the glory of God the Father', not as his rival.

(*iii*) It is generally conceded that this specimen of early liturgy is quoted not as a doxological tribute to Christ but with a hortatory purpose in view. Paul is deliberately recalling the readers to consider what the hymn means in a cultic setting. If—as seems certain—the centre of the hymn's teaching is not kenosis (cf. D. G. Dawe, *SJT* 15 (1962), pp. 337–49; T. A. Thomas, *EQ* 42 (1970), pp. 142–51) or a recital of traits of Jesus' earthly life in humiliation and obedience (but cf. C. F. D. Moule, loc. cit., and G. N. Stanton, *Jesus of Nazareth*, pp. 105f.), but his final and present lordship and the road he took to that office, then we may assume that the confession 'Jesus Christ is Lord' (v. 11) would answer to some occasion in the readers' experience when they joined in this form of words and professed their commitment to Christ's present rule (cf. W. Kramer, *Christ, Lord, Son of God*, ET London, 1966, sec. 45, 50, 52). A cultic setting, therefore, is a likely place to postulate for the origin of the confession, and as verse 11 comes at the climax of a pericope, which, on other grounds, has all the ear-marks of a liturgical or hymnic composition, the conclusion of the *Sitz im Leben* of verses 6–11 in early worship seems irresistible (see K. Gamber, 'Der Christus-Hymnus im Philipperbrief in liturgiegeschichtlicher Sicht', *Biblica* 51 (1970), pp. 369–76).

As to a more precise placing of the hymn, we can only mention the range of possibilities, with the chief suggestions being baptism and the Lord's Supper. For baptism, J. Jervell (*Imago Dei*, 1960, pp. 206–9) has offered an impressive case (a summary in English is given in R. P. Martin, *Worship in the Early Church*, London, 1974 edn, pp. 62f.). The setting in a eucharistic service is championed by E. Lohmeyer (*Kyrios Jesus*, pp. 65ff.), with recent support from Gamber (op. cit.), on the ground of a rhythmical correspondence of the verses with the Hallel psalms (Ps. 112–118), and Ligier (op. cit.), with further parallels drawn with the Passover celebration, especially the emphasis on the name of God and the exaltation based on Isa. 45:23ff. Collange, too, accepts a eucharistic setting in celebration of the New Israel's life in a redeemed community.

PAUL'S FUTURE PLANS **2:19–30**

These verses fall into two sections: a promise of Timothy's visit in the near future, with a commendation of him (2:19–24), followed by an explanatory paragraph dealing with Epaphroditus' service and the promise of his return to Philippi (2:25–30). These features, while they serve Paul's immediate interest, which is to communicate information to his readers, have a standardized 'form' (known in modern discussion as 'travelogue') which is present in most of his extant correspondence (see the chart in W. G. Doty, *Letters in Primitive Christianity*, Philadelphia, 1973, p. 43). The combination of travel hints and promises and the assurance that the apostle hopes soon to come to his readers (in a 'parousia') is notable in these verses: see the study of R. W. Funk, 'The Apostolic *Parousia:* Form and Significance', in *Christian History and Interpretation: Studies Presented to John Knox*, ed. W. R. Farmer, C. F. D. Moule, and R. R. Niebuhr, Cambridge, 1967, pp. 249–68, and its development by J. L. White, *The Body of the Letter*, especially pp. 143ff., on this section of Philippians, which contains, in addition to the transmitting of information of Paul's state, an account of the way Paul plans to deal with problems at Philippi by sending these two men. This section normally, though not always, comes at the conclusion of a Pauline letter, and this is an important factor in determining whether 2:30–3:1 marks the end of a letter.

Another noteworthy feature of this section in 2:19–30 is the question whether Paul's tone and promises of early visits suggest a long or short distance between the place of his captivity and Philippi. Gnilka thinks the answer is clear: 'The proposed plans presuppose a geographical proximity to Philippi, which speaks in favour of the sending of the letter from an Ephesian captivity'. See the INTRODUCTION pp. 40-2, 48-54.

(1) *The commendation of Timothy* **2:19-24**

19, 20. The way in which **Timothy** is mentioned, both here and in 1:1, has suggested to some commentators that the situation at Philippi was full of menace to the Pauline mission. For that reason, Paul associates himself with his colleague (see on 1:1), and now proceeds to praise him as trustworthy, and disinterested in his concern for the Philippian church. Paul plans to send him **soon** and not to wait for his own hoped-for release from prison, so that Timothy can add his weight to the settlement of problems at Philippi and Paul will be **cheered** (Gr. *eupsychein*, a rare word, used in papyri and grave inscriptions of encouragement to be of good heart as a pious wish for the departed or bereaved). But there is no threat of Paul's early death (so Lohmeyer), since Paul expects to be alive to receive news on Timothy's return, even if his more distant prospect for survival is in doubt (v. 23). What he looks forward to is to get news of the Philippians' positive response to his letter, so that he may be enheartened along with Timothy at the success of his mission.

The apostle's colleague is now praised. **I have no one like him** also contains a rare word (Gr. *isopsychos*: see Panayotis Christou, '*Isopsychos*, Phil. 2.20', *JBL* 70 (1951), pp. 293-6), which means 'having the same or equal mind or strength' or 'confidant'. Two meanings are possible. Is Paul saying, 'I have no one *else* in my company of fellow-Christians here who has his qualities' (so Gnilka, Michael), or 'I have no one so like myself in my interests' (so P. Christou, Houlden, Collange)? The structure of the sentence and the sequence in verse 21 suggest that Paul is picking out Timothy of all who were around him, not only because he had admirable qualities, but mainly because no one around him could quite do what he expected of Timothy.

Timothy's good qualities are concentrated in **who will be genuinely anxious for your welfare.** If we take **genuinely** in the strict sense, it means that Timothy is the 'legitimate' (Gr. *gnēsios*) son of Paul (as in 1 Tim. 2:1; Tit. 1:4), and verse 22 will return to the idea of the relationship of father and son (1 C. 4:17). Otherwise the adverb qualifies Timothy's concern

(Gr. *merimnan*) for the Philippians, which was akin to Paul's deep regard for the churches (2 C. 11:28).

21. This verse strikes a sorrowful note, echoing Paul's solitude in his prison confinement. Who are **they all** who **look after their own interests, not those of Jesus Christ**? Is Paul here 'guilty of ungracious petulance' (Michael) and of speaking in a sweeping exaggeration in order to enhance the authority of Timothy (Collange)? If we take the previous verse to mean that Paul has no one in his company who shares Timothy's equipment, it may be that this sentence is to be more softly understood, and it becomes a sorrowful but matter-of-fact statement that there is no one except Timothy available to go. They are all busy about their own concerns.

Barth, however, calls attention to the analogy between the wording here and 2:4, and infers that the same plague of self-centredness had afflicted both Christian groups. Then, it becomes just possible that Paul is making a direct comment, and remarking that, if Timothy's authority is challenged at Philippi, it will be because people there are selfishly motivated and not concerned to promote the apostolic mission, as Timothy is (so Collange). The value of this reconstruction is that it provides a smooth transition to the next verse and makes verse 21 an integral part of Paul's commendation. There is no need to remark that in verse 22 'the train of thought reverts to Timothy' (Gnilka) after an intruding comment.

22. But Timothy's worth—as one 'tested and approved', see on 1:10 which has a cognate verb—is well appreciated at Philippi. Or so Paul hopes. The relationship between Paul and his coadjutor is described as that of parent-child, and this is common in Paul's writings (1 C. 4:14, 15; Phm. 10; cf. Gal. 4:19; 1 Th. 2:11). Timothy held a special place, as his 'dear son' (1 C. 4:17).

The intimacy of this relationship seems to have affected Paul's phrasing. He begins with **he has served** (lit. 'served as a slave', Gr. *edouleusen*), but Paul stops short of saying that Timothy served *him* in this way. Rather, both men are colleagues in the service of **the gospel,** i.e., the apostolic ministry as in 1:5. And both men are slaves of Christ in the honoured sense of that designation (see on 1:1). The Philippians would recall how Paul and Timothy first came to their city. (Ac. 16:3 and 17:14 are indications of the latter's presence in the apostolic party in the second journey.)

23. Paul plans to send his co-worker **just as soon as I see how it will go with me** (a euphemism for the outcome of his present imprisonment). In other words, Timothy cannot leave right away because Paul needs him at his side in view of the imminence of his trial and its outcome (Gnilka), or because Paul is facing pastoral problems at the place of his confinement (Collange). Either way, Paul wants Timothy to carry the latest word of his situation, and at the time of his writing the issue is in the balance (1:19–26).

24. The 'apostolic parousia', already anticipated in 1:8 and alluded to twice (in 1:27 and 2:12), is now explicitly brought to the fore (see R. W. Funk, loc. cit., pp. 261f. [ref. on p. 116]). It is a hope established on his confidence in the Lord that **shortly** (Gr. *tacheōs*, perhaps 'certainly', as in Rev. 22:20, but other uses of the adverb suggest imminence, as in vs. 19, 23, 24) he will come in person to Philippi, that is, soon after Timothy's arrival. The carefully guarded way in which he expresses this hope means that he has no prior knowledge how his fate will be decided. But **in the Lord** assures him that it will be the 'best' decision, and if pastoral needs are a factor, he looks forward to being spared (1:24, 25) to revisit Philippi.

(2) *The return of Epaphroditus* **2:25–30**

25. Timothy's delayed departure will not affect the sending of Epaphroditus. He can be released from his commitment to Paul and there is an element of necessity (**I have thought it necessary,** i.e., to deal with the situation at Philippi) in his return. If **to send** (Gr. *pempsai*) is an instance of an 'epistolary aorist', i.e., the writer puts himself in the position of the reader for whom, when he reads the letter, the writer's actions will be past, then Epaphroditus is the bearer of the letter. Bonnard, however, finds several indications in verses 26, 27 that Epaphroditus had already left Paul's side, though he can hardly have returned to his native city at the time the letter is sent. Otherwise he could be the informant of Paul's circumstances.

Epaphroditus (Gr. means 'charming', 'amiable'; it is a common name in inscriptions and letters) is commended in glowing terms and by a five-fold description. To show his strong

attachment to Paul he is called **my brother and fellow worker.**
The first is a family word, to denote the common place these men
have in the household of God (*familia Dei*); **fellow worker** (Gr.
synergos; cf. G. Bertram, *TDNT* vii, pp. 874f.) denotes that Paul
and his companions are in the same service for the kingdom of
God, but there is no obscuring of the singular place given to Paul
as 'apostle'. Equally descriptive of Epaphroditus' association with
Paul is **fellow soldier** (a word found again in Paul only in
Phm. 2). The background is that of general metaphor, 'sharers
together in the conflict' against evil, rather than of a technical
(Lohmeyer, in reference to Philippi as a *colonia* with a garrison of
Roman troops) or apocalyptic (cf. O. Bauernfeind, *TDNT* vii,
p. 708) term.

Links with the Philippian church are given in **your messenger
and minister to my need.** The first word (Gr. *apostolos*) clearly
marks out Epaphroditus as the courier (in the sense of 2 C. 8:23)
who brought the Philippians' gift to the apostle (4:18). The
second word is more debatable. **minister** is *leitourgos* (see on
2:17), and relates to the way in which, at least, the Philippians'
gift *via* Epaphroditus had helped the service of the gospel and had
been part of the church's 'sacrificial offering' to God and for the
apostle's need (4:16–19; Rom. 12:13). See verse 30 for the same
word.

Perhaps there is a deeper meaning attaching to **minister**, both
here and in verse 30. On the ground that Paul writes **to send to
you** (not 'send back') Epaphroditus, J. H. Michael (ad loc.)
concludes that this man was seconded from the Philippian church
to be a regular, permanent member of the apostolic team.
Epaphroditus had grown homesick and, since his condition was
aggravated by illness, Paul decided to release him from his
engagement. This explains both the fulsome commendation of his
character, the recital of Epaphroditus' circumstances of illness,
and verse 30 where he did his best to 'complete your service to
me'. This assumes that Epaphroditus had come to be with Paul,
and then had fallen sick.

B. S. Mackay ('Further Thoughts on Philippians', *NTS* 7 (1961),
pp. 161–70) and C. O. Buchanan ('Epaphroditus' Sickness and
the Letter to the Philippians', *EQ* 36 (1964), pp. 157–66) argue,
to the contrary, that Epaphroditus fell ill on his journey and that
his coming was the fulfilment of a single, not a double, commission,

viz., to deliver the money-gift and then to return. News of his illness *en route*, which was near-fatal (vs. 27, 30), was relayed to the
Philippian church, and they grew anxious (v. 26). Now that he
has recovered, he wants to return, and Paul writes a 'covering
note' to explain just how serious his condition had been. This is a
plausible reconstruction, but it cannot be proved, since (*i*) we do
not know whether Epaphroditus did fall sick on the journey—
Buchanan's surmise that his illness was caused by a land journey
at a bad time of the year and not by shipwreck pointing to an illness
contracted *in via* is speculation—or during his stay with Paul, and
(*ii*) his risking his life (a strong term; see v. 30) suggests some
deliberate action on his part, not the ill-wisdom of setting out at
the wrong season of the year for travellers. And wherever it was
that Paul faced serious trouble (see Introduction, pp. 36–57), we
know that companions such as Aquila and Prisca (Rom. 16:3) ran
a similar risk for his sake. This would explain how Epaphroditus
could fall sick if his illness were not from natural consequences
caused by sharing Paul's imprisonment.

26. Several communications of news (*pace* Buchanan, loc. cit.)
are in view here. Epaphroditus has been sick; the Philippians
have learned of his sickness, and now Epaphroditus is **distressed**
over this reaction to the health bulletin they received. Not un-
naturally he **has been longing for you all.** These are two
strong verbs, full of pathos and emotion. The first (Gr. *epipothein*),
as in 1:8, is an ardent desire to see one's friends; the second
(Gr. *adēmonein*) denotes a great mental and spiritual anguish
(cf. Mt. 26:37; Mk 14:33; 'the distress which follows a great
shock'; so H. B. Swete in *The Gospel according to St Mark*, London,
1927, p. 342, or literally 'to experience homesickness', a peri-
phrastic tense in Paul's verse). Whatever his sickness was, it was
evidently the cause or accompaniment of a nervous disorder and
was partly occasioned by his anxious solicitude for the Philippians.
There was something very real in his sufferings—he was not
simply worried over the Philippians' worry (cf. Barth, p. 88)—
and this gives rise to the possibility that he was a leader in the
church and was deeply involved in the struggle against persecution
which the Philippian church was undergoing (Lohmeyer). Enforced absence and the tension of being alongside Paul in the prison
had taken their toll, and Epaphroditus' health had been affected.

27. The illness was nearly mortal. His recovery was due to

God who **had mercy on him.** From being near to death (cf. v. 30 for a parallel phrase) he had been rescued by divine grace and his life was spared. By this token, Paul's lot had been eased, for if Epaphroditus had died, the sorrow of bereavement would have been added to the troubles surrounding the apostle, both in his awaiting an outcome to the imprisonment and in his delicate situation in the church where he was confined (see 1:15–18). **sorrow upon sorrow** suggests 'wave upon wave' of trouble which mercifully had been averted.

28. Naturally **I am the more eager to send him,** i.e., 'I am very eager' (BDF, sec. 244, on the comparative). **to send** is another epistolary infinitive: see on verse 25. Paul's readiness to send Epaphroditus on his way answers some questions to do with the reason for his commendation. It cannot be that Epaphroditus had deserted his post at Philippi and overstayed his time with Paul, because they will **rejoice at seeing him again.** Paul takes the initiative in discharging him from his 'service' (v. 25), and this suggests that, in terminating what the church intended to be a permanent commission at Paul's side (so Friedrich) on the ground of Epaphroditus' incapacity to endure any more trial, Paul writes a praiseworthy character-reference of the man in order to answer the implied criticism that he had failed in that commission. This undertone in Paul's commendation also argues for a double commission, that Epaphroditus had come with a gift and also had intended to stay at Paul's side. Paul would hardly have expressed an eager desire to send Epaphroditus home if he had simply travelled as a courier with their gift. The Philippians evidently proposed that he should remain, and Paul deflects any criticism of the man because he is returning. If the Philippians did raise an objection on that score, Paul would feel unhappy as one personally involved. So he appeals in the following verse for a cordial reception **that I may be less anxious** than he would be if Epaphroditus meets a barrage of criticism on his return.

29. The warm reception to be given to Epaphroditus is no more than he deserves. **receive him,** as the Lord would (cf. Rom. 15:7), or as befits those who are 'in the Lord' (Rom. 16:2). Either way, a welcome **with all joy** is envisaged. **honour such men,** lit. 'hold such men in high esteem, regard them as valuable'. The reason for Epaphroditus' claim to this distinction is now supplied.

30. he nearly died for the work of Christ. Just how we do not know, but it is better understood (*pace* Mackay, loc. cit.) as though this is news to the Philippians and not Paul's re-telling of an aspect of Epaphroditus' service which they had heard of previously.

risking his life Gr. *paraboleusamenos*, 'hazarding': cf. A. Deissmann, *Light from the Ancient East*, p. 88 and notes, for a tribute paid to a certain Carzoazus who 'exposed himself to dangers' (*paraboleusamenos*). The Textus Receptus authorities have *parabouleusamenos*, 'not regarding' his life, but this is less preferable. The former is a gambling term. He staked his life for the service of Christ, in fulfilling his commission to Paul on behalf of his church. He was their representative (4:18), and he discharged what was asked of him, says Paul, in a generous estimate of a situation which we can only partly reconstruct. We know that the Philippians wanted to assist him in his need (v. 25). Epaphroditus had been their messenger and *leitourgos* (v. 25). His presence made up for the absence of the Philippians (cf. 1 C. 16:17). And Paul pays a thankful tribute as their delegate is sent back. Throughout the section, as Gnilka aptly says, we are in touch with real men of flesh and blood, and human situations of universal interest.

PAUL'S WARNING AND SELF-DEFENCE 3:1-14

This long section of the letter poses several problems of identity which have been referred to in the Introduction (pp. 22–36). In particular, the descriptions given in verses 2–6 of both the sectarians Paul warns against and his own defensive posture raise the issues of (*i*) who these men were and what fault Paul finds with them, and (*ii*) why he goes to such length to defend himself from the implied criticisms of his opponents. There are also subsidiary matters which this section brings to our attention, such as the effect, if any, of this false teaching on the Philippian congregation, and the relation between the intruders in the opening verses of the chapter and the 'enemies of the cross of Christ' vividly portrayed in 3:18–21.

The entire passage can be divided into smaller units, following the call to **rejoice in the Lord** (3:1*a*). On the word **Finally**, see p. 157.

(a) *An introduction and severe warning* **3:1b, 2**

3:1b To write the same things to you is not irksome to me, and is safe for you. While it is just possible to make the phrase **To write the same things to you** refer back to the preceding section, and be an appeal to joy (so Lohmeyer, Dibelius), it is much more likely that Paul is writing an introductory sentence to what is to follow. The 'same' ideas which he will expound in the verses to be written in chapter 3 are also to be supplemented by oral instructions entrusted to Epaphroditus and Timothy in their forthcoming missions to Philippi (so V. P. Furnish, 'The Place and Purpose of Philippians III', *NTS* 10 (1963), pp. 80–3); or, if chapter 3:1b following is a separate composition (see Introduction, pp. 13–22), the term refers to other communications of which we have no knowledge. **irksome** is to be taken in the sense of 'troublesome', 'a burden to me', to send this warning. Paul is greatly moved by the presence of false teachers on the horizon, and has no hesitation in addressing the Philippians with an appeal for watchfulness. What he has in view is their welfare; **it is safe for you**. The last phrase may be rendered 'and it is (something) definite for you' (Gr. *asphalēs* has this sense in Ac. 25:26), 'something for you to be aware of'. After speaking generally in the first two chapters, he will come now to specific points in his pastoral counsel (so Collange).

2. Look out for the dogs, look out for the evil-workers, look out for those who mutilate the flesh. The threefold repetition of the verb *blepete* is used to great effect and is matched by three participles linked in a series in verses 3, 4a (Gnilka). A weakened sense of the verb 'regard', 'look at', 'consider', is offered by G. D. Kilpatrick ('*BLEPETE* Philippians 3₂', in the volume *In memoriam Paul Kahle*, ed. M. Black and G. Fohrer, Berlin, 1968, pp. 146–8); but if this is so, it is hard to account for the repetition of the call which is couched as a warning.

Κύνες **dogs** were regarded as unclean animals in Eastern society (O. Michel, *TDNT* iii, pp. 1101–4), and Paul's point of comparison may simply be that his enemies are despicable men (Gnilka) and evil characters with dissolute manners (W. Schmithals, *Paul and the Gnostics*, ET Nashville/New York, 1972, p. 83). But since Jews were in the habit of calling Gentiles outside the law by the opprobrious name 'dogs' (cf. Mt. 15:21–28; Rev.

22:15; and SB i, pp. 724f.; iii, pp. 621f.), it is more to the point
if Paul is ironically seizing on a term which his Jewish enemies
were using concerning his converts in the Gentile churches—
uncircumcised Gentile believers, at Philippi and Galatia—and
hurling it back at them with a vengeance (cf. Collange). In the
background may be the idea that these Judaizing, or more
probably Jewish gnosticizing, enemies were like a pack of dogs,
continually yelping at his heels and trying to attack his people in
the Gentile mission churches; or else that Paul is using a re-
proachful term because these Jewish-Christian itinerant missionaries are regarded by him as intruders and scavengers on the
Philippian congregation, like the 'sneaking pseudo-brethren who
intruded to spy out our freedom' at the time of the Apostolic
Council (Gal. 2:3–8). So 'anyone arriving in Philippi . . . whose
program was to subvert these agreements (of Paul's right to
evangelize Gentiles without reference to the law) would be
immediately recognizable as an intruding "dog" ' (R. Jewett,
NovT 12 (1970), p. 386). But see Schmithals' objection to this,
op. cit., p. 84.

   The description **evil-workers** fixes the identity of the opponents
in the same general framework as the men who ranged themselves
against Paul at Corinth (2 C. 11:13). They are Jewish-Christian
gnostic emissaries armed with a propagandizing aim to win over
Paul's converts on the basis of their insistence on circumcision.
Paul here calls them 'evil' because their effect is to undermine his
'work' in the Gentile mission (1:22), and they are in league with the
'evil one' (2 C. 11:14), whatever appearances may suggest to the
contrary, i.e., the claim they profess to be representing the
Jerusalem leaders. There are these undoubted links with Paul's
enemies at Corinth. Yet there are some differences, pointed out
by G. Baumbach ('Die Frage nach den Irrlehrern in Philippi',
Kairos 13, 1–4 (1971), pp. 252–66, espec. pp. 263f.). For example,
Paul's apostleship is not in dispute at Philippi (so Baumbach,
though this assertion may be challenged); there is no emphasis
on apostolic credentials, nor on ecstatic elements, nor is the
controversy a christological one. The last point is well made, since
clearly 'gnostic' used of the Philippian heretics and their teaching
has a different connotation from what was true of the Colossian
teachers whose interest centred in their speculation about wisdom,
the cosmic aeons and the angels; and which led to the practical

effect of asceticism (see *Colossians and Philemon, New Century Bible,* 1974, pp. 9–19), as Baumbach observes, loc. cit., p. 263.

those who mutilate the flesh is a paraphrase for Paul's crisp term (Gr. *katatomē,* 'a cutting'). He is deriding their false confidence in the badge of circumcision (for reasons given in Rom. 2:25–29; Gal. 5:2–4) and his irony in the following retort, 'For we are the true circumcision' ('true' is added to the Gr. *peritomē* to bring out the meaning) matches that in Gal. 5:12. A boastful and misplaced stress on circumcision is not merely regrettable; it is a deadly error, and turns out to be simply a mutilation of the body, not a meaningful sign of God's work in the human spirit (see the background of this spiritualizing of circumcision in Jer. 4:4; Dt. 10:16; Ezek. 44:7; and 1QS 5.5, Vermes, p. 78). See further M. E. Glasswell, *ExpT* 85 (1973–4), pp. 328–32. On the issue raised in this verse of the nature of a Jewish propagandizing movement to compel Gentiles to accept circumcision, see earlier pp. 30, 34.

(b) Paul's life—past and present **3:3–6**

3. This is Paul's direct answer to the Jewish Christians' insistence on the cult of the ceremonial. He opposes it with a catechetical version (the first person plural, **we are**, perhaps shows this influence) of the cult of the Holy Spirit. It is the Spirit who inaugurates the new covenant of inward **worship** and obedience (Jer. 31:31–34; Ezek. 36:26ff.; cf. 2 C. 3:1–18) and leads men to **glory in Christ** alone. The very thing the Jewish teachers were doing—having **confidence in the flesh** (as in 2 C. 11:18, 21ff.), i.e., external religious rites—is excluded under the terms of the new order (see Rom. 3:27–31), since the badge of circumcision takes on a new meaning, not of a meritorious profession of human obedience but of a faith which relies solely on divine promise and grace (Rom. 4:9–12; Gal. 3:1–9, 5:2–12, 6:15).

The anthropological term **flesh** is studiously ambiguous. It may refer in a specific way to the human flesh on which a surgical operation is performed in the rite of circumcision. (So W. D. Davies, 'Paul and the Dead Sea Scrolls: Flesh and Spirit', in *Christian Origins and Judaism,* London, 1962, pp. 145–77.) The more customary sense of 'flesh' (Gr. *sarx*) in Paul is man's lower, unredeemed nature, not inherently bad but the target of sin's attack and the occasion of his becoming a victim under sin's dominion.

(See, on the general usage, W. D. Stacey, *The Pauline View of Man*, London, 1956, pp. 154–73; E. Schweizer, *TDNT* vii, pp. 129f.; and in particular reference to this verse, H. R. Moehring, 'Some remarks on σάρξ (*sarx*) in Philippians 3:3ff.', *SE* iv (ed. F. L. Cross) (1968), pp. 432–6.) The trouble with those who placed their **confidence in the flesh** was simply that, from Paul's point of view, they were trusting in some religious ordinance outside of Christ—and so making a fatal mistake (so Moehring, loc. cit., p. 436, opposing Davies).

4. Though I myself have reason for confidence in the flesh also. This is an aside added to say that if his enemies think (mistakenly) that they have an impressive case for circumcision, Paul can produce a set of valid reasons—from their premise—for trusting in this religious system. Indeed, he can excel them: **I have more** to boast of—if it is a question of parading one's merits and claims and qualifications. This mock contest of comparison is parallel with 2 C. 11:21ff., 12:1ff.

any other man looks in the direction of an anonymous debater with whom Paul now enters into an engagement (Gnilka). His parade of all that he could justifiably claim as proving himself an authentic Jew (Benoit) falls into two parts: those advantages which were his at his birth (v. 5), and those which he acquired in later life (vs. 5*d*, 6).

5. circumcised on the eighth day, which was the correct day in an infant's life for his adoption into the covenant by the rite of circumcision (Gen. 17:12, 21:4; Lev. 12:3). Paul was not a convert to the Jewish faith, admitted to the race in later life as a proselyte. He was *born* a Jew.

of the people of Israel. The claim to be an Israelite, a member of the elect nation, was a proud one (see art. 'Israel, Israelite', in *TDNT* iii, pp. 356–91; cf. Jn 1:47), and evidently this status featured prominently in the hellenistic-Jewish propaganda in Corinth (2 C. 11:22: cf. D. Georgi, *Die Gegner des Paulus im 2. Korintherbrief*, Neukirchen, 1964, pp. 60–3).

of the tribe of Benjamin. In order to show his real Jewishness, Paul alludes to his membership of a special tribe within the family of Abraham (2 C. 11:22). Various reasons may be offered to account for this reference. **Benjamin** was, with his brother Joseph, the only son of Jacob by Rachel (J. H. Michael), and the only son born in the land of promise (SB iii, p. 622, citing the

Midrash on Est. 3:4 (94b)). The ³first king Saul belonged to this tribe (Beare), and the future apostle shared his name before his own name was changed. Benjamin also was a tribe to resist the encroachments of pagan culture, and Paul might well have drawn attention to his membership in this tribe to assert that his ancestry was 'pure', and that he was—and is—a 'full-blooded Jew' (Gnilka).

a Hebrew born of Hebrews. This phrase confirms that both Paul and his forebears were brought up to speak the ancestral Hebrew language (cf. Ac. 6:1 for this distinction between 'Hebrew' and 'Hellenist' as denoting a cultural difference expressed in the use of language: C. F. D. Moule, *ExpT* 70, (1958–9), pp. 100ff.). Again this claim is offered as a badge of his strict orthodoxy, untainted by foreign influence. Cf. 2 C. 11:22. Whatever exposure Saul may have had to Hellenism at Tarsus, he traces his ancestry to a Palestinian source (cf. W. C. van Unnik, *Tarsus or Jerusalem? The City of Paul's Youth*, ET London, 1962).

as to the law a Pharisee. Now switching to those items on his list, as though he were counting all the points in his favour (Barth), he proceeds to comment on his voluntary choices. Like Josephus, when confronted with the several options of the 'sects' of the Jewish people, Paul chose to be **a Pharisee** whose reputation for careful and earnest observance of the Mosaic **law** and its tradition was the distinguishing feature (Josephus, *Life*, 9f.) of their life. (See J. Jeremias, *Jerusalem in the Time of Jesus*, ET London, 1969, pp. 246–67.)

6. zeal was another well-known characteristic of the Pharisees who in part traced back their line to the Maccabees, noted for their zeal for Israel's covenant (1 Mac. 2:24–9). The prototype was Phinehas (Num. 25:1–18; Ps. 106:30, 31; Sir. 45:23) 'who was zealous in the fear of the Lord' (4 Mac. 18:12). See too Test. Asher 4:5; 1QH 14:14 (Vermes, p. 193). In Paul's case he showed his **zeal** by being **a persecutor of the church.** The verb *diōkō*, 'to hunt' and so to persecute by chasing and harrying the quarry, is something of a set expression for Paul's pre-conversion activity in hounding Christians (Ac. 9:4, 5, 22:4, 7, 8; 1 C. 15:9; Gal. 1:13f., 23). In striving to show his earnestness and devotion he opposed fiercely the followers of Jesus in a hatred of Christians (in those days of his life) that was seen later to be directed against their Lord (cf. Ac. 9:4, 5; 1 C. 8:12; 1 Tim. 1:12–15).

Paul acted in good conscience, since **as to righteousness under the law** he professed to be found **blameless.** This is an important datum of his autobiography. In reconstructing Paul's pre-Christian life from this verse, we must allow that there is no evidence of an inner conflict **under the law** or any trace of a bad conscience, such as is sometimes deduced from what he says in Romans 7. (On this question see C. L. Mitton, 'Romans vii Reconsidered', *ExpT* 65 (1953-4), pp. 78–81, 99–103, 132–5, and W. G. Kümmel, *Römer 7 und die Bekehrung des Paulus*, Leipzig, 1929.)

blameless is not meant ironically. He is in serious debate with his Judaizing opponents, and professes to be their match in the way he excelled in his law-keeping fanaticism and its reward. (See M. Goguel, '*Kata dikaiosynēn tēn en nomō genomenos amemptos* (Phil. 3, 6). Remarques sur un aspect de la conversion de Paul', *JBL* 53 (1934), pp. 257–67; W. Grundmann, *TDNT* iv, p. 573, on Paul's profession of being **blameless.**)

(c) The benefits of his new life **3:7-14**

7. The introductory **But** must be given its full force. The time has come, in Paul's telling of the story of his past life, for him to state clearly the reassessment—'the transvaluation of all values' (Gnilka)—which followed directly upon his conversion. He opens this section with a strong asseveration: **But whatever gain I had, I counted as loss for the sake of Christ. gain** (Gr. *kerdē*) is plural, suggesting that Paul gathers all the privileges and claims of the preceding section and puts them into one package, which he then surprisingly dismisses as **loss.** He does not simply take up a neutral or negative attitude to them; he rejects them with disgust (Barth), and treats them as a liability and something to be abhorred (v. 8: 'refuse' or 'dirt'). (Cf. H. Schlier, *TDNT* iii, p. 672.) The contrast **gain** and **loss** is a rabbinic one (SB i, p. 749; cf. *Aboth* 2.1: 'for thou knowest not the recompense of reward of each precept, and reckon the loss through (the fulfilling of) a precept against its reward, and the reward (that comes) from transgression against its loss', and Mt. 16:26).

The last phrase **for the sake of Christ** gives the key to Paul's motivation. In place of the things which he rejects and recoils from, he sets the knowledge of Christ (v. 8). That knowledge began in his conversion, and **I counted,** though a perfect tense

(Gr. *hēgēmai*), includes an allusion to what happened on the Damascus road, when he renounced all his past hopes and came to a personal knowledge of Christ (Gnilka, Michael, Michaelis). The tense may well be explained by his larger purpose which is to include an instructional element as a counterweight to his opponents' arguments, and not simply to speak autobiographically (so Collange, who observes that Paul's autobiography of his conversion in Gal. 1 stresses more divine grace and choice than human decision, as here).

8. Repeating the thought in verse 7 and extending it, he goes on to set the knowledge of Christ in a central place in his life. **Indeed** (Gr. *alla menoun ge kai*: see BDF, sec. 448. 6; M. E. Thrall, *Greek Particles in the New Testament*, Leiden, 1962, pp. 11–16, who notes the progression and emphasis in the particles' use) is his way of preparing the reader for an important announcement to follow. In fact, he says, **I count everything as loss** (Gr. *zēmia*, to be picked up in the verb *zēmioō* later in the verse). The change of tense to the present suggests that he is thinking of choices which confronted him every day when he was tempted to forget the worthlessness of his past religious endeavours to gain righteousness by law. Nor can it be accidental that this notion of moral choice is central in the Christ-hymn he has just cited (2:6: the heavenly Christ did not count equality with God a prize).

The great compensating factor is all that **knowing Christ Jesus my Lord** entails. The background of this rich theological term has been assessed in differing ways. Dibelius relates the term 'knowledge' (Gr. *gnōsis*) to the knowledge of the deity in hellenistic mysticism. He writes of 'a revelation of the god in which the vision (granted in the mystery cults) leads to a transformation of the beholder', quoting 2 C. 3:18, 4:6 as parallel. R. Bultmann (*TDNT* i, p. 710) appeals similarly to a gnostic setting of the term, used however in a non-gnostic way since Paul is conducting a polemic. This view is followed by W. Schmithals (*Paul and the Gnostics*, pp. 91f.). Other scholars such as W. D. Davies, in his *Christian Origins and Judaism*, p. 141, and J. Dupont (in his work *Gnosis: La connaissance religieuse dans les épîtres de saint Paul*, Louvain/Paris, 1949, pp. 34–6) argue for a background in Judaism, while more complex derivations of the term are sought by Lohmeyer ('knowledge' is something peculiar to the martyr's experience) and R. C. Tannehill, *Dying and Rising* *with Christ*, Göttingen, 1967, pp. 114–23 (a combination of mystical and legal language). Gnilka (p. 193) also finds a synthesis of several ideas and remarks on the centrality of the idea in Paul. See for an excellent orientation of the term, B. Gärtner, 'The Pauline and Johannine Idea of "To Know God" Against the Hellenistic Background', *NTS* 14 (1967–8), pp. 209–31.

To enter into this deep communion with the risen Lord, Paul recognizes that the path is long and arduous. Sacrifice is involved (he counts **everything as loss,** and he has **suffered the loss of all things**) and a heavy price has to be paid. Nor are half measures much use: he decided **to count them as refuse** in order to gain the prize of this fellowship.

refuse (Gr. *skybala*) is a vulgar term, meaning either human excrement or waste foods consigned to the garbage heap. A word like 'muck' conveys the sense to a modern reader, though even that does not express distaste in sufficiently strong terms. All past religious and ceremonial privileges are thus contemptuously cast on one side and disowned.

For Paul the choice is worth it. **the surpassing worth** (Gr. *to hyperechon*; see BDF, sec. 263. 2, on the precise grammatical form) of the knowledge of Christ is nothing less than the road to a blissful possession of him. **that I may gain Christ** stands as the goal which beckons him. The verb **gain** (Gr. *kerdō*) is chosen in contrast to verse 7 where Paul's past life's treasures as a faithful Jew were summed up as 'gains' (*kerdē*). These were abandoned as debilitating 'losses', and Paul gets in their place the single good of his Lord's presence and gift. (On the different meanings to be attached to Paul's knowledge of Christ, see J. T. Forestell, 'Christian Perfection and Gnosis in Phil. 3, 7–16', *CBQ* 18 (1956), pp. 123–36, but without reference to the polemical context of this passage.)

9. So 'to gain Christ' is to **be found** (by God, a divine passive: see on 1:29) **in him,** enjoying the new status of a man cleared of guilt and accepted in God's presence. The juridicial flavour of 'being found' in Christ at the last day of divine judgment, now brought into the present as a transformed eschatological act of acquittal, is clear from what follows. 'To be found in him and to be justified are both the same' (Bonnard). Justification here carries the eschatological meaning of vindication at the divine court by the possessing of an acceptable **righteousness,** i.e., right relationship with God, granted by God himself. So 'to be in Christ is nothing else than having the righteousness which comes from God' (Bonnard). (See P. Stuhlmacher, *Gerechtigkeit Gottes bei Paulus*, Göttingen, 1965, p. 99, for this meaning.)

Paul expounds the teaching in this verse largely on an individualistic basis, though elsewhere (in Romans particularly) his concept of justification stemming from the *OT* idea of God's righteousness (Heb. *ṣedāqāh*) includes a cosmic dimension, i.e., the believing Christian in the company of those whom God accepts enters a new world set right with the divine purpose (See E. Käsemann, ' "The Righteousness of God" in Paul', *New Testament Questions of Today*, ET London, 1969, pp. 168–82; B. Reicke, 'Paul's Understanding of Righteousness', *Soli Deo Gloria*, ed. J. McDowell Richards, Richmond, Va., 1968, pp. 37–49; H. Conzelmann, 'Current Problems in Pauline Research, iv: The Righteousness of God', *Interpretation* 22 (1968), pp. 178–82; J. A. Ziesler, *The Meaning of Righteousness in Paul*, Cambridge, 1972, pp. 148–52).

About God's action in accepting men as 'justified' which is 'forensic and ethical at once' (Ziesler), Paul's autobiographical section says three things. One is that such a gift of righteousness stands in diametrical contrast to **a righteousness of my own.** In the context, this means that a right standing and relationship with God cannot be acquired or achieved by human effort on the basis of **the law,** the Torah and its rabbinical interpretation of God's purpose for men. Then, he stresses that such righteousness comes to the trusting person as God's gift. It is **righteousness from God** (the phrase *ek theou* is a genitive of author or origin, in strict parallel with *ek nomou*, **based on law** in the preceding line). The law cannot give righteousness (Gal. 2:16–21, 3:11, 12, 21; 5:20, 21; Rom. 4:13–15; 2 C. 3:6); only God can do that because it is his prerogative in his grace to give what is in fact his nature. (See the origin of the term 'the righteousness of God' in Isa. 54:17; cf. Bar. 5:2, 9.) Moreover, according to one interpretation, the ground of the gift is the faith, i.e., the obedience or work, of Christ (Rom. 5:15–19; see R. N. Longenecker, 'The Obedience of Christ in the Theology of the Early Church', *Reconciliation and Hope*, ed. R. Banks, Exeter, 1974, pp. 142–52, esp. 146f.), and it is this fact which Paul makes use of in his phrase **through faith in Christ,** in which the genitive represented by **in Christ** is a subjective or possessive one. Justification comes because of Christ's faith, i.e., his faithful obedience to the Father. That ground is a further proof of the way in which justification is God's sole gift.

Thirdly, the medium through which the divine righteousness or God's saving power, exercised in liberating his people and setting them in good relations with himself (as in Isa. 46:13; 51:5), reaches men is faith. The variation in the prepositional phrase— now Paul writes 'the righteousness of God' **that depends on faith** (Gr. *epi tē pistei*)—brings in the human response, which is a grateful acknowledging of what God has done, an acceptance of it, and a commitment to live by it in the terms of Gal. 5:6.

For the debate on **faith in Christ** see Ziesler, op. cit., pp. 151f.; and A. T. Hanson, *Studies in Paul's Technique and Theology*, London, 1974, pp. 39f. To the objection that the understanding of 'faith' as Christ's obedience means that we need another word to denote man's response, it may be said that only on this view is Paul's phrase **that depends on faith** (which is man's response) meaningful. Otherwise, if 'faith' is taken in both clauses to be a human reaction to God's gift we do have a tautology and Paul has left the objective ground of God's action unspecified.

10. that I may know him (sc. Christ) is slightly ambiguous, as is the Greek. The construction could be taken as a purpose clause, 'by faith I come to know him', or a consequence, 'since I have faith I know him'. Conceivably the infinitive explains the meaning of, and gives the content of, the faith in verse 9. Faith, Paul remarks in conclusion of his previous discussion, consists in knowing him, in the sense already described in verse 8. And further, that intimacy of union with the living Lord in **the power of his resurrection** is only possible as the apostle first comes to **share his sufferings, becoming like him in his death.**

The three expressions, **know him, the power of his resurrection, share** (lit. the fellowship—Gr. *koinōnia*—of) **his sufferings,** go together in close association. It would be far-fetched, however, to see here a latent trinitarian formula as J. A. Fitzmyer ('To know him and the power of his resurrection', in *Mélanges B. Rigaux*, ed. A. Descamps and A. de Halleux, Gembloux, 1970, pp. 411–25, espec. p. 421) suggests. The knowledge of Christ is personal and intimate, corresponding to the Hebrew *daʿat Yahweh*, 'the knowledge of the Lord'. Possibly Paul goes on directly to relate this knowledge to the resurrection power because his first encounter was with the living Lord on the Damascus road (so M. Bouttier, *Christianity according to Paul*, ET London, 1966, pp. 17–19).

Of the three expressions in this verse the most problematical for exegesis is the last, rendered in *RSV* **may share his sufferings.** The Greek is literally 'the fellowship of his sufferings' (*koinōnia pathēmatōn autou*). The debate turns on the precise category of the genitive phrase. It is generally agreed that the genitive 'of his sufferings' must be objective, i.e., Paul longs to share his Lord's sufferings, rather than that he wants to enter into 'fellowship created by Christ's sufferings'. Lohmeyer (*Kommentar*, p. 139) wishes to interpret the phrase in this second way, commenting that 'his sufferings are the foundation of the fellowship of the believer with Christ or God'. But H. Seesemann (*Der KOINŌNIA im NT*, pp. 83f.) observes in criticism of Lohmeyer that the addition of 'with Christ or God' is not warranted by the context. Seesemann's argument for taking the meaning to be 'to participate (*Anteilhaben*) in the Lord's sufferings' in the sense of Rom. 8:17; 2 C. 1:5 is convincing (op. cit., pp. 85, 86). (See, too, B. M. Ahern, 'The Fellowship of his Sufferings (Phil. 3, 10)', *CBQ* 22 (1960), pp. 1–32.)

We may propose that, as to background, Paul's thought is polemical as he confronts the teaching of those perfectionists (see vs. 12–16) who were arguing that the knowledge of the heavenly Lord was all-important and that Christians are already raised with Christ to new life. Paul is meeting this wrong-headed understanding of the Christian life as a resurrection experienced here and now in baptism and which denies all future hope, as in 2 Tim. 2:18, similar to the theology—seen in 1 C. 15:12—which already was being accepted and applied practically at Corinth (see W. Schmithals, *Gnosticism in Corinth*, ET Nashville/New York, 1971, pp. 155ff., 259ff.). He does so with a forceful statement that the only way to enter into the **power of his resurrection** is by a willingness to **share his sufferings,** and so become **like him in his death.** The last phrase is clearly baptismal (cf. Rom. 6:1–11; 2 C. 4:7–15; Col. 2:12, 20, 3:1; 2 Tim. 2:11), referring to the representative death of Jesus on the cross in which believers participate as they too die to their old life and are raised to new existence. (See the exposition in J. Jervell, *Imago Dei*, Göttingen, 1960, pp. 206–8, 261, 273ff.)

The point of the Pauline counter-argument is that our baptism into Christ is not a passport to mystical experience lifting us beyond the range of sufferings and trial, and transporting us to a state of blessed perfection. Rather, our 'becoming like him in his death'—as the baptismal actions should have recalled to the Philippians—is our entrance upon a life in which we like Paul, in a pre-eminent way (2 C. 4:10), share his sufferings, as in 2 C. 4:7–10; and this costly discipleship is the road by which Christians come to know who Jesus is and to follow him. So 'denial of the bodily resurrection and contempt for the suffering body [on the ground that "redemption extends only to the soul; for the body cannot do otherwise than decay, as is its nature" (Irenaeus, *Adv. Haer.* 1. 24.5)]—in the case of Christ as well as with the Christians —are for the Gnostics just as inseparable as for Paul the "suffering and dying with Christ" and the "rising with him" ' (Schmithals, *Paul and the Gnostics*, p. 93).

11. We have assumed that 'his resurrection' in verse 10 is a present experience, i.e., his power as the risen Lord in human lives (so Dibelius, Gnilka, Collange), and not the future resurrection awaiting believers (as Beare, Bonnard, Lohmeyer suggest). However, in verse 11 the thought does reach out to the future: **that if possible I may attain the resurrection from the dead.** He has already corrected any idea that the believers' past 'risen with Christ' experience in baptism is an end in itself. It is a summons to knowing Christ in a life of suffering service and hardship, such as he himself was undergoing in the course of his apostolic labour. Now Paul expresses the hope that complete conforming to his Lord (3:21) will come at **the resurrection from *among* the dead** (the unparalleled Greek expression— 'intended clearly to express the realism of the resurrection from among the physically dead' [Gnilka]—is probably to be accounted for by Paul's emphasis on the necessity for a future resurrection to complete God's saving plan for his people. His eye is on those who denied the future hope on the mistaken ground that the only resurrection was a spiritualized one, already past). See Polycarp, *Phil.* 7: false prophets say that 'there is neither resurrection nor judgment'.

The element of doubt in the term **that if possible** (Gr. *ei pōs*: BDF, sec. 375: cf. a similar expression in Ignatius, *Smyr.* 4: 'only pray for them, if perhaps (Gr. *ean pōs*) they may

repent') is not in reference to the reality of his resurrection, as
though Paul wondered if he might ever attain it, but in regard to
the way in which it will be his, i.e., whether by martyrdom or at a
more distant time, as in 1:20–26. The last thing Paul wishes to
imply is a hesitation about the full realization of Christian hope
in the resurrection. That hope was being discounted by the false
notions current among his enemies. He is really expressing full
confidence that there is a future resurrection, irrespective of
uncertainty as to how Christians come to it. The entire passage is
slanted polemically (see especially the exposition to this effect by
Peter Siber, *Mit Christus Leben. Eine Studie zur paulinischen Aufer-
stehungshoffnung*, Zürich, 1971, pp. 116–22), and here we touch the
nerve-end of Paul's debate with the heretics (Gnilka), as the next
section will show.

   12. To amplify his preceding teaching on the polarity of the
Christian life—the Christian is 'already raised' with Christ, yet
still awaits the consummation of his faith in the final day—
Paul uses the imagery of a race. **Not that I have already obtained** [**this:** not in the original] (Gr. *elabon*, 'received') what
God promised in the future resurrection, or the prize awarded to
the athlete who is victorious (so Bonnard, Beare, Delling in *TDNT*
iv, p. 7). There is no object explicitly mentioned, though P46 and
D* add 'or am already justified', suggesting 'righteousness' as the
object of the verb, a reading supported by A. F. J. Klijn's discussion, *NovT* 7 (1964–5), p. 281. Perhaps we should understand
simply 'Christ', referring back to verse 8, 'to gain Christ' (so
Dibelius, V. C. Pfitzner, *Paul and the Agon Motif*, p. 144); or else it
may be that Paul is intentionally vague and leaves the object
unexpressed (so Gnilka, Collange, Schmithals, *Paul and the
Gnostics*, p. 97, on the ground that the gnostic initiate claimed to
have attained *everything*, the ineffable bliss, beyond which there is
nothing more to attain. He has reached the goal, which is left
undefined in such documented expressions as 'to be fulfilled', 'to
be perfect', 'to be satisfied'. Paul counters this by consciously
leaving the object of his present limited attainment unexpressed
—as a direct antithesis to the enemies' arrogance).

   More agreement is found in understanding **or am already
perfect** (Gr. *teteleiōmai*). Paul never uses the verb elsewhere; and
it is a very likely conclusion that he is borrowing from the vocabulary of the opponents whose catchword both in this verse and in

verse 15 may be part of Paul's quotation. They claimed to have arrived at a state of blessed perfection; he denies that he has reached that goal, though he is on the road to it: **but I press on to make [it: not in the Greek] my own, because Christ Jesus has made me his own.**

Paul's ambition in life is to **press on** (Gr. *diōkō,* referring back to verse 6, where it means 'I pursued as a hunter', and looking ahead to verse 14). The term belongs to the world of both the hunter and the athlete. It is difficult to decide which meaning is uppermost since the first sense would suggest an admirable contrast between Paul's old and new life. Formerly he hunted Christians; now he 'chases' the vocation of a life in Christ and for him. However, he goes on to explore fully the athlete's metaphor in the following lines, so that we should opt for the meaning 'I press on in my course' to claim in the measure which is possible (Gr. *ei kai*: BDF, sec. 368, 375; Thrall, op. cit., p. 90) the purpose for which Christ Jesus claimed me as his servant. There is an obvious play on the verbs rendered **make it my own** (Gr. *katalambanein*) . . . **Christ Jesus has made me his own** (also *katalambanein*) and the preceding 'I have obtained' (Gr. *lambanein*). That which Paul confesses he has not yet attained at the end of his Christian road he strives to reach. He seeks to lay hold upon the hope set before him with ever firmer grip because (Gr. *eph' hō,* BDF, sec. 235) Christ has laid his hand on him. The last phrase refers to his conversion encounter in which he was forcefully arrested and his life set in a new direction (1 C. 15:8–10: see J. Dupont, 'The Conversion of Paul, and its Influence on his Understanding of Salvation by Faith', in *Apostolic History and the Gospel,* ed. W. W. Gasque and R. P. Martin, Exeter, 1970, espec. pp. 180f., 190f. This article contains a number of interesting observations on Phil. 3).

This interpretation of the verbs in the verse assumes that they are to be taken in a metaphorical sense. It is just possible that we should regard them as verbs of cognition. Then, the sense would be 'I press on in pursuit of a knowledge (Gr. *katalambanein,* 'to understand'; see J. Dupont, *Gnosis,* pp. 501–21; Dupont's later view is to see the verb as having an athletic imagery: loc. cit., 1970, p. 180) of the purpose behind Christ Jesus' knowledge (i.e., in electing and claiming me, as Yahweh did to ancient Israel, Am. 3:2 etc.) of me.' Less preferable is yet another meaning

in which the object of Paul's striving is to attain to the resurrection
(v. 11). Then he sets his sights on the future, and presses on towards
the goal of his resurrection which was the blessed hope implied in
that Christ laid hold of him and assured him of his final destiny.
Not all at Philippi share his convictions. So Paul turns to a fuller
statement of the case, distinguishing himself in the next verse from
others who claimed 'perfection'. 'He is in fact protesting against
the false security' (Lightfoot) wrongly deduced from his teaching.

**13. Brethren, I do not consider that I have made it my
own** is really a paraphrase, and the exegesis given in this rendering
depends on the textual reading 'not' (Gr. *ou*, with P46, BG, and
the TR) in preference to 'not yet' translated in *RV* (Gr. *oupō*,
with P16 [uncertain], Sinaiticus AD*). The choice of readings is
not easy. Notice too that **it** in *RSV* is added to make the sense
complete. If the latter MS tradition is followed, it is possible to
translate something like this: 'Brethren, I consider that I have not
as yet laid hold upon what is before me.' Once more the object is
elusive, since Paul does not explicitly say what it is that he has
not, or has not yet, either attained or understood (for the two
meanings of *katalambanein*, repeated from verse 12, see the note
on that verse).

The object of the verb is either the full knowledge of Christ, of
which a foretaste was given him at his conversion, or the blessedness
of the resurrection still to come.

Whatever the precise details of this statement, their purport is
clear. Paul is opposing both an overconfident assertion of perfectionism on the ground that Christians, now raised with Christ
to new life, are blessed with a share in his immortality, and a
quietism which would lead a person to acquiesce in his present
experience and become forgetful of the eschatological hope set
before the church. The Christian life is one set in the midst of this
tension. The Pauline believer is *in statu viatoris*, on the road
between his starting point (he has been laid hold of by Christ)
and his goal (he has not yet reached the end of the race or received
the prize or attained the full purpose Christ has in store for him).
But the tension is partly resolved in a call to action, to which Paul
now turns.

but one thing I do: literally, 'but—one thing' (Gr. *hen de*).
The terse introduction to what follows is perhaps a sign that Paul
is greatly agitated as he dictates, so that his verbless interjection

is elliptical (BDF, sec. 481). Alternatively, since the **one thing** is left undefined and must be inferred from what follows, some (e.g., A. Fridrichsen, '*EN DE* zu Phil. 3, 13', *Coniectanea Neotestamentica*, Lund, 1944, pp. 31f.) have wished to change the breathing in *hen de* ('but one thing') to *en* (*de*) ('but thereby' . . .) See Moulton, *Grammar* iii, p. 250.

forgetting what lies behind in his past life (vs. 7–9) as a Jew, or possibly regarding his past achievements as a Christian apostle (in v. 8 he mentions his continuing need to renounce all self-confidence), he sets his course, **straining forward to what lies ahead.** The picture is that of the runner who knows how distracting a backward glance can be and who exerts every effort to press forward with the race. Paul has the same double thought in view in 1 C. 9:26, where (he says) the athlete must bend every effort to run and also to 'run without swerving' (Moffatt). The prize which beckons him at the finishing line ahead is the prospect of receiving his Lord's commendation. The next verse elaborates more fully the incentive that spurs him on to 'carry off the prize and to reach the winning-post' (Dupont).

14. I press on toward the goal for the prize of the upward call of God in Christ Jesus. Several terms used in this statement pick up ideas Paul has just mentioned. **I press on** (Gr. *diōkō*) looks back to verse 12, and possibly to verse 6 where the verb was used in a bad sense of persecuting the church. The **goal** (Gr. *skopos*, found only here in the Pauline letters) means the mark on the race track at the finishing post to which the athlete directs his eye; and Paul has already used this idea in 2:4 in the phrase, 'Let each of you look . . . to the interests of others'. The **upward call,** i.e., the summons 'Come up,' to be spoken by the heavenly judge at the victor's crowning when he has run his race, may refer back to Paul's conversion (in v. 12) when the divine voice spoke on the Damascus road and he obeyed. But it is difficult to relate this to the notion of the prize which belongs more to the successful close of a race than to its beginning. J.-F. Collange's suggestion, therefore, commends itself: that Paul is alluding to the custom in the games at Olympia of proclaiming the name and family connexions of the victor and addressing him prior to his crowning, at the behest of the *agōnothetēs*, the presiding judge. Even so, **the prize** is not defined. Is Paul thinking of 'the crown of life' (1 C. 9:25; cf. 2 Tim. 4:8; Jas 1:12; Rev. 2:10), familiar from the Greek games? Or is it Christ's recognition of him at the last day and his assurance of being finally accepted, i.e., not disqualified (1 C. 9:27)? Or, more simply, it may be Christ himself who is **the prize,** so that in reaching the end of his course Paul is grateful to anticipate the fulfilment of the desire 'to gain Christ' (v. 8) that first drew him. The last-named suggestion leads on to his next section.

AN APPEAL FOR UNITY IN CONVICTION AND CONDUCT **3:15–17**

15. Let those of us who are mature (Gr. *teleioi*) **be thus minded** (Gr. *phronōmen*). Paul seems consciously to be using the vocabulary of the false teachers whose influence on the Philippian scene had called out his earlier warnings (v. 2). They boasted of their 'perfection', either as Jews who professed to keep the law in its entirety (Klijn), or as Jewish Christians who 'gloried' (v. 3) in their badge of circumcision as the true sign of being 'full' Christians (Gnilka, Köster), or as gnosticizing Christians who claimed enlightenment as men of the Spirit (Schmithals), or as 'martyrs' whose ready self-sacrifice for their faith brought them to a state of perfection (Lohmeyer). See pp. 23–34 for further discussion.

The difficulty lies in that Paul apparently identifies himself with this group that he had just roundly condemned (vs. 12–14); and further, he has explicitly denied the very thing they claimed to have attained, namely, 'perfection' (vs. 12, 13). He is either using the term *teleios* in a different sense (as *RSV* understands it by its rendering **mature,** as in 1 C. 2:6, 14:20; Col. 1:28, 4:12; Eph. 4:13), or else he is speaking ironically (so Lightfoot). The second suggestion would be a helpful one, if we were to follow the textual reading of Sinaiticus L which gives an indicative (*phronoumen*) for a subjunctive (*phronōmen*). Then, as Collange proposes, the sentence could be an interrogative. 'We who then are "perfect"—so we claim—should we not think like this?' Paul is gently calling for consent with his teaching on the ground that those who profess to be *teleioi* will surely agree with him!

The playful mood continues. **and if in anything you are otherwise minded** (Gr. *phroneite*). The use of the key-verb *phronein* makes it clear that Paul is talking about something more serious than a difference of opinion or a slavish acceptance of his views. From the earlier references in 2:2, 5, and what will follow in 4:8, the sense must be a concern on Paul's part that his readers

will not embrace wrong notions which lead to a practical effect in
the shaping of conduct. The verb suggests a blend of conviction
which results in action; it is more ethical than intellectual.

God will reveal that also to you. It is difficult to know what
the pronoun **that** (Gr. *touto*) looks back to. Paul cannot really be
saying that agreement with his teaching is a matter of indifference
and that those who dispute his statements are entitled to their
views. Paul is never so charitable—as we superficially judge such
matters today. Rather, so confident is he that the truth has been
stated, that he invokes the aid of God to **reveal** (Gr. *apokalyptein*;
see A. Oepke, *TDNT* iv, pp. 582-7, for the term always in Paul
used of God's gracious disclosure of what would otherwise remain
hidden or obscure) **that,** i.e., his statement of true 'perfection', to
his disputants who were claiming perhaps a private access to
divine secrets. On the other hand, it is difficult to give any meaning to Paul's **also,** except on the ground that he is agreeing that
these schismatics have received some revelation from God. That
would imply that Paul is continuing his ironical statement begun
earlier, and saying in effect: if—as you claim—so much has been
revealed to you, then no doubt God will reveal **that** to you also!
(See W. Schmithals, *Paul and the Gnostics*, pp. 101f.)

16. The conclusion reads literally, 'only as far as we have
attained by the same let us walk'. This is once more a tactful and
gentle way of calling the readers to an acceptance of the truth as
Paul has expounded it earlier in the chapter. It is a crisp, pointed
admonition, later expanded by various scribes into a fuller form
which underlies the *AV* reading. On one view the apostle is
confident that a desire to know the truth in full measure will be
rewarded by God's revelation (v. 15). In the meanwhile, he goes
on, until you do see things like this, be open-minded and teachable,
and guide your life by what you know to be true. The final remark
is probably aimed at consolidating wavering Philippian Christians
who were being disturbed by the schismatic teachers on the
threshold of the church's life. Alternatively, he launches out into a
counter-thrust: only this, what we are and claim to be (i.e., men
of the Spirit, as in Gal. 5:25), should govern how we live. This is a
stinging rebuke of the gnostic teachers, since their conduct (3:19)
is reprehensible and so throws their proud claims to 'perfection'
into serious doubt, when judged by that standard.

17. To the objection that the standards of belief and conduct

which Paul is calling his readers to live by are not clear, he replies
with the words **Brethren, join in imitating me.** On the
propriety of the term 'imitation' (Gr. *mimēsis:* Paul's verb here is
synmimētai), see W. Michaelis, *TDNT* iv, pp. 666–74; W. P. de
Boer, *The Imitation of Paul*, Kampen, 1962, pp. 169–88; H.-D.
Betz, *Nachfolge und Nachahmung Jesu Christi im Neuen Testament*,
Tübingen, 1967, pp. 145–53.

The point of calling attention to himself is made because of
Paul's apostolic consciousness as a man of the Spirit (1 C. 2:16,
7:40, 14:37) who opposes those who claim superior knowledge
of God's ways (cf. v. 15). Paul claims to represent the risen Lord
in his pastoral admonitions (1 C. 11:1), and later in the letter he
will indicate how his own life sets a pattern for others to follow
(4:9). There is no suggestion that he means to say, 'Be imitators
along with me of someone else', i.e., Christ (as in 1 C. 11:1), as
W. F. McMichael, *ExpT* 5 (1893–4), p. 287, suggests.

But he is not alone. He draws attention to his associates (e.g.,
Timothy and Epaphroditus, who were well-known leaders at
Philippi) and also to **those** (in the church at Philippi presumably)
who so live following the **example in us.** The passage is really a
call to obedience to apostolic authority more than a summons to
imitate the apostle's way of life (so W. Michaelis, *TDNT* iv,
pp. 667ff., against the view of de Boer, op. cit., pp. 184–7). If this is
so, the injunction which associates Paul with the apostolic message
and tradition may well be a veiled defence of his apostolate over
against the Philippian heretics, who, like the 'false apostles' at
Corinth (2 C. 11:13), had impugned his apostolic authority and
standing. This would account for his switch in thought from **me**
(the repository of authority as apostle *par excellence*) to **mark
those who so live . . . an example in us,** as he then calls attention to his colleagues who are identified with him in his gospel
ministry, even though they do not share the pre-eminent 'status'
which is his by divine appointment. See further on 4:9. This train
of thought links Phil. 3 with 2 C. 10–13 (see p. 125).

live is literally 'walk', and picks up the metaphor of v. 16 (see
the commentary). Both verbs (Gr. *stoichein* in v. 16, *peripatein* in
v. 17) go back to a popular idea in the ancient world, namely,
that human conduct is likened to a journey in which there are
choices to be made and a deportment to be accepted. (Cf.
Hebrew *halākhāh*, 'walking', for 'daily living'; Ps. 1:1, etc.)

Paul has just mentioned his own ambition to set his sights on the goal (v. 14, Gr. *skopos*). Now he encourages the Philippians to **mark** (Gr. *skopeite*) the lives of all those who accept his teaching and to have them as **an example** to follow. So the encouragement he gives to Philippian church-members who wavered because their doubts about his apostolic instruction is intensely personal. He bids them look at the men they know and see the proof of his teaching in their lives. Pointedly his readers should turn away from rival teachers who were infiltrating the church (see Rom. 16:17 for parallel warnings).

SECTARIAN TEACHERS TO BE SHUNNED 3:18–19

18. By contrast, then, his readers are to avoid the bad example of certain errorists who have appeared on the scene. **For many, of whom I have often told you and now tell you even with tears, live** (Gr. *peripatousin:* lit. 'walk', as in v. 17) **as the enemies of the cross of Christ.**

Obviously Paul has professed Christians in view, not Jewish opponents or men in the pagan world who persecuted the Church. If it were the latter, the term **enemies** would be a platitude, as Kennedy, *Commentary*, p. 461 notes. Furthermore, the lives of these people are in direct contrast to the example given in verse 17; and Paul's **tears** (cf. Ac. 20:31) are more likely to be caused by faithless and mistaken Christian leaders than by any other group of opponents.

The chief clue to the identity of these men is, in fact, just the contrast Paul *does* make between these false teachers and his own friends and their adherents. Quite likely, these teachers were setting up themselves as 'models' of Christian leadership and derogating Paul's authority in consequence. Paul is emotionally moved as he writes, **even with tears,** shed perhaps more over defecting Christians in his churches (2 C. 2:4) than over the teachers who misled them, since he has only harsh words to address to those persons.

Such teachers represent a powerful group, both in size (**many**) and influence. (Paul has had occasion repeatedly to warn his converts of their danger.) That danger consists in their disastrous teaching on the cross. **enemies of the cross of Christ** cannot mean simply that they make out that Christ's cross is not sufficient to save (Dupont), or that they oppose Pauline Christians who do place their hopes in the cross (Bonnard). Some more deadly matter is involved. This catastrophic error Collange identifies as a refusal on the part of professed Pauline Christians to understand the eschatological importance of what happened decisively on Christ's cross and in his resurrection, viz., that in the event of Christ crucified and victorious a new beginning to world history was made, and a new life-style created in terms of a call to self-denying sacrifice and service within the Christian community that has found reconciliation through the cross. This description makes their enmity something deeper than a continual adherence to the law (Klijn, Dupont), or a refusal to live on any other plane than the material (E. F. Scott speaks of their error as their looking only to material good; Betz, op. cit., p. 151), or a denial of Christ in time of persecution (Lohmeyer), or even, what most commentators find here, a moral laxity which disowns the ethical demands of the gospel. What is implied is an abandonment of the cross-'side' of the kerygma (as in 1 C. 1:17–2:5) and a proud assertion of moral and religious superiority (as in 1 C. 6:12), based on the teachers' claim to be already risen to a celestial life on earth and on an ethical indifference which treats the body as an irrelevance because the pure 'spirit' is illuminated and protected by the divine spirit. This is a description that would fit the case of gnosticizing Christians, such as were present at Corinth and against whom Paul wrote 2 C. 10–13. For a discussion about their threats to the Pauline message of the cross and the life it entails, see W. Schmithals, *Gnosticism in Corinth*, pp. 135ff.; D. Georgi, *Die Gegner des Paulus im 2. Korintherbrief*; J.-F. Collange, *Enigmes de la deuxième épître de Paul aux Corinthiens*, Cambridge, 1972, pp. 320–4; and especially W. C. Robinson, Jr., 'Word and Power (1 Corinthians 1:17–2:5)' in *Soli Deo Gloria*, ed. J. McDowell Richards, Richmond, Va., 1968, pp. 68–82.

If this is an accurate understanding of the nature of the error Paul exposes—and it is worth observing, as Schmithals does (*Paul and the Gnostics*, pp. 108f.), that gnosticizing libertinism in the early Church took on the two aspects referred to in this passage, viz., sexual promiscuity and disregard of all food restrictions (see Rev. 2:14, 20)—the rest of the section should describe in some appropriate detail the characteristics of the teachers, from Paul's point of view. In this way we can test the validity of the assumptions made on this theme.

19. Their end (Gr. *telos*: at the eschatological judgment, which their 'realized' eschatology—see 2 Tim. 2:18—denied) **is destruction** (Gr. *apōleia*, an eschatological term for the divine retribution meted out in the end-time, which they supposed was already past and done with!). **their god is the belly** (Gr. *koilia*). The term means here not their scrupulous observance of food-laws (J. Behm, *TDNT* iii, p. 788) but their immorality, to which they have been led by their false anthropological notions.

Imagining that the body and its appetites were irrelevant, they have cast off all restraint in the same way that the Corinthian Gnostics played fast-and-loose with the claims of morality on the ground of their being enlightened as 'men of the Spirit' (1 C. 6:9–20; 2 C. 12:21), especially in the matter of eating idol-meats (1 C. 8:1–9, 23; 10:23–11:1). Possibly the term for **belly** is neutral and is equivalent to the ethical word 'flesh' (Gr. *sarx*). Then Paul berates their ethical insensitivity. Professing to be *illuminati* as spiritual men, they are victims of their unredeemed self-life, as in Gal. 5:16–26. Or, again, since *koilia* can mean 'womb' (Gal. 1:15) or navel, Paul may simply be commenting on their egocentricity. 'All they do is fix their eyes on their navel. Their god is—themselves!' (Collange).

It may be too that Paul is using, as in Rom. 16:18, a current proverb, e.g., picked up from Euripides, *Cyclops* 316–40: 'Wealth is god for men of sense ... My god's my belly ... As for those who have complicated life by making laws, they can go to hell' (trans. J. Ferguson). Clearly, in this context, belly-service is a combination of antinomianism and avarice, a mixture found also in 2 C. 10–13.

and they glory in their shame. Obviously **glory** (Gr. *doxa*) is a key-term, but it is not easy to understand. Some interpreters see an allusion to the effects of circumcision. W. Schmithals (*Paul and the Gnostics*, pp. 110f.) refers their shame to their sexual indifference, citing Jude 13. Perhaps the best view is that they were 'glorying', i.e., boasting (contrast v. 3), in their powerful presence as charismatic figures in the church, claiming to be a special breed of Christians who had 'arrived'. They were 'perfect', having attained a nirvana state in a resurrection life already begun as a heavenly existence on earth, beyond the reach of temptation, suffering, and failure (so we infer from 2 C. 10–13). Paul has a different opinion of them. **shame** (Gr. *aischynē*, 'disgrace') is the

F

fate of those who are rejected at the last judgment (Gnilka, citing
Isa. 45:24f.), and who, denying divine righteousness, awake to
God's sentence of 'destruction' (*apōleia*) when it is too late. When
God's 'glory' is manifested in that judgment, they will be covered
with 'shame'. For the present, Paul says, they play the reverse
roles in their ignorance. Their self-esteem betrays their failure to
'glory in Christ Jesus' as his servants.

Finally, **with minds set on earthly things,** they both reason
falsely and are specimens of a sub-Christian way of life, which the
Philippians should shun. Paul returns to his favourite term.
minds set on renders one verb, Gr. *phronountes*.

The charge is that both their wrong-headed ideas about the
cross, the resurrection, and the judgment, and also their practices
which flow from these ideas, are earth-bound, lacking the dimension of the 'upward call' to God which characterizes Paul's
gospel (3:14). That means they lack the hope of the resurrection,
which (*i*) gives to the Christian the anticipation of what lies
ahead when God's purpose will be complete; (*ii*) defines the
nature of the Christian life as a tension set within the 'already
achieved' salvation and the 'not yet' promise of the future. Hence
the ethical seriousness and strenuousness of the Pauline Christian,
found in verses 12–14; and (*iii*) promises that while the believer
has to wrestle with bodily weaknesses and temptations in this life,
since his body is frail and his power limited, the new body, the
'spiritual body' of 1 C. 15:38, 42–50; 2 C. 5:2–10 will be the
vehicle of service suitable to the life of 'heaven'. But that time is not
yet. It is known only in prospect. To consider just that prospect
Paul turns in verses 20, 21.

THE TRUE HOPE **3:20, 21**

This short section has a literary style and content all of its own.
It is set in a rhythmical mould (Lohmeyer even prints it as a piece
of poetry) and is couched in terms which are rare. (The words for
commonwealth, Saviour, lowly body are unusual for Paul.)
Some interpreters think that Paul is making use of an already
existing hymnic period, as in his citation of the *carmen Christi* in
2:6–11. (See E. Güttgemanns, *Der leidende Apostel und sein Herr*,
pp. 240–7; G. Strecker, 'Redaktion und Tradition im Christushymnus', *ZNW* 55 (1964), pp. 75–8; N. Flanagan, 'A Note on Phil.
3:20–21', *CBQ* 18 (1956), pp. 8f.) What is perhaps more probable

(cf. P. Siber, op. cit., pp. 122–6, who points out how the remaining terminology used is typically Pauline) is that Paul is drawing upon traditional matter, current in the churches, to refute the ideas he personally has condemned in verses 18, 19. From the negative assessment which he gave in those verses, he moves on now to a ringing affirmation of what constitutes the true Christian hope.

20. The opening words **But our commonwealth** seem to be chosen in direct contrast to what the heretics were saying. We may compare (with Gnilka) 3:3, where Paul also moves on to the offensive with the same Greek expression (*de*) which introduces a counter-position. **commonwealth** (Gr. *politeuma*) recalls 1:27 and suggests that Paul is consciously reflecting on the civic status of Philippi as a Roman colony. Cf. Moffatt's translation: 'We are a colony of heaven.' There is this undoubted background, brought out too in Dibelius' paraphrase: 'We have our home in heaven, and here on earth we are a colony of heaven's citizens.' If the political colouring of the word is most apparent, we should take note of E. Stauffer's comment (*New Testament Theology*, ET London, 1955, pp. 296f.) that *politeuma* must mean a 'capital or native city, which keeps the citizens on its registers'. There is no denying the forcefulness of this allusion, even if an alternative background in the Judaism of the Dispersion is suggested (e.g., by E. Güttgemanns, op. cit., p. 243, n. 19; Gnilka, ad loc., and especially Siber, op. cit., pp. 133f.) stressing that the contrast lies with the 'realized eschatology' of Paul's enemies who *did* think of themselves as a heavenly community on earth and so were eliminating the element of future hope. The background is set in Jewish apocalyptic, according to which the realities of salvation are already stored up in heaven in anticipation of the end-time of final salvation (P. Volz, *Die Eschatologie der jüdischen Gemeinde im Neutestamentlichen Zeitalter*, Tübingen, 1934, pp. 114–16). Paul is interested in establishing the thought that the Christian on earth has his true future hope and home set in heaven, and is not as a man whose 'mind is set on earthly things' (v. 19). For that reason, A. N. Sherwin-White's contention (*Roman Society and Roman Law in the New Testament*, Oxford, 1963, pp. 184f.) is preferable, viz., the idea behind the word is that of community, not citizenship, and it is based on Jewish synagogues and sanhedrins in Asia. So Christians are not citizens but resident aliens in the cities of the world and their colony has special rules.

from it (Gr. *ex hou*: this should strictly refer back to **commonwealth**, so Lohmeyer and Stauffer; but a construction *ad sensum* may be preferable; Paul is saying that 'from heaven', where our hope lies, we expect the Saviour: so Gnilka, Güttgemanns, Siber, Michaelis). **we await a Saviour, the Lord Jesus Christ.** The verb **await** (Gr. *apekdechometha*) is used by Paul of the Church's hope set on the future (see Rom. 8:19–25; 1 C. 1:7; Gal. 5:5) and specifically bound up with the *parousia* of Christ. Paul is boldly announcing as a future prospect the very article of faith which the heretics at Philippi were despising, viz., a future hope which will complete God's salvation and affect our bodily existence, now weak and frail (Rom. 6:12, 8:11; 1 C. 15:42f.), but then to be redeemed (Siber, op. cit., pp. 127f.).

So it is **the Lord Jesus Christ** (the full title suggests a credal formulary) who as **Saviour** (lack of the article indicates a functional use of this title, so rare in Paul: it is found in the Pauline corpus only at Eph. 5:23; 2 Tim. 1:10; Tit. 1:4; 2:13; 3:6—all texts are held to be deutero-Pauline by several scholars) will bring about a transformation to the Christians' existence in the body. The deliverance implied in **Saviour** is not primarily from oppression and persecution, but from the thraldom of continuing evil and from the frailty and mortality which no Christian can escape in this life (as in 1 Th. 1:10, 4:14–17, 5:9). 'Saviour' suggests something different to Christians today, i.e., redemption from sin; and it may be that, because there were so many such 'saviours' in the hellenistic world, in the imperial cult, and the mystery religions, *NT* writers such as Paul avoided the term in order to obviate confusion with 'many "gods" and many "lords" ' (1 C. 8:5) of contemporary paganism. Paul, however, can use the term without misunderstanding—if verse 20 is Paul's and not the tradition—because its apocalyptic-eschatological significance is clear and that puts the work of the Christian Saviour in a category by itself.

21. The central term is **body** (Gr. *sōma*). Paul's verse, whatever its origin, meets the point exactly. The effect of the Saviour's coming from heaven is to bring a new dimension to human existence 'in the body'. *sōma* here means 'the total earthly existence which is established through corporeality, and that a corporeality of humiliation' (Gnilka). **our lowly body** is less desirable than a full, if cumbrous, translation: 'the body of our humiliation', corresponding to 'body of sin' (Rom. 6:6), 'body of this death' (Rom. 7:24) (Güttgemanns, op. cit., p. 245), since it is precisely Paul's purpose to emphasize that the Christian's existence as a person now—his selfhood—is marked by his feebleness, sinfulness, and mortality. The Philippian schismatic teachers, glorying in their supposed 'heavenly life on earth', were missing this. Their 'glory' was claimed here and now; for Paul 'the body of his glory' (again a better rendering than **his glorious body**) awaits the *parousia*, and the heavenly Lord's transforming power. In the meanwhile, the Christian apostle and the congregation struggle with the 'not yet' handicap imposed by the fact that they have not attained, nor are they perfect (vs. 12–14).

to be like (Gr. *symmorphon*) needs to be read in the light of 3:10: 'becoming like him (Gr. *symmorphizomenos*) in his death'. Paul had earlier alluded to this blessed state of conformity to Christ, and had insisted that only in and through suffering is the Christian able to attain it. Now he sets the eschatological reserve of 'not yet' between what he believes true conformity to Christ to be, and what the deniers of his gospel were claiming. In their view, union with the risen Lord, certified in the new birth of baptism, brought the pneumatic Christian over into a happy state of release from suffering and invited him to live a celestial life here and now. For Paul, the thrust of his argument in 3:10ff., and the evidence of the confessional statement on which he draws, are diametrically opposite. As Gnilka puts it, Paul corrects the idea that 'the new state of the redeemed is already effective and does not await the day of the parousia'. True likeness to Christ the heavenly *Kyrios* comes only through suffering and is a future hope at the end-time. 'This antithesis is the nub of the debate between Paul and his opponents'.

Furthermore, the transformation into likeness to the risen Lord is possible only by his **power**. So the section concludes with a formula of liturgical confession, ascribing all power to him (Norden's *Allmachtsformel*: see *Agnostos Theos*, Tübingen, 1913, pp. 240ff.): **by the power which enables him even to subject all things to himself.** The closing part of what looks to be a fragment of liturgy takes in a wider meaning than the change in the believer's body, even when *sōma* is construed to mean 'whole man'. There is a cosmic sweep in the phrase, linking it with 2:10, 11; and this is only one of several links of terminology which connect 2:6–11 and 3:20, 21 (see Flanagan; and Güttgemanns, p. 241). For instance:

'form' (2:6, 8)	'to be like', to conform (3:21)
'being' (*hyparchōn*) (2:6)	'is' (*hyparchei*) (3:20)
'likeness' (*schēma*) (2:7)	'change' (*metaschēmatisei*) (3:21)
'humbled' (*etapeinōsen*) (2:8)	'lowly body' (*tapeinōsis*) (3:21)
'every knee shall bow', etc. (2:10)	'able to subject all things' (3:21)
'Jesus Christ is Lord' (2:11)	'the Lord Jesus Christ' (3:21)
'glory' (*doxa*) (2:11)	'body of glory' (*doxa*) (3:21)

There is a striking resemblance between these sections (Collange), and if both have a pre-Pauline, credal, or liturgical origin, that fact would unite them and explain their common terminology and similar thought-forms. But, more particularly, the passages are used by Paul to correct false impressions. He intends to show (as in 2:6–11) what it means to be 'in Christ' as a member of his Church and under his rule, and to teach (in 3:20, 21) that the universal lordship of Christ sets the pattern for the Christian's life-style by calling him to live 'in the sphere of that lordship'. Paul also reminds the reader that the road to a future glory is along a path of suffering, and that the believer is never free to escape the paradox of 'what he is now' and 'what he will be' in the future. The ethical ramifications of both passages are especially pointed; and their relevance to the Philippian situation would not be lost on Paul's first readers as they are put on their guard (3:2) against the false teachers, whose doctrine and way of life are a standing denial of what Paul taught and what is exemplified in his apostolic ministry. The root of their error is their entertaining a form of 'realized' eschatology which cuts the nerve of future hope on the mistaken assumption that the Christian is already 'perfect' as an illuminated, reborn soul. This leads to an ethical laxity and a false 'enthusiasm' that has no prospect of a future work of God in delivering his people from their present thraldom to mortal weakness. Most seriously, these sectaries oppose the Pauline message of the cross which gives a new, ethically-controlled relationship to God in Christ, and commits the believer to a life-style in which suffering and hardship are his present lot in anticipation of the day when he will be set free. The Pauline disciple is like a runner in a race, or an athlete at the games. He struggles and exerts himself now, by God's assistance, in hope that he one day will reach the winning-post and gain the prize. He is thus faced with a paradox: already 'saved' and with the race begun, he awaits and strains forward to attain his resurrection, which will be the completion of his salvation under God and the attainment of the prize (1:6, 2:16, 3:11–14).

PASTORAL PROBLEMS AND ADVICE 4:1–9

4:1. Therefore, my brethren, whom I love and long for, my joy and crown, stand firm thus in the Lord, my beloved. The exhortation to **stand firm** is linked with the preceding call (3:17) that Paul's readers should join to imitate him and his colleagues, and so be fortified against sectarian teachers (so most commentators). Lohmeyer is an exception. He regards verse 1 as a solemn and formal introduction to what follows. It is just possible, however, that this verse picks up earlier admonitions, such as in 1:27, 28, and that Paul is reflecting on the need for this church to be united in its common front against a persecuting world around it.

At all events the verse contains some of the most affectionate and endearing language Paul ever used about his churches. **I love** (lit. 'beloved') and **long for** (Gr. *epipothētoi*, recalling the verb in 1:8, expresses Paul's desire to see them again; it is a term found only here in the *NT*) are followed by **my joy and crown,** similar to 1 Th. 2:19, 20, 3:9. **crown** (Gr. *stephanos*) belongs to the world of athletic competition in which the victor was crowned with a laurel wreath and wore the crown as a festal garland (1 C. 9:25). Cf. 2 Clem. 7:3, 'Let us then struggle that we may all receive the crown.' Paul is perhaps going back to the imagery of 3:14. More likely he has the Church in view; then his 'crown' will be the good success that has attended his apostolic labours and the consequent firmness of the Church under trial, as in 2:16. 'Crown' suggesting the joyful recognition of faithful living and service, carries this meaning in Prov. 12:4, 16:31, 17:6 (LXX). The eschatological setting in 3:20, 21 would contribute to the total metaphor of a heavenly reward to be given to Paul if his pastoral work at Philippi is 'crowned' with success (see W. Grundmann, *TDNT* vii, pp. 615–36). Hence the summons to

stand firm in the Lord as his **beloved** friends (repeated from the same verse).

2. That all is not harmony and joy inside the church is clear from the appeal to **Euodia** and **Syntyche.** These were evidently women members of the congregation who had quarrelled. It is well-known that Macedonian women were noted for their strong personality (see earlier p. 8), and the Lucan account of the initial evangelism at Philippi contains two conversion stories involving women (Lydia and the slave-girl). (See W. D. Thomas, 'The Place of Women in the Church at Philippi', *ExpT* 83 (1971–2) pp. 117–20.) Moreover, the names **Euodia** (meaning 'pleasant', the same Greek word as in 4:18) and **Syntyche** are attested in extant inscriptions and were evidently common names (AG, *s.v.*). For these reasons there is no need to take seriously the Tübingen school's notion that the names were used here allegorically to represent two factions, Judaeo and Gentile, of church life. Nor should we speculate further as to the reasons for their disagreement. W. Schmithals (*Paul and the Gnostics*, pp. 112–14) thinks that their quarrel was caused by gnostic agitation and even that they may have broken the church's unity by giving hospitality to intruding false teachers (cf. 2 Jn 10). We do not know the precise background of their dispute, though it is likely that it formed part of the general malaise in the church, referred to in 2:1–3, where the same Greek expression rendered 'being of the same mind' (*auto phronein*) (in this verse it is translated **to agree**) is used. And just possibly it had to do with church leadership, if 2:14 relates to a trouble-spot at Philippi involving the leaders, 'the overseers and deacons' (1:1). At any rate, the call is 'be of a common mind' in the Lord, i.e., as members of the body of Christ. The disappearance of these two women from the scene suggests that Paul's plea was heeded (Collange).

3. Paul's pastoral counselling is both tactful and tactical. He enlists the service of a third member, called **true yokefellow,** in a ministry of 'encouragement' (so Michaelis) to these offended ladies. The designation **true yokefellow** is curiously roundabout, perhaps suggesting that Paul does not wish to refer to this individual by name. If such is the case, we can dispense with some speculative suggestions that Paul is referring to *Epaphroditus* (Lightfoot), *Silas* (G. Delling, *TDNT* vii, pp. 749f.), *Luke* (T. W. Manson, *BJRL* 23 (1939), p. 199; and, more recently, Milan

Hájek, 'Comments on Philippians 4:3—Who was "Gnésios Syzygos"?' *Communio Viatorum* 7 (1964), pp. 261–2, who also argues for Luke since he remained in the city of Philippi during the second missionary journey), and we can think, even more imaginatively, of *Lydia* (Paul's wife? see Collange, and cf. E. Haenchen, *The Acts of the Apostles*, ET Oxford, 1971, p. 494, n. 8) or, last of all, of *Timothy*, who is certainly so described in 2:20 as having a 'genuine' (Gr. *gnēsios*, as here) interest in the Philippians (cf. 2 C. 8:8; 1 Tim. 1:2; Tit. 1:4). It is not clear whether Paul included his name in the first draft of the letter and Timothy, the scribe, struck it out on grounds of self-effacing modesty and replaced it with this descriptive phrase as he wrote it (cf. W. Schmithals, *Paul and the Gnostics*, pp. 76f., 252, who argues that Timothy's name stood in the missing prescript to the hypothetical fragment which begins at 3:2, along with other community leaders mentioned in 1:1).

We must rest content with what little we do know for certain. The name refers to a Christian who was evidently a person much valued by Paul as his 'companion'; 'sharing the same yoke' suggests a partner in the apostolic mission. Lohmeyer thinks that he may have been a 'brother in suffering' sharing Paul's imprisonment, although it is hard to see how he could then help the women at a distance.

The alternative is that the Greek for **yokefellow,** *syzyge*, conceals a proper name, and the preceding word is Paul's commendation of him, 'Syzygos (comrade), rightly so called', by making the play on the word somewhat similar to his practice in Phm. 11 regarding the name 'Onesimus', meaning 'profitable' (see *New Century Bible*, 1974, p. 164). In this event Paul is playfully reminding him to be true to his name, and be a real 'yokefellow', by assisting in the coming together of the estranged women. (So Gnilka.) But 'Syzygos' is nowhere else attested as a proper name.

Euodia and **Syntyche** are known as close associates of Paul. They, as with the women in Rom. 16, **have laboured side by side with me in the gospel.** Others too share the work with him. **Clement** is the name of a Philippian Christian otherwise unknown. Attempts have been made to equate him with Clement of Rome, the author of a letter to the Corinthians in AD 96 (see Lightfoot's note), but this identification is not successful. Clement was a common name in the Roman empire, and at Philippi, a colony, its popularity would have been obvious (*Corpus Inscript. Latinarum* III, 633, gives the evidence). Other unnamed helpers are given honourable mention as **the rest of my fellow workers** (as Epaphroditus was, 2:25). Unknown to us as they are, and not singled out by the apostle as were some of his co-workers (cf. E. E. Ellis, 'Paul and his Co-Workers', *NTS* 17 (1970–1), pp. 437–52), they find a place in God's record, **the book of life,** a term in late Jewish apocalyptic literature (cf. Rev. 3:5, 20; 15:21, 27; Apoc. Baruch 24:1), and at Qumran (1QM 12:3; Vermes, p. 139), which is drawn from Exod. 32:32; Ps. 69:28, 139:16, to denote God's register of his people. Cf. Lk. 10:20.

4. Rejoice in the Lord always. This is addressed to the entire congregation, as an appeal going back to 4:1, or even to 3:1, which contained a similar admonition to rejoicing (Michaelis). That would explain the formula **again I will say, Rejoice**, as though Paul were making a point of his reiteration.

Paul's appeals to joy are not founded on natural optimism, as though he were inviting his people at Philippi to see a silver lining in the ominous clouds of opposition and hazard that are approaching (1:28, 29). Nor is it a joy shared peculiarly by martyrs (Lohmeyer), nor based paradoxically on his fear that he may not see them again (Gnilka), nor does the modern idea of 'joy in the Lord' as meaning 'openness to the future' (Collange) help much to clarify Paul's sense. The key is **in the Lord**, which is the governing factor in the exhortation. It is the Philippians' faith **in the Lord** (i.e., the exalted Jesus) which makes the call to rejoicing both practical and realistic when they are facing persecution. Bonnard comments: 'The Pauline appeals to joy are never simple encouragements; they throw the distressed churches back on their Lord; they are, above all, appeals to faith.'

5. The steps to a realization of this confidence are now given. The background is clearly that of a congregation facing opposition and threatened by danger from the hostile world. Paul proceeds to describe the resources by which Philippian Christians may win through. **Let all men know your forbearance** is a call which prevents the church from being too preoccupied with its own interests (Gnilka); it is also a reminder that the church's setting in the world should summon it to a life of winsome influence on its pagan neighbours. **forbearance** (Gr. *to epieikes*) is a disposition of gentleness and fairmindedness to other people in spite of their faults, and inspired by the confidence Christians have that after earthly suffering will come heavenly glory, referred to in 3:20 (see H. Preisker, *TDNT* ii, pp. 588–90). ⁊ノ

Perhaps the best English equivalent of the Greek term (used in Wis. 2:19 of the 'righteous sufferer', a forerunner of Messiah; used of God in Wis. 12:18 as well as in the 'catalogue of virtues' in 1 Tim. 3:3; Tit. 3:2; Jas 3:17, in regard to the Christian's attitude to other people) is 'graciousness'. In this context, it will stand for a spirit of willingness to forgo retaliation when Christians are threatened or provoked because of their faith.

The reason for such an unabrasive spirit is not found in weakness or an unconcern to stand one's ground. Such a cowardly attitude is denied in 1:27, 28. Rather, the readers will be gracious since their Lord is coming to vindicate their cause—**the Lord is at hand**—and, therefore, they do not need to be over-anxious to defend themselves in a way that could cause increased offence. The recall of the Lord's nearness may be an allusion to Ps. 145 (LXX, 144):18 (so Michaelis). Lohmeyer takes it in reference to the special privilege of the martyr to be 'near the Lord'. But most likely it is an eschatological watchword, as in 1 C. 16:22 (*Marana tha*, meaning 'Our Lord, come') and Rev. 22:20, imploring the arrival of the *parousia* (Gnilka, Bonnard, Dibelius, Beare). Then, at the Lord's coming, he will both reward the faithful (cf. Barn. 21:3) and vindicate their case to a disbelieving world (cf. 2 Th. 1:7f.). The latter part of the verse is thus a call to patience (cf. Jas 5:7, 8).

6. The assurance of what lies ahead has a practical bearing on the present. So **Have no anxiety about anything.** In this context it has to do with the threats from the surrounding world. **anxiety** betrays a lack of confidence in God's protection and care for his people, and the sentence of admonition recalls the words of Jesus in Mt. 6:25–34. (Dibelius suggests that Paul is giving a commentary on this set of logia, while Lohmeyer, less successfully, relates it to Mt. 10:19, spoken to banish anxiety from persecuted disciples.)

On the positive side, the Philippians are counselled to make their **requests** (i.e., specific petitions, as in Lk. 11:9, 10) **known to God. prayer** and **supplication** are sometimes distinguished. The former (Gr. *proseuchē*) means prayer in general; **supplication** (Gr. *deēsis*) stresses the sense of need and a specific request. But no fine distinction seems intended in this context (Gnilka). (See comment on 1:9, and G. P. Wiles, *Paul's Intercessory Prayers*, pp. 19f.)

One additional factor, however, is significant. It is **with thanksgiving** that requests are to be made, and **in everything**, directed over a wide range of needs, i.e., not 'in every prayer but in every situation of life, both pleasant and adverse'. This is Paul's injunction in 1 Th. 5:18: 'give thanks in all circumstances'. Doubtless, if they recalled what happened in the Philippian jail (Ac. 16:25), Paul's friends in the church there would know that he exemplified the teaching he passed on to them. Furthermore, 'the passage epitomizes much of the joyful mood of the whole letter' (Wiles, p. 288), linking rejoicing-in-suffering with the call to patience-under-trial and a reminder of the *parousia* hope.

7. As a consequence, **the peace of God, which passes all understanding, will keep your hearts and your minds in Christ Jesus.** This promise closes the section and is its climax. **the peace of God** carries the overtone of his saving and preserving power (implied in the Hebrew *šālôm*: see W. Foerster, *TDNT* ii, pp. 411ff.), and Paul's use of a military verb (**will keep,** Gr. *phrourēsei*, lit. 'stand guard over', as in 2 C. 11:32; Gal. 3:23) shows that he is thinking of the security of the church and its members in a hostile environment and surrounded by foes. The divine **peace,** which is almost personified (as in Jewish literature: Lohmeyer and Gnilka cite the comment (*Siphre* §42) on Num. 6:26, 'Great is peace . . . the name of God means peace'), is such as 'transcends every human thought' (Gr. *nous*), 'surpasses all our dreams' (cf. Moffatt's translation). Alternatively, it can 'perform more than human plans can accomplish'. Both ideas are possible from the Greek participle, *hyperechousa*, rendered **which passes.** Gnilka argues for the second; cf. *NEB* marg. Nor should we fail to observe Paul's fondness for the verb (*hyperechō*) in this epistle (2:3, 3:8, and here, three occurrences out of four times in all his writings). It may be deliberate that he employs a polemic against his enemies in 2 C. 10–13 by denouncing their claim to superior knowledge (Gr. *noēma*, 2 C. 10:4–6; 11:1–3), which would be a link with the sectarian teachers in Philippi and suggest that they are similar, if not the same, persons. (See J.-F. Collange, *Enigmes de la deuxième épître de Paul aux Corinthiens*, p. 93.)

in Christ Jesus describes the 'sphere' in which the believers' inner life is set. By union with Christ, in obedience to his authority and submission to his will, they will discover the security of their lives as they are assured of the divine protection, 'God's peace'.

8. Finally, brethren. There are several ways to take Paul's **Finally** (see C. F. D. Moule, *An Idiom-Book of New Testament Greek*, Cambridge, 1953, pp. 161f.). It may be no more than 'and so', or it may be logically connected with the preceding section and be a transition from what Paul has just said: 'it follows then, in this connexion'. In this case **Finally** continues the thought of the peace of God in verse 7, and verses 8, 9 are a further extension of the way to the enjoyment of that peace. Alternatively, there may be a distinct break at verse 7, and Paul's **Finally** marks the conclusion of a separate letter (see Introduction pp. 16–22).

The present verse is governed by the verb, **think about these things,** Gr. *logizesthe* which means more than 'keep in mind'. The sense is 'take into account (*logos*)' or even 'make these things the *logos* of your personal universe' (see John A. Hutton's discussion in the book referred to on p. ix, pp. 240–7), that is, 'reflect upon and allow these qualities of living to shape your conduct'. There is a close connexion between 'think' (v. 8) and 'do' (in v. 9), as Collange indicates: 'the dynamic of Christianity derives from the union of these two imperatives'. And such imperatives are embodied in the collection of ethical qualities (v. 8), apostolic traditions (v. 9a), and teachings exemplified in Paul's own life (v. 9b).

The use of ethical lists was a feature of Stoic religion (see A. Vögtle, *Die Tugend- und Lasterkataloge*, Münster, 1936). Several scholars confidently assign this verse to a contemporary pagan source: 'it is almost as if he had taken a current list from a textbook of ethical instruction, and made it his own; these are nothing else than the virtues of the copybook maxims' (Beare). While it is true that these ethical expressions are 'terms of popular moral philosophy' (Dibelius) current in Paul's day, and that there is, on the surface, nothing specifically Christian in the items mentioned, Lohmeyer and Michaelis have shown that the influence of the Greek Bible is significant (*pace* Gnilka). Another line of investigation into the background of this verse has been taken by J. N. Sevenster (*Paul and Seneca*, Leiden, 1961, pp. 152–6). He maintains that Paul has indeed borrowed a series of terms drawn from Stoic moral philosophy in verse 8, but that verse 9 adds something

of a corrective. He treats the earlier verse as provisional by noting
how Paul is calling upon the Philippians to be mindful of the best
features in the world around them, which set a minimum standard.
Yet the distinctive elements in Paul's moral teaching are not to be
seen in his adoption of contemporary idioms, such as 'what is
excellent' (lit. a 'virtue') or 'what is praiseworthy'. Rather 'Paul
takes into account their environment in order to obtain every
possible support and understanding for what he wishes to say in
verse 9' (op. cit., p. 156). In this way, Sevenster is able to account
for the use of terms such as 'virtue' (Gr. *aretē*), which is not found
elsewhere in Paul, and at the same time the undeniable fact that
his ethical emphases are placed ordinarily on the transformed life
of the Christian who belongs to Christ and possesses the Spirit,
and not on the appeal to some pagan religious ideal. For another
reason for his use of this ethical appeal, see p. 32.

whatever is true (Gr. *alēthē*) can mean 'truth' as opposed to
what is unreal, insubstantial (the Greek idea) or 'truth' as opposed
to falsehood or error (implied in the Hebrew *'emet*). R. Bultmann
renders the term here by a more general sense, 'upright' (*TDNT*
i, p. 248). **honourable** (Gr. *semna*) means simply what is morally
good and is so defined in the Stoic Epictetus; perhaps a translation
such as 'dignified', 'elevated', catches the sense here and in 1 Tim.
3:8, 11; Tit. 2:2, the remaining *NT* references. **whatever is just**
(Gr. *dikaia*) is again a rare emphasis in Paul who does not
normally place 'righteousness' in a series of virtues as one among
many (so S. Wibbing, *Die Tugend- und Lasterkataloge im NT*,
Berlin, 1959, p. 102). But we may compare 1:7 for a 'neutral'
flavour given to the word.

whatever is pure (Gr. *hagna*) recalls 1:17, where it has to do
with motivation of conduct, although a sexual reference is intended in 2 C. 11:2; Tit. 2:5 ('chaste').

lovely (Gr. *prosphilē*) is found only here in the *NT* and is
absent from contemporary ethical lists (Wibbing, op. cit., p. 101).
The same singularity is true of **gracious** (Gr. *euphēma*), but the
noun *euphēmia*, 'good repute', is found in 2 C. 6:8. Both terms go
together. The former means 'pleasing', 'attractive'. But, as L. H.
Marshall (*The Challenge of New Testament Ethics*, London, 1947,
p. 304) says, since 'we may perversely find evil things attractive,
the rendering "beautiful" is to be preferred'. AG give 'pleasing,
agreeable, lovely, amiable'.

euphēma means not so much 'well spoken of' as 'speaking well of', though AG offer both meanings in their list; 'auspicious', 'well-sounding', 'praiseworthy, attractive, appealing'. Moffatt's 'high-toned' is just right.

Paul in making this list is obviously being selective and his choice is 'more or less accidental' (Wibbing, op. cit., p. 102). Rather than continue his selection he now sums up: **if there is any excellence** (Gr. *aretē*, lit. moral virtue), **if there is anything worthy of praise** (Gr. *epainos*, either 'what deserves your praise' or 'what commands the divine approbation'). Both terms are inclusive of the earlier list, and describe in general terms the kind of qualities that should mark out the Philippians in their attitudes and actions. *aretē* is not usually employed in this comprehensive way to sum up a series of qualities (Wibbing, op. cit., p. 103); perhaps we should give it a more particular application, as Collange suggests: 'honour', rather than 'virtue'. 'What was deserving of public acclaim' is the sense of *epainos* (Preisker, *TDNT* ii, p. 587, and L. H. Marshall, op. cit., p. 305). If this is the case —rather than 'what pleases and is approved by God'—this term with its distinct civic associations would appeal to the Philippians who lived in a Roman *colonia* and were proud of their citizenship in the empire.

9. The rhythmical format of verse 8 with the last line closing with: 'think about these things' (so Lohmeyer, Gnilka) is matched by the final line in this short strophe: **do.** Clearly both imperatives go together, just as both verses are clamped by a common subject-matter. The series of virtues is succeeded by a list of verbs: **what you have learned and received and heard and seen in me.** These elements comprise all that the Philippians may be expected to have known as part of the apostolic instruction. The combination of teaching, tradition, the spoken word, and the living example, is impressive. We should perhaps see the clue in the term **received** (Gr. *parelabete*) which is a technical term for the receiving of an authoritative tradition handed down from Church leaders (1 C. 11:23; 15:3). Frequent reference to these 'traditions' (see F. F. Bruce, *Tradition: Old and New*, Exeter, 1970, pp. 29–38) or 'ordinances' in Paul (1 C. 11:2, 15:1ff.; Gal. 1:9; Col. 2:6; 1 Th. 4:1, 2; 2 Th. 2:15) reminds us of the importance of catechetical instruction in the early Church as part of the educational ministry of 'teachers' and 'prophets' in the earliest communities. But what is striking here is the close tie-in between the word and the person who speaks it (Gnilka). Paul has clearly (3:17) held himself up—perhaps defensively so, if his apostolic authority has been challenged at Philippi—as an example to follow. This he repeats: **in me** strictly relates to the verb **seen**, but the zeugma unites his person with all the elements of apostolic instruction and paves the way, as Lohmeyer remarks, for Paul's writing to become canonical, i.e., authoritative as Scripture, and his person to be regarded as apostolic (2 Pet. 3:15–17; cf. *Acta* of the Scillitan Martyrs where in the church's box are the 'Gospels' and the books of 'Paul the righteous').

the God of peace will be with you might be seen as the completion of a circle which began in verse 7, in a form of *inclusio*. It could conceivably mark the conclusion of a letter (see the Introduction, pp. 14–22.)

THANKS FOR THE PHILIPPIANS' GIFTS 4:10–20

The literary problems associated with this section of the letter have already been discussed (see Introduction, pp. 14–22). The main point to be decided is whether these verses are in their proper place at the close of a single letter to the Philippian church, or represent a 'Thank you' note, complete or in part, sent earlier than the preceding sections of what is now our letter and forming the first in a series of letters. Either way, the purport of the section is plain. It is to acknowledge the gift which Epaphroditus (2:25–30) has brought (4:18). On the whole paragraph, see O. Glombitza, 'Der Dank des Apostels: Zum Verständnis von Philipper IV 10–20', *NovT* 7 (1964–5), pp. 135–41, who also tackles another issue raised in these verses, viz., does Paul consciously employ a set of commercial terms drawn from the contemporary banking scene, or does his main emphasis fall on the Philippians' response to his preaching and on his assertion that 'we live all the time by grace'? (p. 140)

10. There is a connecting particle (Gr. *de*) not translated in *RSV*. If this section belongs integrally to the foregoing, this word 'but', 'and so', is a transition-point.

I rejoice in the Lord greatly that now at length you have revived your concern for me. This is Paul's way of saying 'Thank you'. Its roundabout and oblique allusion to the church's gift has given rise to some speculation among interpreters. Why is

Paul so reticent to come out boldly with a word of appreciation, and have we any justification, in company with Dibelius, Lohmeyer, and Gnilka, to talk of Paul's 'thankless thanks' (*danklose Dank*)?

One reason for a guarded expression would be found if we could accept J. H. Michael's view ('The First and Second Epistles to the Philippians', *ExpT* 34 (1922-3, pp.106-9), shared by E. F. Scott, that in an earlier letter to the church Paul had said something, namely, that he was not in need of a money gift, which had caused resentment at Philippi. This sentence is Paul's attempt to clear up the difficulty. C. O. Buchanan (*EQ* 36 (1964), pp. 161ff.) thinks that Paul is really upset that the Philippians have disobeyed his order about his refusal to accept financial assistance from the churches (cf. 1 C. 9:15-18). But we may question whether this firm policy of refusing help applied to all his congregations. Probably the truth is that Paul felt a certain embarrassment over money matters, and that his ambiguous way of writing reflects something of a conflict between his desire to express gratitude for the gift received both recently and earlier (v. 15) and a concern to show himself superior to questions of depending on others for financial support.

Certainly Paul has an unusual way of acknowledging the gift, whether in money or kind, from the church, and not least in the idioms he uses. He places all stress on his joy **in the Lord,** and not on the Philippians' generosity—a trait to reappear in verse 18. **you have revived** (Gr. *anethalete*, found only here in *NT* but present in the LXX of Ps. 27:7; Wis. 4:4; Sir. 46:12; 49:10, of plants 'blooming again' after the dormant season). The verb may be either transitive, a meaning found in *RSV* and accepted by Dibelius, Bonnard, and Beare—'now at length you gave effect to your concern'; or better, factitive (see AG, who give this meaning 'to cause to grow' found in LXX at Ezek. 17:24; Sir. 50:10). The alternative is to regard the verb as intransitive: 'you have revived as far as your concern for me'. So Gnilka and N. Baumert, 'Ist Philipper 4, 10 richtig übersetzt?', *BZ* 13 (1969), pp. 256-62 (260). This is preferable, if it is true, as Gnilka asserts, that Paul's writing of acknowledgement sees the matter entirely from the Philippians' side; and this interpretation is supported by what follows.

Your concern for me uses the key verb in this epistle: Gr.

phronein, cf. 2:3f., and 1:7 which has a parallel expression. Paul has a deep concern for the Philippians. Now he pays tribute to their involvement and active interest in his affairs. **you were indeed concerned for me, but you had no opportunity.** The first part of the sentence stresses the willingness and readiness of the Philippians to send help (picked up in vs. 15f.: so Baumert, loc. cit., pp. 260f.). What stood in the way of their help reaching him was not the Philippians' lack of interest but unfavourable circumstances. 'You lacked the right moment (*kairos*) to help', Paul comments in his verb (Gr. *ēkaireisthe*).

The reason for the absence of a favourable circumstance is not stated. This fact has some bearing on the dating of the letter. (See the Introduction, pp. 52f.) Whether it was the apostle's situation in some inaccessible place, or the Philippians' own poverty, or their preoccupation with the collection for the Jerusalem saints, no blame attaches to this remissness. It was something outside their control.

11. In any event, and whatever the cause for the delay, Paul maintains a detached attitude. **Not that I complain of want.** So Paul's appreciation of the Philippians' assistance is not expressed out of a sense of need (**want** [Gr. *hysterēsis*] is found only here and in Mk 12:44 in the *NT*). He has no reason to feel abandoned: **complain** is inserted in *RSV* to make smooth reading of an elliptical phrase (see BDF, sec. 480. 5). He can maintain this reserved stance for one reason: **I have learned, in whatever state I am,** whether of unfavourable circumstances such as 2 C. 11:23ff. (so Bonnard), or with what meagre possessions I have to hand (so Glombitza, loc. cit., pp. 136f.), **to be content.** The last word is Gr. *autarkēs*, an important quality describing a person's independence of things. It is an assertion of self-sufficiency taught by the Stoics. It was in fact their fundamental virtue in the moral life. See J. N. Sevenster, *Paul and Seneca*, pp. 113f., citing Seneca, 'the happy man is content with his present lot, no matter what it is, and is reconciled to his circumstances' (*de Vita Beata*, 6.2). But the term had a wider currency than simply that of a technical expression in the Cynic-Stoic school (G. Kittel, *TDNT* i, pp. 466f.). Even if Paul did borrow it, he quickly transformed it into something quite different. The Stoic 'self-sufficient' man, of whom Socrates is held up as prime exemplar, faces life and death with resources that are all found within himself. Paul finds the

secret of life in his union with Christ (1:21), whom he came to
know in the hour of his conversion (**I learned** is an aorist tense,
suggesting a specific time when this truth broke upon him; he did
not acquire it through patient discipline and concentrated effort).
He can, therefore, proceed in the following section to declare that
true liberty is his as he depends on God and is committed in
obedience to a new Lord (v. 13). (So Glombitza, loc. cit., p.137.)
His freedom also disengages him from dependence on human
resources, as though he were a hired worker of the church
(Gnilka, quoting E. Peterson, 'An apostle is no employee of the
church').

12, 13. What that detachment from earthbound conditions of
apostolic ministry means is set out in a rhythmical passage, which
we may attempt to reproduce:

a **I know how to be abased,**
b **and I know how to abound;**
c **in any and all circumstances I have learned the secret**

a **of facing plenty and hunger,**
b **abundance and want.**
c **I can do all things in him who strengthens me.**

In the last line the TR MSS and Origen have 'Christ' in place of the
pronoun, but this is a secondary reading.

This two-stanza, six-line poetic piece is a tribute to Paul's
apostolate. His 'humiliation' (Gr. *tapeinousthai* recalls 2:8) is more
than economic deprivation and his lot as a martyr (Lohmeyer); it
reflects his entire outlook on and disregard of personal comforts
in life. Cf. 1 C. 4:11; 2 C. 6:3–10, 11:23ff. 'Abounding' (Gr.
perisseuein) has been taken to mean spiritual elation (cf. 2 C.
12:1ff.), when as a man full of power and the Spirit Paul exercised
authority in the churches (1 C. 4:18–21; 2 C. 13:5–10). The
contrast **plenty** and **hunger** is normally used of physical supply
and lack (Lk. 6:21), and again the best illumination is provided
in Paul's *apologia pro vita sua* in 2 C. 11:21ff.

The closing line gives the inner meaning of the whole. Paul's
learning (Gr. *memyēmai*: a technical expression in the Greek
mystery religions to denote initiation and insight into the symbolic
acts practised by the hellenistic cults: see AG, 'initiate [into the
mysteries]'; but they also give a general sense of the verb: 'to

learn the secret') of the secret of independence and self-containment is matched by his indebtedness to his Lord and his utter reliance on him. So **I can do all things** has to be taken in context, i.e., the **all things** are those tasks and responsibilities that belong to his apostolic office and commission and that he can fulfil only in so far as he is dependent on the Lord (Gnilka). Mention of this 'strength' (Gr. *endynamounti*) will recall what he said in 3:10, where the 'power (Gr. *dynamis*) of his resurrection' is the driving force of Paul's ministry.

14. Yet it was kind of you to share my trouble. This is perhaps the closest Paul gets to saying 'Thank you'. By using an idiomatic expression (lit. 'you did well', as in Ac. 10:33; 2 Pet. 1:19; 3 Jn 6), he congratulates them on their thoughtfulness in this 'good work' of support for his ministry, especially at those times when he had been in distress. **my trouble** (Gr. *thlipsis*) is left undefined; but it can hardly refer, in this context and in the light of verse 11, to Paul's personal needs and trials. In 1:17 and 2 C. 1:8 the word relates to Paul's prison experience, but even there an eschatological sense lies in the background. *thlipsis* is the tribulation to come on the earth at the end-time in apocalyptic literature (cf. Mk 13:19; 2 Th. 1:6), and it may well be that this is in Paul's mind here. The Philippians had supported the apostle by their gifts and made possible his continuing ministry. They had stood by him in his apostolic labours and he is praising them for their support of him as 'eschatological apostle', destined to promote God's purposes in the spread of the gospel to the Gentiles and so to prepare the way for the dénouement of history (for this estimate of Paul, see A. Fridrichsen, *The Apostle and his Message*, Uppsala, 1947; J. Munck, *Paul and the Salvation of Mankind*, ET London, 1959, ch. 2). This understanding would at least throw some light on Paul's strange reticence in saying 'Thank you' for the gifts to him personally, and it explains his use of the verb, **to share**, i.e., they shared with him in his work, in the sense of 1:7: Paul and they are joint sharers in divine grace.

to share (Gr. *synkoinōnein*), then, signifies not sharing with Paul as a private individual, but sharing in his apostolic task (so Glombitza, loc. cit., p. 137; H. Seesemann, *Der Begriff KOINŌNIA im NT*, pp. 33f., referring back to the usage of the verb, meaning 'sharing in something outside of oneself', p. 5).

15. And you Philippians yourselves know that in the

beginning of the gospel, when I left Macedonia . . . This is
an obvious reminiscence of Ac. 16:12ff. when the church was
first formed. **the beginning of the gospel** refers back to Paul's
first preaching mission in the city of Philippi (1:6), and it is not
unnatural that he should wish to call these church-members by
their Roman nomenclature, **Philippians** = Latin *Philippenses*
(cf. W. M. Ramsay, 'On the Greek Form of the Name Philippians',
JTS 1 o.s. (1900), p. 116). He did so, not to soften a blow in an
earlier sentence which had censured them (J. H. Michael; see
on 4:10) but to give them their true name by which Philippian
citizens dignified their civic status. The term **gospel**, moreover,
takes on a kind of personal significance, as though to mark the
intimate character of Paul's evangelism (see P. T. O'Brien,
'Thanksgiving and the Gospel in Paul', *NTS* 21 (1974–5),
pp. 144–55 [espec. pp. 153f.]). But in what sense could his initial
evangelism in Macedonia be called **the beginning** of his apostolic
work? We are not to suppose that he considered this work in
Macedonia of such importance as to call in question his earlier
ministry (Ac. 13–14; so Glombitza, loc. cit., p. 140). But there
may be a sense in which Paul felt that, when he stepped on to the
Greek mainland and moved in a westward direction *en route* to
Rome, he was at the beginning of a new phase of his ministry,
with Silas as companion, for which his earlier evangelization in
Asia Minor had been preparatory. At all events, the crossing to
Macedonia is described in Acts as a 'decisive turning-point'
(E. Meyer, *Ursprung und Anfänge des Christentums* iii, Berlin, 1923,
p. 80, cited in Gnilka), and thereafter Macedonia remained in the
foreground of Paul's mission strategy (mentioned in the Pauline
corpus some thirteen times).

Paul is apparently reminding his Philippian friends that they
occupied a unique place in his missionary procedures: **no church
entered into partnership** (Gr. *ekoinōnēsen*), i.e., in the work of
the gospel, **with me** (Seesemann, op. cit., p. 33) **in giving and
receiving except you only.**

It is clearly Paul's intention to single out the Philippian church
as the community which held a special place in his affections and
esteem. He was willing to receive gifts (not necessarily in money:
possibly other items are included). But unless the phrase **giving
and receiving** is an idiom and its strict meaning is not to be
pressed, it looks as though there was a two-way transaction

involved. The Philippians gave and they also received, presumably spiritual good, from Paul (as in 1 C. 9:11; cf. Rom. 15:27). They had begun to support him and his apostolic labours right from the start. Even before he left Macedonia the Philippians were involved in this double ministry. That it was not simply a matter of their supporting Paul which made them rank in a class apart is seen from 2 C. 11:8, 12:13, where other churches sent help to the apostle. What stamped the relationship of Paul and the Philippians was that they both gave and received—and, we may surmise, raised no objections such as Paul encountered at Corinth, because of which he determined to receive no payment for his ministry there.

16. From Philippi the apostolic missionaries came to **Thessalonica** (Ac. 17:1–9). **even** there the Philippians began their generosity by sending help. *RSV* simplifies this text by translating a shorter reading. The better textual tradition (Sinaiticus, Vaticanus, etc.) adds 'for my need'. There are several issues raised by this reference to help received during Paul's ministry in Thessalonica; **for even in Thessalonica you sent me help once and again.**

Paul refers to his 'labour and toil' (1 Th. 2:9; 2 Th. 3:8) during this period, and it may be surmised that in a time of economic stress, partly relieved by his manual work, the gifts from Philippi came at an acceptable time. That these gifts were repeated is suggested by **once and again** (see L. Morris on this phrase, *NovT* 1 (1956), pp. 203–8; B. Rigaux, *Les épîtres aux Thessaloniciens*, Paris, 1956, p. 461). If the first word in the full phrase *kai hapax kai dis* is not part of the expression (it is not translated in *RSV*) but rather a connective word, then the sense will be: 'Both when I was in Thessalonica and more than once when I was in other places' (so Morris, loc. cit., p. 208). A frequent sending of gifts to Paul, probably while he was in Thessalonica—during a longer period than Ac. 17 envisages (see E. Haenchen, *The Acts of the Apostles*, pp. 511f.)—is implied by this phrase (Gnilka, Michaelis Collange).

17. **Not that I seek the gift, but I seek the fruit which increases to your credit.** If Paul has come near to an explicit acknowledgement of material gifts, he withdraws from it now. First, with a disavowal, **Not that I seek the gift**; then with a twist in his thought which places the emphasis in a new direction,

but I seek the fruit which increases to your credit. The verse is full of commercial terms (see H. A. A. Kennedy, 'The Financial Colouring of Phil. iv, 15–18', *ExpT* 12 (1900–1), pp. 43f.). **seek the gift** is perhaps 'a technical term for the demand for payment of interest' (Gnilka); **fruit** is 'profit' or 'interest': see Moulton-Milligan, *Vocabulary*, *s.v. karpeia*, a variant of Paul's *karpos* in this verse; **increases** (Gr. *pleonazein*: a regular banking term for financial growth; **your credit** (Gr. *logos*) means 'account'. The whole sentence is a playful attempt at putting his hope into a commercial key: 'I am looking for the interest which is accruing to your credit', so that Paul will at the last day of reckoning be satisfied with his enterprise at Philippi (2:16). See 1:11 for a similar eschatological hope.

18. He continues this vocabulary of mock finance. **I have received full payment, and more.** The non-literary papyri shed some light on Paul's first verb **I have received** (Gr. *apechō*, a technical expression used for drawing up a receipt for payment in full in discharge of a bill; AG render 'to receive a sum in full and give a receipt for it'). Paul has more than sufficient: he claims to have enough and more (Gr. *perisseuein*, 'I abound', as in v. 12). **I am full** (Gr. *peplērōmai*) because the Philippians have faithfully and unstintingly, and not without cost on their part (see v. 19), sent these gifts which he has received from Epaphroditus. This matches the description in 2:25 where Epaphroditus is the church's 'minister to my need'. See, too, 2:30 for this service.

What is interesting is the threefold designation in sacral terminology of so mundane a matter as the conveying of a material gift: **a fragrant offering, a sacrifice acceptable and pleasing to God.** The first term is borrowed directly from the *OT* and is literally 'the odour of a sweet smell' (Gn. 8:21; Exod. 29:18, 25, 41; Lev. 1:9, 13; Ezek. 20:41; cf. Eph. 5:2 for an allusion in this way to Christ's self-sacrifice). The spiritualizing of the Levitical sacrifices had already begun at Qumran (1QS 8:7–9; Vermes, p. 85) as part of the sectarians' critique of the Temple cult at Jerusalem (1QS 9:3–5: 'and prayer rightly offered shall be as an acceptable fragrance of righteousness . . . perfection of way as a delectable free-will offering'; Vermes, p. 87; 1QS 10:6: 'all my life the engraved Precept shall be on my tongue as the fruit of praise and the portion of my lips'; Vermes, p. 89). **sacrifice** has already been used in a symbolic sense in 2:17, where it has also to do with the Philippians' service rendered on behalf of the apostle. See on that verse.

acceptable and pleasing to God are again cultic terms found in association with the *OT* sacrificial system. They are given a spiritual connotation in Paul's writings (see Rom. 12:1; Col. 3:20; Tit. 2:9) as part of his general teaching on the ideal of Christian living, viz., to be both accepted by God and seeking to please him in daily conduct (see *Colossians and Philemon, New Century Bible*, 1974, pp. 52, 120).

19. If we give an importance to the connective particle rendered **And** (Gr. *de*), there may be a slight adversative force, better conveyed by 'but'. That would imply that as the church had helped the apostle in his need, so God would relieve the church in its need (Gnilka). The link term is **every need of yours** which corresponds with 'my need' (in v. 16, if this reading is accepted, as it should be). The form of the verse is a wish-prayer (see G. P. Wiles, *Paul's Intercessory Prayers*, pp. 101–7) and the verb **God will supply** is more a prayer request than a simple statement. **supply** (Gr. *plērōsei* links with v. 18: Paul says that 'he is filled', using the same verb to denote a sufficient supply): Paul is evidently wishing to stress that the Philippians' giving has been observed by God, whose work, entrusted to his hands, they have helped forward. Now, in a reciprocal way, **my God** (the personal pronoun is very rare in Paul; cf. 1:3) will make up the supply of the Philippians' needs, evidently at a time of economic stringency (if 2 C. 8:2 is germane in its account of the Macedonian Christians' financial straits at this time, as Michaelis believes).

The giving of God is **according to his riches in glory in Christ Jesus,** where the prepositional phrase (Gr. *kata to ploutos autou*) signifies that 'the rewarding will be not merely *from* His wealth, but also in a manner that befits His wealth—on a scale worthy of His wealth' (Michael). And to that there is no limit. The phrase **in glory** is a teaser. It may be construed as an adverb qualifying the verb supply: 'he will supply in a glorious manner' (Collange). The preposition **in** takes on the same meaning as the Hebrew *be*. Or, the phrase may point forward to the future kingdom of glory (Lohmeyer, Michaelis). Or else **in glory** is to be connected with **riches** and used adjectivally: 'glorious riches', or perhaps 'riches which consist in the gifts of his glory', in which 'glory' characterizes the life of believers in Christ Jesus (Gnilka).

Then it must have a futuristic reference, since the life of the Christian *hic et nunc* is never called 'glory' in Paul; rather it is a condition of lowliness and frailty (3:21; 2 C.4:7–12). Perhaps here again we should suspect an anti-perfectionist polemic (see p. 150).

20. glory, an elusive biblical term (see H. Kittel, *Die Herrlichkeit Gottes,* Giessen, 1934), reappears in this doxology. The tribute of praise to our God and Father comes as a splendid climax, and 'flows from the joy of the whole epistle' (Bengel), i.e., it is Paul's fitting response, borrowed from the liturgical practice of the primitive churches, to all the things which cause him joy in his prison experience.

for ever and ever. Amen are no conventional terms to round off a doxology. The Greek behind **for ever and ever** simply puts into that language the Hebrew idiom *leʿōlām waʿedh* with its time-division between 'this age' and 'the age to come'. God's praise endures into the future ages. The **Amen** response is a confessional endorsement of what has been said, and an acclamation of the worshipper's acceptance (see H. Schlier, *TDNT* i, pp. 335–8).

FINAL GREETINGS **4:21–23**

21. Greet every saint in Christ Jesus. Ancient Greek letters usually conclude with a farewell (Gr. *errhōsō*) or a wish for good luck (Gr. *eutychei*). Paul's practice includes a greeting (see Rom. 16:3–23; 1 C. 16:19–21; 2 C. 13:12, 13; 1 Th. 5:26) and is rounded off with a Christian benediction (v. 23).

The form of this greeting is unique. **every saint** virtually means the same as 'all the saints' (2 C. 13:13), i.e., all Christian people who comprise the congregation. But there may be a special point to Paul's way of writing. Instead of greetings 'in the Lord' (as in Rom. 16:22; 1 C. 16:19) he describes the Philippians as **in Christ Jesus.** And **every saint** (Gr. *panta hagion,* a neuter) may be designed to appeal to the inclusive company, and so to be a final appeal for the church's unity as God's 'holy ones' (1:1). Then, who is the subject implied in the verb, **greet**? The best guess is that the Philippians are to greet one another, and so cement cordial relations as they are brought together by Paul's letter.

The brethren who are with me, such as Timothy (1:1, 2:19–24), join in the salutation.

22. All the saints probably extends the circle of 'brethren' in the preceding verse to include the church-members present in the place of Paul's captivity. The phrase matches that of 2 C. 13:13, and may conceivably refer to the same group of Christians in Rome or Ephesus. The totality of 'all the saints' may well be a pointer away from Caesarea where we have no independent knowledge of a large Christian community (see earlier, p. 47).

especially those of Caesar's household. The occasion of this part of the greeting may well be the link of special interest between the Christian members of the imperial staff on government service at the place of Paul's imprisonment and the citizens of Philippi which was a Roman colony (so Michaelis, E. F. Scott). Certainly the phrase **Caesar's household** (Gr. *hoi ek tēs kaisaros oikias*) does not refer to the emperor's family (Herod Agrippa is called 'a member of Caesar's household' in Philo, *In Flacc.* 35) as the Latin *familia Caesaris* might superficially suggest. Nor does it necessarily mean the members of the imperial court at Rome (see on 1:13).

'Imperial slaves' (Moffatt's translation) unduly narrows the group to the slave class by omitting other members of the freedman class, unless 'slaves' is taken in the broader sense of 'servants', i.e., civil servants.

What is intended is a greeting from those in the imperial services, whether as soldiers (Gnilka thinks of those to whose guardianship Paul was committed and whose greeting is meant as a reassurance to the Philippians naturally solicitous over Paul's welfare, 1:12; 2:19–24) or government officers in the praetorium. Centres of administration were found in the provinces as well as at Rome; and there is inscriptional evidence of the way that in Ephesus members of the civil service, both freedmen and slaves, formed themselves into *collegia* or guilds of the emperor (*curam agunt collegia lib[ertorum] et servorum domini n[ostri] Aug[usti] i[nfra] s[cripta]*). See J. T. Wood, *Discoveries at Ephesus*, London, 1877, referred to in G. S. Duncan, *St Paul's Ephesian Ministry* London, 1929, p. 110.

23. A final prayer calls down **The grace of the Lord Jesus Christ** on the Philippian congregation. The full expression of the name and title suggests a liturgical formulary, though there is an appropriateness of the term **Lord** in a letter which has set this christological emphasis at a central point (2:11) and worked out its implications for the church's life and relationships (2:5: see commentary).

The grace of the Church's Lord is invoked on **your spirit** (Gr. *pneumatos*, a singular noun, to stress perhaps the unity of the body of believers in which one spirit is to be found, 1:27). **spirit** replaces 'with you' (Rom. 16:20; 1 C. 16:23; Col. 4:18), or 'with you all' (Rom. 16:24; 2 C. 13:13; 2 Th. 3:18; cf. Eph. 6:24), but Phm. 25 repeats it. **spirit** means the entire person (E. Schweizer, *TDNT* vi, p. 435) of the several believers who make up the assembled congregation (**your** is plural). Paul's own agreement may be heard in the 'Amen' (found in a strongly attested textual tradition, P⁴⁶, Sinaiticus, ADKLP Lat. Syr. TR) as he confirms ('Amen' = 'it is true') the benediction; or else it is the scribe's witness to what he thought was the congregation's most suitable response, as it indeed is.

INDEX OF SUBJECTS

INDEX OF MODERN NAMES

τὸ ἐπιεκής